THE STARGATE CHRONICLES

Other Books by Joseph McMoneagle

Mind Trek

The Ultimate Time Machine

Remote Viewing Secrets

THE STARGATE CHRONICLES

MEMOIRS OF A PSYCHIC SPY

JOSEPH McMONEAGLE

HAMPTON ROADS
PUBLISHING COMPANY, INC.

Copyright © 2002
by Joseph McMoneagle
All rights reserved, including the right to reproduce this
work in any form whatsoever, without permission
in writing from the publisher, except for brief passages
in connection with a review.

Cover design by Steve Amarillo
Cover art copyright © 2000 by D. Falconer/Photolink/
Photo Disk: bottom image
Cover art copyright © 2000 by Photolink/
Eyewire:top image

For information, write:
Hampton Roads Publishing Company, Inc.
1125 Stoney Ridge Road
Charlottesville, VA 22902

434-296-2772
fax: 434-296-5096
e-mail: hrpc@hrpub.com
www.hrpub.com

If you are unable to order this book from your local
bookseller, you may order directly from the publisher.
Call 1-800-766-8009, toll-free.

Library of Congress Catalog Card Number: 2002100965
ISBN 1-57174-225-5
10 9 8 7 6 5 4 3 2 1

Printed on acid-free paper in the United States

Dedication

This book is dedicated to the people who died during Project Star Gate while exploring remote viewing at Stanford Research Institute, Science Applications International Corporation, and Fort George G. Meade, Maryland. They participated at great personal cost while being subjected to incessant and baseless ridicule by others. They did so quietly and without fanfare in the defense of their country and in the pursuit of knowledge. They did so with undeniable personal courage, intelligence, and resourcefulness. They did so with good humor and a clear focus on the benefits they always hoped humankind would derive from such an effort. They were and always will be fine examples of what explorers should be. And they will not be forgotten.

Pat Price
Jackie Keith
Hartleigh Trent
Gemma Foreman
Martha Thompson
James Salyer
Robert Cowart
Hella Hammid
Larrisa Valenskyia

Table of Contents

Foreword by Brig. Gen. L. Robert Castorr ix
What Is Remote Viewing? xi
Preface xiii
Acknowledgements xxi
Introduction xxiii
Chapter One: Childhood: Troubles and Experience 1
Chapter Two: From Enlistment through School 25
Chapter Three: From My First Assignment
           to a Near-Death Experience 38
Chapter Four: Reaching the Top .52
Chapter Five: The Special Project 71
Chapter Six: A New Remote Viewer 84
Chapter Seven: A Crisis 101
Chapter Eight: Fighting the System 109
Chapter Nine: Downward Spiral 125
Chapter Ten: The Army and Bob Monroe 139
Chapter Eleven: End of the Line 156
Chapter Twelve: Retirement 167

Chapter Thirteen: Exploring New Territories 187
Chapter Fourteen: Research 207
Chapter Fifteen: *Mind Trek* and Searches 223
Chapter Sixteen: Put to the Test—on Live TV 230
Chapter Seventeen: The AIR Report 237
Chapter Eighteen: Going Public 243
Chapter Nineteen: Curtain Call 255
Final Words 266
Appendix A: Parapsychology in Intelligence:
                A Personal Review and Conclusions 269
Appendix B: "Psi Conducive States,"
                Journal of Communications 285
Appendix C: Legion of Merit and Certificate 287
Works Cited 289
Index 293

Foreword

The Stargate Chronicles is a brilliantly written documentation of a very provocative subject. Its author demonstrates a superb in-depth psychic undertaking of paranormal activities of the mind. His humble beginning in life, coupled with many obstacles and sacrifices made during his military career in addition to death-threatening health conditions, may have given him this incredible, phenomenal gift, the ability to tell this story of bringing the unknown into reality.

It is a must for all to read and then to pause and reflect upon the mystery within.

Those who do not possess an adventurous mind open to the challenging or the unusual, and those who are not willing to explore it, may classify *The Stargate Chronicles* as an exercise in futility. The unsophisticated or uninformed leave the mysteries of life as simply that—mysteries. But for those who have inquisitive minds, the paranormal experiences described by the author lead to the exploration of baffling questions. Joseph McMoneagle should be recognized as being as much a pioneer in this field as were our astronauts traversing the unthinkable far reaches of outer space.

Brigadier General L. Robert Castorr
United States Army Infantry Retired
OWE, VM, GCSTS, GCPR, CMWS, MV, BSML, OSJ
Ambassador-at-large, The Order of St. Stanislas

What Is Remote Viewing?

Remote viewing is a human ability to produce information about a targeted object, person, place, or event, while being completely isolated from the target by space, time, and other forms of shielding. This isolation is guaranteed by following a very specific scientific protocol. This protocol was developed at Stanford Research Institute in the early 1970s and has become more rigorous and specific since then.

Remote viewing can be considered to have taken place only when the remote viewer and anyone else in the room with the remote viewer are completely blind to the specifically targeted object, person, place, or event of interest. They must remain blind to the target of interest prior to and during the production of information. In scientific terms, this is called a double-blind condition. That is, the viewer and all the people associated with the viewer are unaware of the target material. There are no exceptions to this protocol.

A specific technique or system used to produce the information is called a "method." Specific methods have been designed for use within a remote viewing protocol. However, regardless of the method used, a method is never considered an acceptable substitute for the protocol.

In common parlance, some of the methods developed for use within a remote viewing protocol are sometimes referred to as "remote viewing." This is not accurate or appropriate. Utilization of such methods outside a valid protocol not only violates the definition of what makes psychic work "remote viewing," but it also violates both the design and intent of the methods themselves.

If any exception to a protocol is made during training in any technique or method, then it is considered a "training method" and not a valid remote viewing protocol.

Psychic functioning, clairvoyance, extrasensory perception, and other methods or techniques are considered to be remote viewing when the person using these methods and everyone in the room with that person during information production has been guaranteed blind to the targeted object, person, place, or event. If everyone is blind to the target, they are fulfilling the requirements for a remote viewing protocol.

Preface

I've been accused of a lot of things in my life, but ducking an issue isn't one of them. I entered the army in 1964 when it wasn't a popular thing to do. I did twenty years service to my country as an Intelligence NCO and officer, and spent more than twelve continuous years overseas in some places most people wouldn't have volunteered to be in, doing things most wouldn't do. I did this at a time when many of my own countrymen, people I defended and supported, disliked what I was doing. When I was first exposed to the possibility of remote viewing as an intelligence threat, I took it very seriously because the evidence already extant was significantly compelling to demand attention.

I have now spent 23 years of my life carefully studying remote viewing within research laboratories and applying it in hundreds of intelligence collection circumstances. I have visited other countries and met with remote viewers who are participants in both research and applications, in both civilian and military labs. And whether you want to call it paranormal or not, I'm more convinced than ever that there is something going on that we should be very concerned about.

Most in America were outraged by the events involving the World Trade Center disaster and what happened in our nation's capital and on a small field in Pennsylvania. Since my retirement from the military in 1984, I've come face to face with evil acts that I knew would eventually occur within our borders. It is an inescapable fact that terrorist activities and the efforts of terrorists across the world have more than tripled in a little less than two decades. I've been dealing with it for 28 years and it's only getting worse.

While these facts are not new to much of the world, they are new to many in America who must now deal with them. I find it silly and irrelevant, stupid and ignorant, to continue to ignore a proven intelligence capability that might be used in our defense. A lot of commentary has revolved around the percentage or degree of reliability associated with remote viewing. The fact is, this is no better or worse than the dependability of most agents in the field, another area in which we now find ourselves deficient. While much of the argument revolves within science, scientists—who are supposed to have open minds—continue to shift the goalposts around. They automatically treat the investigation of remote viewing as they would some kind of "circus entertainment" or "magic stunt" because it's far easier to ridicule the phenomena than to deal with it. These scientists are aided and abetted by a majority of the media, who are looking for one-line sound bites to sell more television or radio time, contributing nothing of value to our cultural data bank.

Even parapsychologists, who have spent the better part of their lives investigating the paranormal and who are quick to react to microparanormal events or anomalies, will usually walk away when they are confronted by a macroevent—like an in-your-face demonstration of an excellent double-blind remote viewing. I've personally witnessed this on at least three occasions within the very organizations to which I belong.

Why?

Maybe because they don't want to have to seriously expose themselves in the defense of something they cannot yet explain, or perhaps they enjoy the mental challenge as long as it doesn't cost them a greater degree of exposure. I believe, they, like many they call their enemy, are just as afraid of what might happen to their reputations and credibility as anyone else. If the Wright brothers had been sensitive to this same issue, humankind would never have gotten off the ground.

Since the exposure of the military Star Gate project on *Nightline* in November of 1995, there are now dozens of people in the culture running amok with claims of being or having been associated with that project. They are creating websites and developing teaching centers that cater to mostly innocent people who are conned into paying sometimes large sums of money to learn—or be deluded by—whatever is thrown at them. Many of these self-proclaimed experts are teaching *brands* of remote viewing that have no direct relationship in reality to what was originally demonstrated at SRI-International or within any effective portion of the Star Gate program. These people have no respect for the rules and ignore the simplest part of what differentiates remote viewing from psychic functioning—the *protocol*. They push things totally unrelated to the reality of remote viewing as it was originally discovered, developed, or applied. Many of these people make claims connecting remote viewing to themselves and every kind of bogus operation that can be sold and taught, or that will entice a buck in through the door. Their produce is slung like hash onto metal trays in feed lines being filled by the uninitiated, those who should deserve more respect, those who are hungry for spiritual growth and development. By their nature, these unwitting victims are simply humans looking for a better way, something positive in their lives to balance out the newest threats to their social and cultural framework, something to soften their fears.

Many of the *brands* of remote viewing are psychic methodologies that claim to teach remote viewing. Some mimic, directly or indirectly, supposed training methods now many generations removed from the originally conceived concepts people attempted to develop for the Army within Project Star Gate. The success of the project did not depend on any of the training methods used (and there were more than a few), but instead was dependent on following the SRI-developed protocol, the skill in its application, careful analysis of the results, and the talent of all the individuals involved. This is true for all the remote viewers involved in the project. A near cultlike situation has now developed that is very disturbing to me and others, a direct result of the new initiation rites wherein the novitiates are being indoctrinated with "the inside track to remote viewing" when there is none. This is having a substantial effect on people's belief systems and is the antithesis of the responsible, scientifically based approach to remote viewing that brought real-world success in its application in the first place.

Psychic ability has been within the world of humankind since the dawn of time. World-class levels of talent appear to be very rare and it has been demonstrated that while most individuals have some degree of talent, they do so only if remote viewing is pursued within the proper protocol and practiced repetitively and diligently over a long course of time. There are no "tricks." I've provided the rules very straightforwardly in my book *Remote Viewing Secrets: A Handbook. The rules are: Protocol, Practice, Talent.* In that order.

Once again, I find it necessary to state that it is unfair to the point of fraudulence for "remote viewing"—a term coined in the science lab to mean "psychic functioning within a specific protocol"—to be taught without the critical points of that protocol. Most selling "training" refer publicly to their *methods* as "protocols," even though the training lacks most if not all relevant knowledge of any real remote viewing protocol or conditions within which remote viewing must be done. This seeming confusion of terms is deliberate and used to blur the meanings within the minds of the public.

It took a great deal of effort and work to bring legitimate human PSI out of the dark ages, strip it of its cultism and mystification, as well as its sometimes fraudulent framework. As soon as knowledge of Star Gate hit the public market, all of these negative aspects historically associated with the term "psychic" immediately reattached themselves.

Herein, I once again, clearly and emphatically state that there is only one protocol in remote viewing. There is a clear and distinct difference between remote viewing *methods* (whether they are used for teaching or application), and the remote viewing *protocol.* This one protocol is:

> *The remote viewer and everyone in the room or in communication with the remote viewer prior to and during a remote viewing must be totally blind to the target.*

Anything other than that is bogus, and should not be considered remote viewing. There are training "methods" in which the teacher is not blind to the target. Those training methods might be and can be acceptable in a training-only circumstance, because it is a "training method." Because it is considered a training method and a training session, what happens therein is not and cannot be considered a demonstration of remote viewing.

If someone wants to claim a demonstration of remote viewing, then it has to be done within the *protocol,* and the protocol demands that the target is blind to everyone involved in all of the data collection.

There are people within local, state, and federal governments who would like to use remote viewing, however limited its capabilities might prove to be, in their efforts to protect their citizens, thwart crime, or pursue terrorism. That's an appropriate and recognized desire. But it has taken decades for people who study the use of remote viewing to learn to use it appropriately, especially within the forms of application that can maximize its use and do so within the protocol. Learning how to use it properly is in some cases even more difficult to do than the remote viewing itself.

With this caution well known, many still choose to exercise this desire to use remote viewing both inside and outside the government, but not by going through appropriate channels or with proven researchers and people experienced with the information-collection techniques. They are doing it under the cover of darkness, through direct contact with anyone who comes along claiming expertise. This is a very dangerous practice and there is even a name for what can happen if this practice goes unchecked—it's called self-delusion. Being self-deluded into thinking you know all there is to know about remote viewing and applying it on criminal or terrorist cases without years of expertise is not only foolish, it only damages and discredits the previous work that's been done and further trashes any possibility of its continued use within appropriate boundaries. At best this is a display of grand ignorance.

It almost goes without saying that working within aboveboard channels would require

- having the courage of one's convictions
- following the historically established rules
- setting appropriate and verifiable goals
- determining specific guidelines for a proper evaluation of the results
- managing the problem openly, under the direct observation of one's peers and superiors alike

In many cases, this would almost guarantee a requirement for taking ridicule and dealing with it, not to mention having to stick one's head above the ridgeline and defending yourself as well as the protocol you are using.

There's a lot wrong with what's going on in the remote viewing world, but some things have been demonstrated—over and over again, and within protocol. Remote viewing has been appropriately applied and used, has already proven itself valuable to presidents, the National Security Council, and the services or agencies tasked with the protection of our nation, contrary to whatever disinformation purveyors inside and outside the government would have you believe.

If one takes but a minute to focus through the clouds of defensive and egotistical posturing, the personalized embarrassment, and the politically motivated reputation enhancements taking place on either side of the argument—one of the first things that one will notice is that the face of war and the world is changing. We are moving into a period when new methods of warfare are being developed, and these will be and are already being used against us—and I'm not talking here about some shiny new technology constructed from nuts, bolts, and stainless; I'm talking about a "transcendent form of warfare"—a warfare of the mind. It is already being applied in new ways, ways that are hardly recognizable. It's a style of warfare where the battles are fought with information and mental constructs along seams of weakness never before recognized, and these deal first and foremost with how we conceptualize threat and go to belief itself. These are commodities our own people, media and self-proclaimed skeptics (better termed "debunkers") in particular, are far too willing to sell, trade, or profit from at the expense of rational action.

I'm really tired, very tired, of demonstrating what's right about remote viewing and why people should be paying attention to it. Enough is enough. Either climb on the cart or get the hell out of the way. If we don't find a way to use what we already know about remote viewing and its proper application to our own advantage, someone else will—and that's a very easy prediction to make. All it takes is courage and a will to follow the rules.

So, having said all of the above, why would I do it? Why would I trash a perfectly good career as an Army intelligence officer, put up with so much ridicule and irrationality, and take on such a challenge as this?

Was it just to become known as a psychic spy? So I could call myself Remote Viewer #001 of Project Star Gate? Hardly.

The reason for this entire book is to talk about how, in the face of overwhelming odds, paralyzing fears, crushing difficulties, stupefying roadblocks, and the advice of just about everyone closest to me—and why, based on what I read in a classified document one morning back in late 1977, I felt the reality of remote viewing was too important not to pay attention to.

It was then and still is, in my opinion, the greatest threat to my nation and possibly the single greatest discovery in our species' history. Remote viewing, when used appropriately, has a capacity for extensively destructive and creative contributions in our development.

Back then, I had a sworn responsibility to my commander, to the United States Army, and ultimately the population at large that I was sworn to defend—I chose to carry out that responsibility in spite of the issues I knew loomed on the horizon. Maybe reading this book will give some insight as to why I made that decision, and why I feel even now that it was a good one.

Acknowledgements

This book would never have been possible if it were not for the contributions and efforts of a number of my closest and dearest friends. I need to thank Edwin May, who is my colleague and the brother I never had. Barbara Bowen, who is not only my friend, but is also about the best agent and editor one could ever hope for. And, to Palyne Gaenir, I owe a special thank-you. Your friendship can only be equaled by your frank and open honesty. Please don't ever stop being the person you are.

Once in a great while someone comes along who can do magic with written words. I am eternally grateful to Frank DeMarco for working his magic on my manuscript. I will always envy your power with words and try to learn from you.

Of course, no writer on the planet could or would ever finish a manuscript without the never-ending support of their significant other. My lovely wife, Nancy, and her unconditional love and emotional nourishment are the only reasons this book now exists in time/space form. Thank you for always being there. I could not have done it without you.

And finally, I give thanks to all of you out there who continue to investigate and pursue remote viewing within the appropriate boundaries and protocols, and with a healthy skepticism. It's a difficult task you set for yourself. You constantly walk the razor's edge, somewhere between oversell and undersell, reviled by those who believe too much about it and criticized by those who lack the gift of an open mind.

Introduction

By Edwin C. May, Ph. D.

During my career as a research scientist, which now spans three decades, I have encountered many psychics. They range from self-professed yogis in India or New Age hopefuls to self-denied individuals who would never admit to being psychic yet can "knock your socks off" in double-blind laboratory tests or field operations. A precious few survive the rigors of scientific validation and among those that do, Joseph W. McMoneagle is the best, by far.

I first met Joe in 1979 when he was part of a team of six people who were sent by the U. S. Army as part of a "technology transfer" program at SRI International. What that actually meant, when stripped of its military jargon, was that we were to test all six people for their possible remote viewing ability using a double-blind (that is neither the viewer nor anyone in contact with the viewer knows the target), scientifically valid protocol. When it was Joe's turn, my colleague Hal Puthoff served as a "beacon" person and for each of six days stood at a different randomly chosen location for about 15 minutes. Joe was supposed to describe the surroundings where Hal was standing using only his mental impressions.

Determining whether Joe had any remote viewing ability required a fair and independent judge who was required to pick the target from a set of six locations, only one of which was correct. Naturally, the judge must not know the answer until after his or her assessment. I was that judge for Joe. The results were far different than chance would allow, and the series of six remote viewings were the best of that set of Army people. That began what is now a 24-year-long partnership in trying to understand how psychic abilities work and how they may be improved.

In the very beginning of *Stargate Chronicles,* Joe expresses frustration over the lack of good scientific protocols, which is unfortunately all too common with some of the material that purports to pass as valid remote viewing that can be found on the World Wide Web. Joe is especially qualified to speak on these matters because in addition to his contribution as a test subject, he has also evolved to be a fully qualified, contributing researcher. To my knowledge, Joe is the only "subject" to qualify as a full member of the Parapsychological Association, or PA for short, an affiliate of the American Association for the Advancement of Science. The PA is a professional organization with rigorous and strict entrance requirements.

I found reading *Stargate Chronicles* a special treat. Joe gives us a remarkable and candid glimpse into not only his multifaceted career but equally as important, he shares an intimate view of the many trials, tribulations, and successes of his personal life. It is clear from Joe's writing that there are many more interesting, important and sometimes quite funny stories to be told, but we will have to wait for further books.

From my perspective as Joe's close friend and co-researcher, two things emerge from the *Stargate Chronicles.* First and perhaps foremost is the very complexity of psychic functioning that range from technical details for a good experiment to critical psychological factors. We have seen all too often that some people become consumed by the process and in some way "go off the deep end." In this regard, Joe is as comfortable with his failures as he is with his successes and takes the psychic process in stride. We joke together about being on "ego" watch, and Joe has given me permission for the two-by-four cure: That is, a whack on the head if I ever see him losing it.

Second, while not directly stated, *Stargate Chronicles* displays for us the immense personal and physical sacrifice and hard work that is required to become the top in your field. Of course, we would expect that this is true for nearly all exceptional-human performance. Consider a football star or a virtuoso violinist.

What separates Joe as a psychic from the pack is the detailed and independent evaluation, both in the laboratory and in the field. To be scientifically valid, it is insufficient to hang out a shingle as a self-declared practicing psychic. Rather, the psychic material must be submitted for critical analysis and the results published in peer-reviewed journals.

In the real world of intelligence applications, scientific evaluation is much more difficult. Joe gives two examples where a military client tested an intelligence operation where 100 percent of "ground truth" was known. Joe scored exceptionally well on an electron accelerator target and support activity and on a high-energy microwave device. The best testimony for his excellence in real operations using remote viewing is Joe's Legion of Merit Award. At his retirement from the army, he was given this honor for providing a vast amount of accurate and useful material to the intelligence community.

In short, Joseph W. McMoneagle is the most tested and certified psychic in history. In *Stargate Chronicles*, Joe tells the sometimes-tortured, sometimes-joyous, but always fascinating story of how he got there.

—Edwin C. May, Ph. D., president,
The Laboratories for Fundamental Research,
Palo Alto, California

Chapter One

Childhood: Troubles and Experience

I'm selecting 1962 as a starting point, but only for describing the things as far back as I can remember, which occurred much earlier. If I tried a point of recall further back than that, the complexities of detail would become mired in the fog of developmental childhood emotions. I do remember things from earlier, but my relatives disbelieved this, convinced that I had to have been too young.

One of my favorite people was my twin sister's namesake, my Aunt Margaret. One afternoon in the summer of 1962, just past my sixteenth birthday, we were talking about memory, and how much one could or could not remember, a more than interesting topic to me now, because much later in life, she suffered from Alzheimer's disease.

I said that I could remember when she held me as a small baby, something she said she could not believe. I told her my memory included being held in her arms while lying on my back, which would have made me less than a year old. I distinctly remember looking up at her face and her gentle smile. I remember having a feeling that this was someone who was protection, someone who loved me a great deal. To underscore the event, I remarked that I also remembered seeing her dressed at the time in a totally white outfit with a very large wide-brimmed hat made of white straw. This was unusual, because otherwise I had no recall of ever seeing her wearing a hat of any kind at any other time. I said the hat was distinctive, because the sparkles of sunlight were coming through the small woven holes, reflecting light as through the facets of hundreds of diamonds.

She laughed and accused me of inventing the memory. I insisted that the event took place out of doors, because I remembered the bright sunlight as being directly in my face at times. She humored me, while impressing on me the fact that she had never even owned an all-white straw hat.

Some weeks later, I received a phone call from her. She said if I would stop by for a few minutes, she had something she wanted to share with me. She wouldn't tell me over the phone what it was, which of course made it all sound quite mysterious—especially as I didn't even recall our previous discussion.

I arrived at her house after school the following day and she made a big deal out of pulling a small suitcase down from the upper shelf of a closet. Then she retrieved a photograph from the large pile contained within. She told me she had come across the picture quite by accident while looking for something else. She passed it to me with shaking hands.

I was stunned by what I saw. She was standing in the center of the photograph, holding my twin sister and me in her right and left arms. The photograph was in color, which was unusual for the period, and my aunt was dressed completely in white, wearing a wide-brimmed, finely woven, straw hat, which was also entirely white. A penciled note on the back said it was the day my sister and I were christened. We were a little less than three months old. She said it had been noon when the picture was taken and someone had loaned her the hat in order to keep our faces in the shade.

I think this shocked my aunt more than it did me. But what it did to me was interesting. Seeing the picture was like having a lightning bolt discharged through my head. It woke up a part of my mind I had never experienced. Suddenly I was filled with dozens if not hundreds of images, flashes of things remembered, and flashes of things that made absolutely no sense to me. Images that I had not had until that moment. Many of these images were commonplace, but some were frightening in their context. It was as if the doorway to my earliest memories was suddenly opened. As if by magic, I had sudden recall of events previously blocked from my perception.

I know that for some this would not be a significant event. But for someone who had nearly a complete block to memories prior to age five, this was a significant development.

I suddenly found myself recalling with near-perfect and vivid imagery my time as a three-year-old on my grandfather's farm in Stone Mountain, Georgia. I could remember the colors of the walls in the small wood-framed house, the floor layout of the farmhouse, even the direction you needed to walk to get to the truck garden, the barn, and cornfields. I vividly remembered the smell inside the barn, the odor of my grandfather's mules, the stink of the chicken coop—even the open and rank septic field behind the farmhouse. I had instant recall of the sound of the hand-cranked corncob stripper, the kindling popping in the wood stove in the kitchen, picking bugs from the spinach plants in the garden, collecting doodlebugs in the warm sandy soil under the porch, and my grandmother's homemade pies—especially rhubarb. I could even see, floating in front of me, the bent nail on which my grandfather hung his hat by the kitchen door.

Memories of fishing off an old dock in a mountain pond behind my aunt and uncle's cabin in Franklin, North Carolina, jumped into sparkling clarity: the long, tall timbers that supported the rear room 25 feet up the slope; me, sitting on the dock, holding a small stick with a couple of yards of white cotton string and a safety pin for a hook. I spent a lot of time feeding small balls of bread dough to the tiny fish I now know as bream, until I fell asleep. When I had woken up, they were cooking fish in the kitchen, fish they told me I had caught. (I was four when we visited there the first time, so I believed them.)

At one point I remember being given a small plastic shovel, a hoe, and a rake. They told me to go out and dig for gold along the circular drive in the front of the cabin. (Unfortunately, I have no recall of finding any.)

There were other images and feelings, not quite so comforting. I remember being less than four years of age and being forcefully held down and tied by my ankles and wrists, spread-eagle on my back, while faceless beings with large eyes operated on me. The pain was incredible and indescribable. I remember screaming until I blacked out, then awakening to find them still working on me, and screaming again to unconsciousness. I woke up in a box, very much like a cage. There were bars all around me and heavy netting was stretched across the top. I could pull myself up, but was unable to break out. My legs were wobbly and weak, I hurt terribly, my small body awash with pain, and I screamed until I was too hoarse to scream any longer. Beyond that the images fade.

Of course, I didn't speak of these images to my aunt. They were too disturbing, too terrifying to contemplate. I tried to rebury them, but was unable to do so. Those images haunted me for years. I would have repetitive nightmares in which I was reliving those images and memories. Huge entities, wearing one-piece suits, with no faces and large eyes, would come in the night and take me screaming to a brightly lit room, where I would be secured spread-eagle on my back. Large nails would be driven into my arms, then I could feel the excruciating pain. My body would be awash with it until I blacked out in my dream, or awoke from the recurring nightmare soaked in sweat.

It wasn't until I returned from my first tour to Southeast Asia that I finally brought it up with my parents. My mother was shocked. She said the doctors had promised her that I would never have recall of the experience because I was far too young when it happened. She then related the events surrounding major surgery I had had when I was less than four years of age. It was corrective surgery, a result of being born more than two months premature.

When I came into the world, I weighed in at around a pound and twelve ounces, while my twin, Margaret, tipped the scales at a pound and a half. Back in January of 1946 we were not supposed to survive. If it were not for the heroic efforts of our family doctor, Robert Mayer, we probably would not have. In any event, I ended up needing surgery. Back then there apparently were questions in the minds of some doctors regarding how much pain medication should be given to such a tiny child. The consensus was, far better too little than too much. The belief was that really young children would never remember the experience anyway. Well, guess what? They were wrong.

The immediate effect of these recalled memories was terrifying, mystifying, as well as mind-expanding. Before long, I was recalling whole periods and events. I found that I was also linking the events I was remembering to their long-term effects, events occurring at ages when I was too young to understand, or too young to know.

Was this an effect of reevaluating memories with an adolescent mind? Or was this psychic knowing kicking in early? Back then I didn't know anything about psychic functioning. I only knew that I was having large amounts of recall, some good and some bad. So, I shared it with the only person I could wholly trust, my twin.

My mother was a complex person. Originally she wouldn't touch alcohol. I could see from a very early age that she understood the effects that alcohol had on a person, and she was determined to protect her children from it. She was also extremely intelligent. A straight-A student throughout high school, she should have gone to college and become a teacher or pursued a career in the humanities. She had so much natural talent with art and literature, and in the early years so enjoyed music. All through high school she was a majorette, and was very involved in music and the arts. I still have all of her state merit and honor roll pins for writing and dissertation. I thank her for whatever smarts or natural abilities I was born with.

Anyone who knew her would tell you that her only problem in life was falling deeply in love with my father. She had just turned eighteen, and my father was 27 when they married. He met her at Burdines Department Store in Miami, where he worked in the furniture department. They met one Christmas season while she was working part-time as a gift-wrapper. They fell passionately in love and were married almost immediately. As a result, my sister and I arrived within a year.

As a new mother, she was terrified. I think she realized too late that she was never going to be able to change my father. Because he lacked a formal education and was an alcoholic, he was never going to do any better than he had already done—stock clerk in a department store. There is nothing wrong with that, except that it guaranteed a permanent minimal income, living in "the projects" (what most call slums), and ugly battles over booze. I believe it was in the middle of this realization that she suddenly found herself a brand-new mother of twins.

For years I truly hated my mother. I hated her for her relentless and dogged pursuit of discipline and control, and for her overly protective attitude. She watched me and my twin like a mother panther watches her young. As a result, she was always tougher on us than she would have been with a stranger's child.

Being young, with no understanding of what was really going on, I couldn't see the fear in her eyes every time my sister or I went out in the yard to play. Five-year-olds have little appreciation for the dangers associated with growing up in a slum. The metal framework in the duplex windows was designed to prevent easy access to our bedrooms. Those invulnerable barred windows and the heavy door bolts and crossbars at the points of entry to our abode were meaningless to me. I thought everyone lived that way.

Living in a hovel has its privileges. The poor don't call the bug exterminators, so our home was always filled with Florida roaches. I viewed these large palmetto bugs—three to four inches long and capable of self-powered flight—as simply an irritant. If they walked across your mouth while you were sleeping, it might wake you, or it might not. The trick was learning to sleep with your mouth closed.

We also had what we called swamp rats. They weighed in at an average two pounds plus, and traveled in and out of the street gutters facing the house. They looked a lot like small, narrow-hipped groundhogs. As a kid who was usually hungry, I always thought they'd probably make a great meal. While somewhat ugly, these were simply troublesome pests, something you just dealt with. We kept a broomstick in a corner by the front door. I didn't know it at the time, but that was why most people living in the projects didn't have cats for pets: The hunter could become the hunted. If they had dogs, they were big and nasty, capable of defending themselves. Of course my mother always viewed these rodents as a direct threat to her young. I didn't know about rabies at the time, or any of the other diseases they carried.

There were other problems. At five years of age, I couldn't equate the cast on her arm to her unsuccessful defense of a week's food money from a drug-addicted street bum. How could I fathom that she lived in terror for herself, and must have worried about us? This was far beyond my ken at such an early age.

So, when I disappeared from the front porch for twenty minutes, struck up a conversation with a stranger, or chased my ball into the street, there was no way I could comprehend the rage it would seemingly generate within her. There was no way I could see that it was really love buried within fear that drove her to punishment.

Sometimes her fears, further aggravated by my lack of comprehension for why she might be demanding a certain behavior from me, would only fuel the fires within her. Early on, this resulted in severe spankings across the buttocks with either her hand or a long-handled hairbrush. Later, when I was larger, harder to handle, and seemingly more callused or unaffected by her early choice of tools, she upgraded to a belt, and quickly from there to an open-handed strike across the face. It must have hurt her more than it did me, as she quickly switched to a backhand. I remember as a teen being struck so hard and so many times that I had ringing in my ears and my nose or my lips would bleed. It's odd that I can't seem to remember the offense that resulted in such abuse.

In any event, I learned that the best way to deal with it was to stand there and stoically take it. I mistakenly thought that by not crying or reacting in an overt way, I was demonstrating my ability to "take it like a man." In fact, my lack of reaction only generated a greater sense of fear, which increased her internal conflict, resulting in more frequent and more violent strikes. Our relationship quickly went from one of love to one of a contest as to who could dominate the other through sheer force of will. She may have had the muscle and the size, but I quickly developed an ability to read her.

Herein is where I discovered the birth of my natural ability as a psychic. I believe, as steel is forged in fire, my ability to read humans was forged in pain as a child.[1] Over the years, I began to display an almost uncanny ability to read my mother's actions long before even she knew what she was going to do. In hindsight, I'd have to say it was the natural evolution of a survival skill.

Some may feel that I am betraying my mother by writing this. But what I am reporting has nothing to do with how much I loved or didn't love my mother. It has everything to do with understanding what drove her, and hence what might have driven me. It is terribly difficult to understand where someone's psychic behavior might have bubbled from, so I offer this history as a possible origin.

My sister Margaret and I were twins in every sense of the word. She seemed to always know what was on my mind as I did hers. She, of course, being female, was always just a bit more mature than I was at just about any age. But she wasn't having the degree of detail in recall I was having. So, we talked about it. Sometimes, on what we considered "bad nights," we would talk into the wee hours of the morning. It was the way we kept our sanity.

Sanity was a premium around our house at times, a direct result of parents that were at best emotionally—and at worse, physically—abusive. They were alcoholics. I am saying this without any rancor whatsoever. It is purely a reflective statement based on fact. It was of course a whole lot more complicated at the time we were experiencing it. My perceptions were certainly quite different as a child. On a really bad night, alcohol reigned, and reason didn't.

---

[1] Since my involvement with PSI research, I have learned that many very psychic people have a history of severe abuse, especially during childhood. So, I believe it could be that psychic development can be generated out of a need to survive, or is a natural and unconscious development that stems from the ability to disassociate during an uncontrollable or unavoidable situation, or perhaps during repetitive abuse.

I recall many nights as an early teen, lying in bed and praying for something to happen, for some stranger to come along and adopt me and my sister, and take us away to live somewhere else. Anywhere would have been nice, anywhere but there. To my child's mind, even a stranger would have been preferable to my parents.

I've long since grown out of that desire, and in retrospect I can see how pressures suffered at the early age of thirteen or fourteen can be dramatically different from those we endure in later adulthood. We are better armed to deal with them at a later age. But, back then it seemed more than just a reasonable request. If parents truly understood the stress they bring into their children's lives, they wouldn't be so "flip" in some of their responses. If they knew how it could drive their kids to even accepting a stranger in preference to them, well . . . best to not go there.

On really bad nights, my sister Margaret always took it much worse than I did. Being a male provided some degree of protection that females don't automatically get in the American culture. In America, it is assumed that males are tougher by nature—males usually don't reflect the intense and internalized damage that is done when struck violently across the face with the back of an adult's hand. Nor do we react the same to a belt across the backs of the legs as a small female would.

I am talking about my mother, not my father. I'm not sure if it was the alcohol or the differences in their relationship, but the child-to-parent connections within our household differed significantly from what one might normally expect.

My father was always a gentleman, given only to very short fits of incoherent rage when numbingly drunk. His own father had left him when he was in seventh grade—sometime around 1925. Since he was the oldest, he felt responsible for his mother, brothers, and sister, and quit school to become the man of the house, the primary wage earner. His situation was somewhat complicated as a child, because he had polio and wore braces on his legs. I was never convinced that he actually quit school because the family required support. It might have been because he was tired of being called a cripple or "The Crip." In any event, that's what he told me once while he was warmly enveloped in a refined cloud of bourbon vapor.

He did numerous jobs, but the one he truly liked the best was being a caddy at the Palm Beach and Miami country clubs. I think he liked carrying the golf bags for the gangsters who frequented the

South during the winter months. He said, "They were never threatened by a young kid with braces on his legs, who could keep his mouth shut."

I never pointed out the "playing with fire" aspects of his comfortable involvement with gangsters. He always left me with the impression that he felt his lack of formal education didn't allow equal opportunities when it came to employment. This is somewhat stunted logic in my own mind.

My father once told me about being on the fourteenth green at Palm Beach with Al Capone and a couple of his men, probably his bodyguards, when they suddenly heard the sound of a car coming up the lawn. As it approached, the engine began backfiring. Everyone dove into the sand traps, pulling guns out of their golf bags.

I laughed.

He didn't. He never smiled. Continuing his story, he told me how a year later they machine-gunned someone to death on the next green over. Whether it was true or not was never material, at least not to me. My father discovered early on that he could make a lot of money carrying gangsters' golf bags.

My dad also made a lot of money making bets with hoods. He would bet that he could outdrive them off the tee. Now, he never weighed more than 145 pounds soaking wet—the result of having only half the normal muscle mass in his legs. And, everyone who's a golfer knows that distance off the tee is almost always attributed to weight shift in the hips and legs. But my dad had enormous strength in his upper body from hauling his leg braces around. Also, they didn't know that my dad spent almost all his spare time on the driving range hitting free balls. As a result of his betting, he was driving his own car by age sixteen, and carrying a flask full of booze in his hip pocket. During the early 1930s, he was walking around with a wad of twenty-dollar bills jammed in his pocket, which was very unusual—especially for someone his age.

Somewhere in that period, he decided to throw his leg braces away—a mistake he paid for dearly later in life. It resulted in significant deformity to his left foot, which was causing him almost unbearable pain by the time I was in my teens. This was the primary cause for his alcoholic stupors. He was always lost in his own vapor cloud before sundown, especially after work on weekdays, and beginning with sunrise on most weekends.

Whenever I feel like I'm having a hard time, I think about my dad, and his lifetime.

Over the years I've come to understand that one of the greatest reasons for alcoholism in the poor is the use of booze for self-medication. As a nation, we cannot continue to ignore the need for free medical support to the poor and expect them to not fall as victims to alcohol and illegal drugs. It's a vicious cycle with a very simple remedy. I watched my dad destroy himself and those around him with that cycle, and I've seen other good people fall victim as well.

There were good days, too. I remember when I was nine, when we lived in the Miami projects. They were old government duplexes built after the war, located just off of 79th Street and NW 2nd Avenue, an area they now call Little Haiti. One night, my dad brought a stranger home with him. Dad had been working a second job over on Miami Beach, where he had met the man, and one evening he decided to invite him home to share a meal with us.

The stranger was a short, heavyset man with dark hair. When I first saw him, I immediately felt sorry for him. I remember looking at his face and wondering where he had gotten all the scars. His nose was only a suggestion of what it had been—it was sort of just flattened in place. His ears were really ugly, covered with hardened lumps of scar tissue. He would have been a frightful fellow, except for his very kind and giving nature. He was as gentle and loving as any human I've ever met. When we first met, he got down on his knee and looked me directly in the eyes, and spoke very softly to me. He treated me with a great deal of respect, something I wasn't used to as a very young child. He left me with an impression of incredible strength and surety; he had an innate confidence and there was a genuine core of kindness in him. The stranger was introduced to me as Rocco Francis Marchegiano. Of course, back then he was known to many as "The Brockton Blockbuster," and most of the world knew him as Rocky Marciano—the undefeated world heavyweight champion boxer.[2]

What I didn't know at the time was my dad was working parttime as his sparring partner over on the beach where he was training. Over spaghetti and meat sauce in our kitchen, Mr. Marchegiano told me that my Dad was a small man, but he was quick and could take it as well as dish it out. I didn't understand what he meant at the time. I didn't understand what boxing was.

---

[2] I was eight years old at the time. Rocky Marciano was 29 and had won his heavyweight championship two years earlier by knocking out Joe Walcott in the thirteenth round, on September 23, 1952, in Philadelphia.

Despite his size and weight, and obvious problems with his legs, my dad was an excellent fighter. (This was something I didn't find out about until much later.) Most who knew my father always commented on how gentle and quiet he was. I suppose that comes with being confident that you can take care of yourself. Long after I joined the Army he finally admitted to bare-knuckle fighting for money in some of the back parking lots of the projects on Saturday nights. It was a secret he kept from a lot of people. I'm not sure he won all his fights, but I seldom saw him with a black eye or cut lip. But I can't say the same for the condition of his hands. Later in my life, it began to make sense to me.

I remember once when I was about ten years old a couple of the local gang members beat the hell out of me. I came home with a broken nose, my eyes blackened, swollen, and filled with tears. My dad refused to let me into the kitchen, blocking the screen door with his body. Looking down at me, in a stern voice he said, "Come back when you have blood on your knuckles, then I'll let you in." This was followed by him slamming and locking the inner door.

It took me almost an hour to find one of the kids who had jumped me. I came up on him from the rear, his blind side, and just piled on. I pounded on him till I was out of breath. I returned home with the blood on my knuckles. My father let me in. While treating my wounds in the bathroom, he told me: "It's not about winning or losing. It's only important that you stand up to them. If they get hurt whenever they pick on you, they'll stop." As distressed as I was that night, I found out that he was right. From that point on, I never backed down from a fight. The number of fights I got into seemed to mysteriously slow in numbers, eventually stopping altogether.

The man who made almost as great an impact on me as my father was my dad's brother, William Thomas McMoneagle. Because of his hair color, to me he was Uncle Red. He served in the Navy during the big war—WWII—piloting the landing craft that put the Marines ashore. My dad told me on one run his small boat took a direct hit from a shore battery and went down without reaching the beach. Uncle Red crawled ashore with the survivors and spent quite a bit of time in the jungles before being evacuated to some place in Borneo. I once saw a black-and-white photo of him standing between two very dark Borneo women, both more than four hundred pounds, with bones through their noses, and wearing woven grass. It was the kind of picture that went way beyond anything your imagination could produce.

I always thought he was "different" in a strange kind of way, but could never put my finger on why I felt that was so. After serving in Southeast Asia, I understood those differences.

He was hypervigilant, prone to sudden and extravagant expenditures, and almost obsessive about having enough food. On Sundays, he would barbeque three or four chickens with all the trimmings and open up his house to family and neighbors. He had a heart as big as the ocean and was kind to everyone he met, although to a casual stranger he might have appeared loud and angry most of the time, even belligerent. He always seemed to live as though he might die at any moment.

Later, when I joined the Army, he pulled me aside and told me to never trust in luck. He told me to listen to my gut, pay attention to the little voice I had buried down in there, and to never doubt its authenticity. He also told me if I wasn't sure if I should shoot or not, shoot first, shoot to kill, and sort it out later. I can still remember the look in his eyes when he told me that. It was like looking straight into the eyes of a tiger about to kill its lunch.

My second sister, Mary, was born a few months before my eighth birthday, a few months before I met Mr. Marchegiano. Today I could never express the love I carry in my heart for my sisters, but back then I felt that her birthday was the worst day of my life. At the time, the only thing good about it was the fact that I got to spend more time with my father while my mother was in the hospital, and I wasn't being controlled. When she returned home, carrying Mary in her arms, I climbed the tree in our backyard and told everyone that I would not come down until they gave my sister Mary back to the doctors. I sat huddled high in the tree for hours, until finally darkness closed in around me. Eventually hunger and the dragonfly-sized Florida mosquitoes changed my mind. I figured I could live with "it" being in the house, as long as I didn't have to look at "it." If I had known then how the next three years would eventually turn out, I probably would have left home.

To put it succinctly, in her first few years, my sweet little sister Mary was a major screamer. She screamed for her bottle when she was hungry. She screamed to have her diaper changed when she was wet. She screamed to be picked up whenever she saw another human. But for some strange reason, whenever she saw me, she'd suddenly stop. So it was a no-brainer as far as the rest of the family was concerned: Mary and I got to spend a lot of time together. Wherever I went, Mary went. She became a permanent fixture riding on my hip. As a boy in a tough neighborhood, that meant I had to be a whole lot tougher to get by with it. In retrospect, I'm now sure that Mary never opened her eyes until she got home from the hospital. When she did, like a newborn little bird, the first thing she saw she imprinted on—and it happened to be me.

Mary had an almost insatiable curiosity. Whatever I was doing, she would bury her nose in it. Margaret was my actual twin sister, my other half, my companion child, whatever—but Mary was my shadow, always right there in my face.

In truth, Margaret *acted* much more the shadow. Of all the people I've ever known, she was the most intelligent. She never had her IQ formally measured, but had it been, my bet is they would have found it to be somewhere in the 150s. Whatever I didn't know—and that was a lot—she did. By age seven, she was reading books out of the teen area of the local library, something my mother actually encouraged. Before she was twelve, she was designing, cutting, and sewing her own clothing, a relief to my mother, who made almost everything we wore.

Psychically she was far more gifted than I. We used to discuss visions of a secret world within our own. But we always kept these discussions to ourselves. She almost never spoke in front of my parents, or any other adult. She'd always stand in the shadows and observe.

From day one, she was my mother's favorite. Always obedient, always one step ahead of everyone else, always doing the right thing, and never a problem. I couldn't see it at the time, but she was absolutely, perfectly tuned to her entire environment, something one can only do paranormally. The down side, of course, is that in being that way you quickly lose your identity.

From the very beginning there were two Margarets: the one everyone experienced and the real one, the one I alone knew about. We were connected spiritually, emotionally, and in many cases mentally. When she hurt, I hurt. When she laughed, I laughed. And we didn't have to be together to do the sharing.

We shared our deepest secrets with one another. Some of these secrets I cautioned her to never reveal to others, especially adults. I intuitively knew that some of these secrets would frighten people into actions we would both regret. People don't want their child walking around telling others they can see people no one else can see, can converse and interact with them, or can have those invisible friends tell when things are going to happen before they actually do. Margaret told me about these experiences. I on the other hand would only tell her about a small rabbit that would come in the night to comfort me when I felt alone or afraid. The point being, I understood that these were serious secrets between siblings and not something adults should hear.

Unfortunately, Margaret was unable to live with those secrets cooped up inside her. Around our twelfth birthday, she began her quiet revolt against parents, church, and society at large . . . but more on that later.

My mother converted to the Catholic religion when I was eight. I now believe this sudden change was predicated by a number of major events in her life.

First, she was severely maltreated (at least emotionally) by her own brothers and sisters. This was not really clear to me. I didn't realize until much later that her entire side of the family had an intense dislike for my father. I suppose it was primarily because of his alcoholism and his inability to improve the family situation financially. These were viewed as weaknesses, and rightly so, but should not have been a cause for cutting her off emotionally. The fact that all of my relatives were Methodist and my father was Catholic probably only added gasoline to the fire. I believe that this smoldering dislike for my father always weighed heavily on my mother. As children we were blind to the effects this was having on our mother, but it was certainly felt energetically.

Second, our mother recognized that if she were going to provide the best education she could for her children, she was going to have to get us out of the state-run neighborhood school that sat next to the projects, and into the closest Catholic school, which was miles away from the poverty-stricken area in which we lived.

Saint Mary's Catholic School sat adjacent to the site for the newly planned Miami Cathedral, and was located well outside the slum area in which we lived. St. Mary's parish would also make deals for those who couldn't afford to pay tuition, by having the kids work around the school or church after hours.

For me the change of schools was really aggravating. I was suddenly forced to walk more than a mile to school each day, going and coming, and later had to act as escort and protector for my little sisters. That may not sound like much, but believe me, it was a major pain in the ass. For example, Mary would sometimes walk the entire distance with her eyes squeezed shut, simply so I'd be forced to hold her hand. Of course this was a total embarrassment for me with all the guys in the neighborhood we had to walk through. To this day, she still claims this was because her eyes were sensitive to the sun, which was in our face both going to school and coming home. She is sincerely definite about this claim and it remains unarguable, but *I* still think it was because she got to hold my hand. In any event, I no longer view it as having been a pain in the ass. (I guess I've matured since then.)

Like Margaret, I've always thought of our sister Mary as being a lot smarter than I ever was, mostly because whenever Mary decided to pull the wool over my eyes or shine me on with something, it always seemed to work.

My third sister, Elizabeth, was "the good child." In every family there is a child who can do no wrong. That was Beth. She was always smiling and always glued to my father's side. She learned one of those basic family truths while still wobbling around the house in diapers—if you control the alpha male in the family you control everything. Why she gravitated so quickly to my father's side, I don't know. I do know that she and Dad had a bond that was unique. For some reason, the glue in their relationship just set up that way.

One of my fondest memories of Beth was watching her enter a room as a tiny child. She always reminded me of a small fawn gently tiptoeing into a clearing. In fact, for years, when barefoot she'd only walk on her toes. She'd tiptoe into the room with her large eyes scanning everything, and always seemed to be in control of her decision to stay or not stay, participate or not participate, depending on her mood.

Beth always sat within reach of Dad. He'd move, and she'd move right along with him. I think for her, he was always a sense of protection. She shared his field of energy. It's true also that this was very good protection against Mother. By the time Beth was born, our mother had given up fighting my father's alcoholism and had joined him at the bottle. As a result, there were bottles hidden throughout the house. They even hid them from each other.

I always worried about Beth's vulnerability. But in later years she showed me what true strength was all about. She married very young, as my mother had, but missed all the minefields my mother didn't. I remember first meeting her husband-to-be—long hair in the latter sixties, a sure sign of "instability." Yet Jimmy is still her husband today. A more solid bond would be difficult to find. She has raised a fine family of kids and has always been there for them. She may appear soft and is certainly a gentle soul, but she is also a rock, much like one you'd find only in a much older and wiser foundation.

My mother did eventually fall in the battle against the bottle. In the beginning of such an environment, my youngest sister, Kathleen, was born. Kathy was very small and very independent. She was also very much the tomboy. She did extremely well in track and field, and to just about everyone's dismay (and usual panic) was always demonstrating her acrobatic skills in the overly congested living room, doing maneuvers like reverse somersaults over the glass coffee table on the faux marble floor. She was also probably the toughest of my sisters. Not many knew that from an early age Kathy always carried a straight razor. I had no idea, until she showed it to me once after I returned from my first overseas tour. Would she or could she use it? Yes, in all probability, I believe she would have. Where did she learn to do that? Well, unfortunately it was probably from me. I carried one once as well. In my early teens I hung out with a couple of guys, spending a great deal of time on the streets. The guy I hung out the most with advised me to carry a straight razor for protection, so I did. He said no one would ever stand up to a person with a straight razor.

This young man had a severely abusive father who would use his fists as punishment for the smallest infractions. My friend was really quick and could usually avoid him, but he was trapped in his room one night and had nowhere to run. He pulled the razor on his own father in a desperate act of self-defense. His major mistake was not being able to use it. He spent about a week in the hospital and was really messed up. I learned from that incident that if you carry a weapon and pull it, you'd better be ready to use it. If you know you can't use it, don't carry it. I pitched my razor in a dumpster and only carried steel knuckles in my jacket pocket. Those I had no problem using.

It took a while, but my violent tendencies finally caught up with me. My sister Margaret came home from school one afternoon with her blouse badly ripped. She finally told me that one of the local gangs had molested her. Without going into an absolute rage, I quietly pulled my size 33 Mickey Mantle hardball bat from my closet and set off across the neighborhood to the gang leader's apartment building. I rang his doorbell and, when he opened the inner door, I swung the bat through the screen door. What probably saved his life was the decorative ironwork in front of the screen. I left him unconscious and caught two more members of the gang before the police caught me. One minute I was standing there with a bat in my hand and the next I was flat on my back in the parking lot seeing stars, looking up at a very large policeman.

The cop who disarmed me was an ex-Marine, an all-Okinawa jujitsu champion, who, thank God, also had a sister. In exchange for not being arrested and charged, I had to agree to start taking martial arts classes from him. I agreed because it sounded really cool. But as he started my instruction, he started me on my way to understanding open-hand defense and what a warrior's code of honor meant. I quickly learned that because you *can* do something doesn't always mean you *should*. It sometimes takes more courage to walk away than to make a bad situation worse.

I took to the training like a duck takes to water. It was the kind of training I always wished existed for my sisters as well. Now young girls are encouraged to pursue that sort of training. Then, they weren't.

Our parents' drunkenness had numerous effects on us kids. When only one parent was drunk, the other was always angry and was someone we avoided at any cost. There were a few times when they were both sober, which were pleasant and enjoyable. However, it was the easiest when they were both drunk together. During those times, we were pretty much on our own and could go anywhere or do almost anything we wanted.

Being on our own meant having to provide our own food and clothing, caring for each other when we were sick, and—during the short time that I was home while my sisters were growing up—providing what protection I could within the neighborhood. None of this was an easy task, at least from my point of view, and most of the time it left me depressed, exhausted, angry, and enraged with life in general. Somehow we managed. Because I was male, I always felt that my sisters had it harder, and there was very little that I could do about that. I sometimes felt helpless about what they were experiencing and have always felt like they deserved better. While I know this is a product of finding myself in a part-time parental role, it is nevertheless difficult to shake. And to be perfectly honest, I'm not sure I really want to.

High school was probably the hardest time of my life. Entering my teen years, I was not prepared for what happens at that age, either hormonally or emotionally. Neither was my sister Margaret.

One day, Margaret suddenly and unexplainably decided that the visions we shared within our secret world of knowing were something she should be sharing with others. Since it included what some might consider strange, this was a major mistake. (I had to beg her not to say anything about my imaginary rabbit friend, from whom I derived comfort.) It immediately resulted in an appointment with a psychiatrist, followed by other appointments, and the eventual prescription for drugs to control what they called "her delusional mental state." The doctor said it would help to shut out her visions, and that all-invasive *knowing* that she proclaimed. The situation worsened for her around the end of the tenth grade when they discovered she was pregnant.

I knew who the father was, because she told me. But, because she asked me not to tell, I never shared the information with anyone else. I won't share it today. Who he was isn't really material now. What was important and should have been noticed back then, was the fact that she needed an outside source for her self-esteem.

When our parents found out, they sent her away to live with our mother's sister, who lived in Baltimore. My twin lived there until she gave birth, at which point they forcibly took her baby away and put it up for adoption. This was the last straw for Margaret. After the pressure on her, the inappropriate responses from others, the years of serious antipsychotic drugs, and the taking away of her child, she collapsed. At that point she really did need to be hospitalized for a mental condition. The way she was treated, at least from my point of view, was cruel, unjust, and unusual punishment. From that point on, she was continually running away or spending time in one facility or another.

My mother told me they were locking her up for her own protection, because she was seriously mentally ill. I, of course, never believed this. In my own mind, it was because they couldn't control her. But then, from the time she was a little child, Margaret was never under anyone's control.

Many years later, Margaret told me they first diagnosed her as bipolar, which resulted in her taking some very powerful medications, most of which she said only made her condition worse. Whether she was or not isn't really material to me. I just know that over the years I watched the light in my sister's eyes slowly dim until it eventually went out. My heart aches for the years of loneliness and despair I know she suffered, and even now when I think about it, I become enraged by some people's views of psychiatry.

In retrospect, she probably did have a biochemical imbalance that needed some form of medication to help keep her centered. But back then, it was a new science and no one really knew what that meant. I wish she could have had the benefit of today's sophisticated medicines and the more enlightened counseling that's available. It would have been a completely different story and ending. I think it's one of the reasons I've always had a very soft spot in my nature for those who suffer mentally.

As I've already said, my years in high school were not good. Attending high school at Archbishop Curley, an all-boy school in Miami, was difficult. Our family had moved again, this time to the outer edges of Opalocka City. It was a brand-new project for the poor, the city's way of cleaning up the inner-city areas—and providing real estate to businesses needing space. The new project was built in the extreme northwest of the city, about thirty miles north of downtown Miami. It was different from the other places I had lived, mostly because it was new. Until then I didn't know you could live in a "new slum." It was way out on the very edge of town, backing onto what was then swamp.

There weren't many gang symbols spray-painted on the walls yet, and all the outside lights still worked, but it made for a long commute to school every day—a little less than twenty miles in one direction. There was only one other kid, Frank, who lived as far away from school as I did. On most days, he would pick me up on his motorcycle and we'd meet up with the other guys we hung with at what we called the "Corner." It was a small gas station on the corner across from the all-girls school, Notre Dame, which was our sister school. The station didn't open until school started, so we could hang out there and exchange love letters, do a little smooching (that's kissing, for my younger readers), and smoke cigarettes unhindered.

We'd spend a lot of time talking and socializing with our girl-friends till their first class bell. I was usually acting as a courier—that is, carrier of messages from other guys to their girls or vice versa. (I didn't have a steady girlfriend until much later in my high school years.) Hanging out at the corner gave me time to sneak in a few cigarettes before my first class.

It was actually a Catholic priest who got me started smoking. I was 15, running errands at the parish rectory one Saturday to work off some of my tuition, when Father Neil came in and threw a carton of cigarettes at me. They were unfiltered Chesterfields. I asked him what he wanted me to do with them. His response was "Smoke 'em. That's what men do." So I learned, erroneously, that cool men smoked. I took up smoking because I thought it made me look cool. I didn't understand at the time cool was living your own mind. Now I wish I hadn't.

Father Neil also loaned me his car for dates in my junior and senior years. He'd throw me the keys on Saturday night and ask me to please bring it back with as little sin on the backseat as possible. He was an intimidating kind of guy. I mean, who'd mess around on the backseat of a priest's car?

The nuns of Notre Dame must have known about us guys meeting their girls out on the corner, even though we were just out of sight of the school. They always rang their first bell about ten minutes before our own, which gave us just the right amount of time to get to our homerooms six blocks down the road.

On afternoons and mornings when Frank didn't show up, I was forced to get myself to and from school any way I could. Sometimes I'd hitch a ride to a bus stop ten miles farther south with the man who picked my dad up for work. He drove an old Ford and smoked a pipe. He was always leaning forward and stuffing his pipe or messing with it in heavy traffic, while driving with his elbows. More than once I left nail prints on his dash when he was slamming on the brakes to avoid a rear-ender on the newly finished freeway. No one else would ride in the front seat for that reason.

I had sworn an oath to my parents that I wouldn't hitchhike, but that's about the only way I could make it to school on time. In hindsight, I have to say this was probably the dumbest thing I've ever done. For four years, I caught rides from total strangers, sometimes after dark, always in the worst possible parts of town. That's probably where I first started to hone my psychic abilities. I relied purely on instinct when deciding whether or not I should get into a car that would stop to pick me up. If I got a certain feeling deep in the pit of my stomach, I'd wave them off and back away from the car.

But not every system is perfect. At least half a dozen times I didn't follow my own rules and found myself in a situation that could have led to serious trouble. The least problematic of these resulted in a broken bone in my wrist from bailing out of the front seat onto pavement at 45 MPH. I had accepted a ride from a man who seemed at first to be polite and nice. But when he made a sudden turn down a dark street and reached over grabbing at my crotch, I knew it was time to bail. After that, I always climbed into a car carrying a Coca-Cola, or nursing a cup of hot coffee.

The judo and jujitsu I was learning from my cop/ex-Marine friend was worth it. The solution to many of my problems grew out of my increasing familiarity with the martial arts. My friend taught me how to apply it on the street. Combining what I learned from him about self-defense with my growing natural instinct for smelling out trouble before it began, my problems seemed to fade. There is also a confidence that is bred from knowledge, and I'm sure body language played a great deal in addressing any potential problem. If you study animals you can see it in the subtle way they change their posture. Like in cats, a slight alteration in their stance shouts loudly to other cats—don't mess with me.

My high school years weren't very exciting. My twin essentially disappeared from my life. No one would even tell me where she was after they had sent her up to Baltimore to have her baby. I suppose they felt they were protecting me in some way. I instinctively knew something was wrong, but just couldn't quite figure it out on my own. After that, with her hospitalizations and supposedly protective incarcerations, her whereabouts became a state secret.

As I got older, I was beginning to understand the rage my mother had within her. It didn't make the abuse right, but did explain it. My father had deteriorated to the point that I really wasn't sure he was even going to survive. I have no memory of him sober during my high school years. He was usually half in the bag by the time he got home in the evening and he always passed out very soon after dinner, which meant he was unconscious when I got home.

My mother was beginning to suffer from thyroid, liver, and kidney problems (a result of alcohol, I'm sure). She also had a heart problem, but kept it hidden from everyone. I could tell that her health was deteriorating by the way she cooked our meals. Things were either undercooked or burned to a crisp. No in-between. And because so much money was going out for booze, the meals were barely enough for two adults, never mind my three sisters, and me. So I actually stopped eating at home. I'd do odd jobs at a couple of local restaurants in exchange for a meal, or would wash a car or two for food money.

I wish I could say that my social life was like everyone else's in my high school years, but it wasn't. I was always the kid that came from "those projects." I kissed my first girlfriend through a screen door on my eleventh birthday—her name was Theresa Lammington, and she was also a twin. Her brother's name was Bruno. They were from the French-speaking area of Quebec, in Canada, and neither could speak English very well. I think her language was the primary turn-on for me at the time. That sexy French accent, well . . . you know what I mean. But then, what does an eleven-year-old know? I remember she had very soft lips and dark eyes, and something turned over in my stomach whenever I was close to her. That was a long time ago, but it's something you just don't forget.

My first passionate love affair was in eighth grade, with a dark-haired little vixen named Ann, whose last name I can no longer recall. She actually let me undress her in the backseat of an empty station wagon. Of course what's good for the gander is good for the goose, but nothing ever really happened beyond satisfying our very young curiosity about what the other sex might look like sans clothing. We went steady for about six months, and I got to exchange sodas and ice cream for a soft warm kiss on occasion, which seemed a fair trade for exposing ourselves to one another at such an early age. I stopped seeing her when her stepfather threatened me. I knew in my heart that he was probably abusing her, but there was little I could do about it, as he was nearly six times my size.

After that brief experience with unbridled nudity, I dated dozens of different girls for one reason or another all through high school. I think I dated so many for a lot of reasons. First, I was looking for love. I knew I had little of it in my life, but really didn't know what it should look like in the first place. Secondly, I was intrigued by the opposite sex. They were so completely different, one from the next.

Some of the girls I dated couldn't speak a word of English. One very beautiful girl from Venezuela had long straight blond hair down to her waist and blue eyes that were very pale and looked like cracked marbles. She only spoke Spanish and my Spanish really sucked. Her grandmother always went on the dates with us, and her English was passable. We'd walk hand-in-hand to a movie, with her grandmother always strolling along ten paces behind.

I also double-dated with a guy who must have been seeing Al Capone's granddaughter. What nights those were! Driving around town with one large black limo to the front of us and another one to the rear—each carrying two huge guys with dark hats. I always thought the guy had a lot of *cojones* to be necking with some Mafioso's granddaughter under the watchful eyes of "The Hulk" and his brothers. The shadows never spoke, never interfered, and were never more than ten feet away.

I met my first serious love purely by accident. My buddies talked me into going to a dance at one of the other Catholic high schools. The dance was sponsored by a local chapter of the CYO (Catholic Youth Organization). I saw her standing across the dance floor when I first walked in, and I knew she was the one for me. The fact that I was only fifteen didn't seem to matter. I didn't let the fact that I had never learned to dance stand in my way either. Her name was Arlene Jackman. We went steady for nearly two years, then I went by her house one Saturday morning and her father told me that she had eloped with another guy she had been seeing for some time. I was absolutely crushed. I never saw it coming. So much for being psychic, I guess. I have since learned that you can be psychic about almost anything except yourself.

In revenge, I skipped around from girl to girl for nearly six months, then fell passionately in love a second time with a young lady named Marcia Benedict. She occupied nearly my entire senior year. But as much as I loved her, it was hard being with her. If you can imagine two people totally from opposite sides of a street in all ways—we were certainly those two people. We fought like cats and dogs over the dumbest things, but we also loved each other deeply. It gave me even more insight into the relationship that existed between my mother and father, at least at the outset of their lives together. Being a lot older and wiser now, I know that none of these relationships could have worked out. The kind of love I was searching for then was not the kind they were capable of giving. They were safe harbors in a time of need, and for that I am eternally grateful. Real love was a lifetime away and beyond my comprehension then.

Marcia's father was always noncommittal, but her mother was into subtle sabotage. I was fine with her until I arrived one Saturday evening to take Marcia to a drive-in movie. By then I was driving a 1952 Ford I had bought from a junk dealer and had fixed up. Marcia's mother was standing next to the car saying what mothers do when their daughters are going out on a date, "be careful, be home early," etc., when I started the engine to leave. As women do when wearing a short skirt, Marcia put her feet against the car floor and pushed to pull her skirt down further, and the entire front seat suddenly flipped over backward, forming what I'm sure looked like a perfect bed. I tried to explain that I had repaired the front seat with a bad bolt, which fell on deaf ears. From that point on, her mom always seemed to be in the way. It was really tough to have a private moment. The good part was getting to drive her mother's car to the movies all the time. It was a brand-new Thunderbird with bucket seats.

I finally graduated in June of 1964 with two partial scholarships to universities. I eventually chose the one closest to home—the University of Miami—simply because I couldn't afford an apartment.

"What a zoo!" Those were my first words on sitting down in my orientation class for freshman year. I had a stack of textbooks on the desk in front of me that I had busted my buns for nearly two weeks to pay for. And there I sat, not being able to make out what the professor at the front of the hall was saying. Everyone was shouting and talking to everyone else all at the same time. The professor, apparently oblivious to the commotion going on around him, continued to speak and simultaneously write something on the blackboard that I couldn't see. It looked like he was carrying on a conversation with the air. The last straw was a lanky, thin-boned kid with freckles, dropping an IBM punch card on my desk and telling me to memorize the number on it, that was my student identification number. I realized that, as difficult as high school had been for me, at least there I could see and speak directly to my teacher. I stood up and slid my stack of books over to the kid sitting next to me, and said something like, "Help yourself." Then I walked out. No way could I endure four years of that.

At the same time, I knew that I couldn't go back to my summer job, which had been working in a warehouse unloading boxcars under the beautiful Florida sunshine. I'd have to come up with a better plan.

Chapter Two

From Enlistment through School

I loved Miami, especially in my earlier years. I was in the unique position of being a fifth-generation Miamian. So I knew things about Miami that most didn't at my age. The first house I lived in as a small child was my grandmother's old house, which stood very close to the Miami River. (Where the house was now sits an expressway off ramp.) The exterior wood of the house was weathered a splotchy brown from countless years of neglect and hurricanes. It was the same house her mother and her mother's mother lived in. A two-story structure, it had originally been a saloon and dance hall back in the early 1800s. I remember playing in the front yard, which was filled with old statuary of seminaked women in fanciful Greek costumes. By the time I was playing in the courtyard, the statues had become embedded deeply within the trunks of very old live oaks surrounded by mimosa trees—the trees having encapsulated most of the statues, at least partially.

While living there, I remember my dad reading something in the evening newspaper that noted the population had finally broached 100,000, and saying to my mother with a bit of surprise, "The whole city is going to hell in a handbasket!"

Now here I was a high school graduate, the only one in my graduating class who wasn't going to go to college. An interesting quandary: If not college, then what?

Everyone was subtly aware of the increasing possibility of war in Vietnam. Many who could read the handwriting on the wall were doing what they could to avoid the situation. I didn't really have any serious thoughts about it one way or the other. I don't even recall knowing where Vietnam was on the map.

So, what to do?

Surprisingly, I didn't have long to wait for the answer. It came while standing at a bus stop about a week after I had quit my job. I had approximately half a dollar in my pocket excluding the bus fare. It was most definitely one of those times I made a decision that was totally intuitive.

It was very late, sometime past eleven, and as I stood there, I looked up at the moon. It was one of those sultry Miami moons, not quite full but awash with a deep orange glow—what I've since learned to call a "blood and sand" moon, larger than life.

A small voice in the back of my mind said, "I wonder if that's the way it looks on the other side of the world right now?"

It was at that point I knew that I was going to have to leave home, leave Miami, and even leave Florida. I knew in my heart that I was going to strike out on my own. The bus arrived soon after I made the decision, and I bought a ticket to its last stop.

The last four miles I had to walk in order to get home. In that four-mile walk, with the moon for company, I came up with a number of plans for leaving home. I can now say that most of them were pretty stupid.

If you've ever been to Florida, you'd know initially the hardest obstacle to overcome is just getting out of the state.

Back then, with a 55 MPH speed limit, it took the better part of two days by car. I needed to find a way out of town that would guarantee a quick trip, otherwise I'd probably lose my courage . . . old patterns are the hardest to break.

What I eventually settled on was simple: I'd just sign up for one of the military services. I was eighteen, so I wouldn't need my parents' permission. Vietnam wasn't yet a great concern. Besides, the only people they were sending there were Special Forces, or at least that was the rumor.

Early the next morning, I called a couple of my buddies and we agreed to meet downtown, in Courthouse Square right after lunch. Courthouse Square was the tallest building in Miami at the time and that is where the military recruiting offices were located.

Not surprisingly, the recruiters were all pretty much the same. Any one of them could and would talk the fuzz off a tennis ball. I mean, after all, they'd have to be at least that good if they were going to talk someone into being voluntary cannon fodder. I still had a young mind back then, and couldn't see the forest for the trees. So, I spent nearly half an hour with each recruiter and seriously listened to their pitch. Boy, did they lay it on thick! Initially I had a strong leaning toward the Navy, because my Uncle Red and many of my distant relatives had done their time with the Navy back in the Big War. But it was clear to me that the Navy recruiter was spinning a superlative fairy tale, if not outright lying. And he wasn't even trying to hide it! "Oh yes, and a girl in every port, travel to exotic places, any job you want."

The Air Force recruiter was just as bad. He promised things like a private room with your own bath during basic training and everyone could try out for flight school. I guess he simply forgot to inform me that to fly, you needed to start with a four-year college degree, and an advanced degree was even better.

The Marine Corps recruiter, on the other hand, was offering what sounded like a Club Med membership, with maybe a few glorious battles to round out your tour of duty. Do you know how many famous battles Marines have been involved in since the beginning of time? He probably told me, but I've since forgotten. I just remember there were an awful lot of them, and he made it all sound like it was fun to be shot at in the company of good comrades, under the protection of Mother Corps.

The recruiters made their best efforts to turn me on by bending reality. The truth would have been better. I learned from the Brothers of the Holy Cross and Jesuits that sometimes the truth is bitter, but it's a whole lot easier to deal with. The fact of the matter is, it doesn't matter for what branch of service you wear a uniform. An honorable man is an honorable man, and anyone who serves his country should be respected for it. And there are a lot of ways to serve one's country that don't include a uniform.

The Army recruiter took me by surprise. He offered no fancy sales pitch, didn't dress up the facts or touch only on the good points. He looked me right in the eyes and asked me if I knew what a "bullet launcher" was.

Of course, I didn't. I think I might have muttered a gun or something like that. He reached over and tapped me gently on the chest with his right index finger and barely whispered, "You. You're a bullet launcher. And, a bullet catcher."

I could feel the cold wind of death brushing past the hairs on my arms. At the same time, I felt indirectly challenged. The feeling I was having is kind of hard to describe. But I knew at the time, this man was telling me the truth. If I joined the Army, the very least that I could expect was being shot at, and without a doubt having to shoot back.

It was enough of an adrenaline rush to get me into a seat next to his desk, where I took the Army entry tests, after which I signed on the dotted line. He told me I had two weeks to clear up any personal business and then I would be headed for basic training in Fort Jackson, South Carolina. More important to me, I'd soon be headed out of state and away from home, which was my entire focus and plan.

When I met with my buddies a bit later, I found that my best friend, Jimmy Powers, had signed with the Navy. The rest had chickened out altogether.

To say that my mother was terribly upset would be a complete understatement. She was absolutely livid with rage. She told me in no uncertain terms to go back down to the Recruiting Center and give them their damned papers back. I refused, of course.

It was a Kodak moment, frozen in time, one I'll never forget. Suddenly I found myself face to face with her never-before-revealed fears. Seeing the light in her eyes change was like watching an ember slowly dying in the face of a cold north wind. As that light slowly faded from her eyes, I knew that all the rage she had expended up until that point was her way of dealing with her life's frustration. I just stood there and watched as she slowly let out her breath, turned, and walked away. I could feel something breaking deep inside me that day, but I have never been able to identify what that might have been. I just knew that some meaningful connection between my mother and me was severed forever. Could that have been the apron string snapping? In hindsight, I'd have to say that it was more like a major feed line to my heart.

Surprisingly, my father didn't seem to be upset at all. While seemingly somewhat confused by my decision, because he had always thought that I would join the Navy, he was otherwise very supportive.

Why the Army?

I tried to explain my reasons, but knew in the voicing of them they fell on already-deafened ears. In a sense he was proud of me, I suppose, maybe even a little bit jealous.

He had tried to join the Army back in the beginning of the Second World War, but they had caught him in his third week of basic training trying to hide his polio-deformed foot. As a result, he was honorably discharged for the good of the service and sent home. It forever distorted the view he had of himself. This was further complicated by the fact that most of his childhood friends and boot-camp buddies were killed in a bus accident while moving from basic training to their first assignment.

I can understand the military viewpoint in discharging him, but I've always wondered why they couldn't create a special category for people like my dad. They could always use people like my dad to fill in a stateside job, which would further relieve an additional able-bodied soldier to serve overseas, especially during a time of war. It would relieve some of the shortfalls the military suffers in some of its more menial job categories, or, by filling such categories, the shortfalls they suffer in the combat units.

In a visit to Russia in 2000, while standing in a rehabilitation center in a veterans hospital outside of Moscow, the Russian commanding general and I were discussing a man who had lost both his legs to a mine in Chechnya. I was amazed, watching him playing tennis on artificial feet, and I commented on his rehabilitation. When the general told me the man was about to be discharged from the hospital, I asked if he would receive a disability pension. The general said it wasn't necessary, because he was going back to full service with his original unit. In even more amazement, I asked why. He told me that they felt it was more humane to demonstrate to the man that he was just as valuable after he was wounded as before. He added, "We don't throw people away like they do in many countries." While many will find that comment arguable, I can see the value in continuing to use a well-trained man for a job that he understands. Of course, the man will be working in a noncombat role, but his pride is intact, and he can share with those around him valuable knowledge that would otherwise be lost forever. I believe that my dad and many other fathers who were denied this possibility were unjustly categorized and suffered for it.

But back then, what worried both my parents, and of course remained unspoken, was the ever-growing threat of a full-blown war in Southeast Asia. My dad sort of accepted my decision with a mixture of pride and well-hidden fear. The difficult part for me was telling my sisters. When I enlisted I automatically assumed that Kathy was so little that she wouldn't remember much about it, which I later found out was totally untrue. My twin sister, Margaret, was in a hospital/school for out-of-control young women somewhere in central Florida. Mary and Beth were the ones that I worried the most about. Who would protect them if I were no longer there? Who could they lean on when Mom and Dad were three sheets to the wind? Leaving my sisters was the hardest part of all. But I knew if I stayed, it would only be a matter of time until I was ground under by the neighborhood, or found myself wedded to a job that could only promise the same kind of life my parents led. I needed to leave. I had to go out and find my own way in life, and I needed to do that somewhere other than Miami. (This first step, while intuitive, was also very scary, taken somewhat in ignorance.)

Of course I learned much later that the survival of my sisters was never in question. They were as adaptable as I was to the circumstances of our lives, and while I might have made a difference with some things, they, too, had to find their own way in life, as well as their own way out.

I started my first day away from home in a singularly spectacular way. Just how much trouble can a person get into while riding a train from Miami to Fort Jackson, South Carolina?

Throw in six other recruits looking for a little action their first time away from home, and the answer is: a lot.

The train made its first stop, just a bit longer than ten minutes, just north of Miami in what was back then a small, sleepy burg called Fort Lauderdale. This was just long enough for the oldest-looking recruit in our group to slip into a liquor store and purchase half a dozen quarts of vodka. We had pooled our money, but the best he could do was the cheapest brand he could find. With vodka, cheap is relative, but at least he found bottles with labels. Once back on board the train, we discovered we had nothing appropriate to drink it with. So, we bribed one of the conductors to bring us something we could mix. He brought us a couple of large jugs of orange Kool-Aid.

To make a long story short, it must have been very disturbing to the military police to be carrying unconscious bodies off the train in Columbia, South Carolina, all six with large, bright-orange smiley faces curling up at the corners of their mouths. Blessedly, like the others, I have absolutely no memory of our arrival. However, I can tell you that no matter how hard you scrub, it takes about two days for orange Kool-Aid stains to fade. Never have I been as sick as those first few days at Fort Jackson. Welcome to manhood.

It doesn't take much in the way of an intuitive nature to get through basic training. You simply do as you are told and keep your head down. Everyone has heard that whatever you do, you should never volunteer for anything. Well, it's true. They asked once if anyone knew anything about steam and engineering. I raised my hand because I had done some work on a boat in Miami outfitted with steam engines. I ended up running a steam hose inside a dumpster while scrubbing it down with a wire brush. It was the last time I volunteered for anything, at least in basic training.

I graduated easily, earning an expert badge with a rifle and a bayonet, and making sharpshooter with a Colt .45 automatic. I never actually finished the bayonet course. I broke the stock off two M-14 rifles before they gave me a third and asked me to quit and go sit in the shade. Surprisingly to me, I had made expert by scaring the hell out of the arms repairman.

The week I graduated, they passed out orders sending everyone else in my platoon to Advanced Individual Training (AIT). I received nothing. Instead, my company commander called me into the company orderly room and informed me that the Army had decided to delete my weapons system from inventory. (I was originally supposed to receive AIT in the 106-mm recoilless rifle, specifically a weapons system called the Sidewinder, which had six barrels mounted over open tracks.)

I didn't know at the time, but found out much later, that my records and test scores had been reviewed by Army intelligence and, as I had scored in the upper three percentile, a decision had been made to recruit me. They didn't tell me that directly of course, they simply told me to go out and search for another military occupational specialty (MOS). For some ungodly reason, military intelligence needs to be so very clandestine about everything, even recruitment. Had they known how well I could hold my liquor I'm sure they would have made a different decision.

Anyway, I spent a few days combing the grounds of Fort Jackson, looking for something I'd like to actually do in the Army. While searching out this new MOS, I spent one afternoon sitting in the post exchange beer hall, drinking 3.5-beer from a pitcher. I was eventually joined at the table by a stranger dressed in civilian clothes. After a couple of beers spent ignoring one another, we finally struck up a conversation. When he found out I was looking for a new MOS, he slipped me his card and asked me to drop by his office for a chat. After a week of sitting around waiting for a callback from a number of possibilities that never seemed to materialize, I took him up on his offer.

Of course it never occurred to me that he might be the reason no one was calling, and that our chance meeting was anything but. I was still quite naïve back then.

So I eventually stopped by his office for a chat, he pitched me, and I accepted. But the decision wasn't as easy as I now make it seem.

Originally I had volunteered for two years of service, with four years in the reserves to meet my six-year obligation. Military intelligence wanted a commitment for a minimum of four years' active-duty service time. This requirement was primarily because AIT in intelligence was about four times as long as any of the other AIT schools. Depending on what I was qualified for in intelligence, I could be spending another two years going to classes.

I agreed to the additional two years and was allowed to pick my new job by throwing a dart at a wheel that was broken up into individually sized, pie-shaped segments with job titles. It looked unsophisticated, but it was just the opposite. They knew the percentages of fill rate they required for each MOS, and broke the wheel up into exactly that percentage of coverage, some pie shapes being quite a bit larger than others.

He spun the wheel and I let the dart fly. My dart nailed the very thin line of purple that divided the different MOSs. I laughed and started to throw the dart again, but he stopped me, informing me that the purple lines segregating the other colors was also an MOS. But all he would tell me was that it was in signals intelligence. A week later I was on my way to AIT in sunny Fort Devens, Massachusetts, where the leaves were already changing colors in the early fall.

Back then, on entering the grounds at Fort Devens, one saw a beautiful, albeit small, Army base in quaint New England. The older red-brick three-story school buildings surrounded an open and paved parade ground situated across the street from a larger now-turning-brown turf-covered parade ground. This was fronted by rows of large red-bricked manor houses, which were field grade officer housing. It was the perfect picture of peace and tranquillity.

Of course, one would soon discover the antiquated two-story wooden barracks in which we privates resided. Thrown together for

World War II, the structures had been meant to serve as temporary billets only, no longer than four or five years at the most. Did I mention they put no insulation in the walls back in the 1940s? With Vietnam looming on the horizon, they were putting new coats of paint on the buildings, hoping they'd continue to serve their purpose without falling down.

When I arrived in the late fall, the weather was still wonderfully brisk, but you could sometimes taste the bite of winter in the air. You could also tell that the base was gearing up for the Vietnam War because they had just started running classes night and day, or in today's vernacular, 24/7, to push twice as many soldiers through as normal. I was assigned to a night platoon. As a night school student I attended classes from four in the afternoon until midnight.

Ask anyone who ever attended school at Fort Devens what it was like, and they will tell you it was about as difficult a learning environment as any could be. During my third week I personally witnessed the first of two suicides in our student group. Someone—I assume a private, because of his slick sleeves showing no rank—did a near-perfect swan dive off the upper-deck railing, hitting the pavement with a loud pop, very much like you'd expect to hear if you dropped a watermelon three floors to concrete. Another student hung himself in the barracks latrine with a couple of web belts a few weeks later. Both scored perfect tens on the suicide scale. (I always wanted to know how these were reported to parents. "Your son gave his life in service to his country by . . ." I probably shouldn't go there.)

It's difficult to understand why someone would want to commit suicide, especially in a training environment. But, having been through the same training I can now say that suicide is not only possible, it is a viable choice.

One of the primary things we were expected to learn early on was how to accurately copy and understand International Morse code. Initially they began by familiarizing us with individual letters of the alphabet, which we listened to with headphones at about three words per minute. That would be a string of fifteen characters, one character every four seconds, not difficult at all. Translating "dit-dah" into the letter *A* was a piece of cake, especially at that speed. Later they added special symbols like the "&" sign or characters specific to different languages. Cyrillic was a pain in the butt, but some of the special characters in other, more bizarre, languages were even more difficult. All the while they would be increasing the speed of transmission. As the speeds increased, the level of difficulty rose exponentially, especially when they added cut numbers and started differentiating between letter/number groups and international Q&Z signals, all intermixed one with the other.

Q&Z signals were abbreviated three-letter codes for things like "You're using too much transmission power," "Please repeat—your last transmission was garbled," or "Over and out," that sort of thing. What makes them difficult to understand is that they are normally sent so fast the letters all run together and you can only understand them by their individualized cadence or rhythm, which is totally out of cadence with everything else being sent. A difficult system to initially learn.

Almost everyone developed some proficiency at speeds up to eight words per minute or forty letters every sixty seconds. Producing copy with virtually no error made it a bit more difficult, but that too was expected. Eventually everyone reached ten words—fifty characters per minute.

Beyond that, the degree of difficulty was nearly overwhelming. Above ten words per minute you no longer have the leisure to listen to the actual transmission and then translate it to the appropriate character through formulation. It has to become second nature, something you don't even think about before doing, kind of like driving a manual shift car after twenty years.

Like many around me, I was stuck at ten words per minute for nearly four weeks. After sitting eight hours a day in front of a typewriter doing nothing but trying to copy more than ten words a minute in Morse code, I can tell you that suicide begins to look like the lesser of two evils. However, eventually I intuitively discovered the solution to my problem.

The small town of Ayer, Massachusetts, lies just outside the main gate of Fort Devens. As in most military towns, the downtown part of the small city contains numerous bars that cater to the soldiers. Most are dives, where drinking and brawling provided the Friday and Saturday night entertainment. Anyone who has ever been to Fort Devens has gotten a black eye at the Wagon Wheel Bar and Grill on a Saturday night. And, if not there, there were plenty of other places to choose from.

I had heard that if you visited the Hotel Ayer bar while wearing your uniform, they wouldn't ask you for an ID. So, that is where I went on Wednesday noon, toward the end of my fourth week. I had every intention of getting completely potted and skipping classes that night. The result, of course, would have been an immediate reassignment to a combat arms unit and duty in a hot and wet place somewhere in Southeast Asia, but I was past the point of caring.

By 4:00 P.M. I was pretty drunk. I had been drinking and shooting pool all afternoon, and had lost any desire to cut classes because I had forgotten why I was even there. So, I caught a cab to the school building and slipped in with the rest of my platoon when they arrived for night school. Stumbling into class, I quickly took my seat along the wall and braced my body so it wouldn't fall over when I fell asleep.

A surprising thing happened. Because I was still feeling the major effects of the alcohol, I was unable to keep track of what I was hearing in the earphones and following along with my fingers on the typewriter keys was an impossibility. In fact, it was actually quite comical and made me laugh. Suddenly, it was as if someone had reached inside my head and flipped a switch. My fingers began responding to the sounds of the Morse code I was hearing, without my thinking about it, and suddenly I was running on full automatic.

That night, I passed speeds ten, twelve, fifteen, eighteen, and twenty words per minute—all in one evening. From that point, it was a piece of cake. By Friday of the following week I was working twenty-five wpm with ease. Another two weeks went by and our class finally graduated: 33 out of 48 who started had stayed the course. I graduated first in my class. As proud as I was, I didn't know at the time this was not a good thing.

Seven days later, everyone in my class was on the way to their overseas assignments, the majority, of course, headed for Saigon. I was reassigned for further training in a place across the post we called Area G. I had heard about Area G. In fact, most students had. The nickname for the place was "Little Korea," because almost all the training took place outside and not inside the buildings, which in a typical Massachusetts winter, made any form of training quite nasty. The Area G training compound was circled with a double fence topped with razor wire, and filled with all kinds of equipment mounted on the backs of trucks and Jeeps. There was also an area filled with dozens of different antenna systems. We students had always thought that Area G was where they sent you if you couldn't hack it in the main school building, but it was just the opposite. Area G and a number of other special schools were skimming the cream off the top.

The class size in Area G was surprisingly small. In my class there were eight others assigned; four were Special Forces buck sergeants, two civilians (at least, two without uniforms), and two Navy personnel. Another surprise was my promotion to specialist four. So, I was feeling pretty good that first day, until they started the class. That was when they told us that everything we had learned to do with a typewriter, we would now learn to do with a pencil, or as they called it, "a stick." Not only that, but we would be expected to learn how to transmit Morse code as quickly as we could receive it. If you want to understand the level of difficulty involved, sit down and try to write 100 characters a minute by hand, never mind translating them from or into International Morse. Or try to tap the tune to a song on the right side of your thigh while driving a military Jeep cross-country and off road, or better yet, while jogging.

Besides learning to send as well as receive, we were taught everything anyone could ever want to know about transmitters, the use of encryption systems, and how to identify and locate them. The course even included two weeks of applied slide rule and the use of logarithm books.

It was a grueling ten weeks, but I again graduated first in the class, and once again watched as my classmates packed and departed for overseas assignments, all in the Saigon area, while I was under orders to sit and wait.

Ten days later, my orders finally arrived. They didn't make any sense. I was asked to turn in all of my military-issued clothing and was then taken by car to a Worcester, Massachusetts, men's store, where I was ordered to spend $250 on civilian clothes. By dark, I found myself sitting in the rear shadows of a C-123 military transport plane headed to points south, and I still did not know where I was actually assigned.

The plane made two stops en route, both in progressively hotter climates. At one stop we picked up a pallet of equipment destined to the same place I was traveling to. The equipment was covered with canvas and sealed, so it was impossible to see what it was. No one on board would volunteer where we were headed, so I didn't ask. Eventually, as the sun cracked the Eastern horizon, we set down on a very small runway bordered on both sides with what appeared to be ocean. They unloaded me and the pallet, and then quickly taxied back out onto the runway and lifted off. I found myself sitting alone with some sea birds, on a rock in the middle of nowhere, next to a tin shack. It was hot, humid, and devoid of human life.

I didn't have to wait very long. After sitting in the heat and humidity for about ten minutes, a Ford Econoline pickup pulled up and I was greeted with a warm hello from my new boss, Chief Warrant Officer Sal Corrado. He was appropriately dressed for the occasion in a white T-shirt, tan shorts, and beach sandals—back then they were called flip-flops. He had a baseball cap to cover his thinning and receding hairline. The good news was that he wasn't armed.

"Welcome to Eleuthera in the Bahamas," he said, reaching out and shaking my hand.

My sense of frustration was almost overwhelming. I had spent considerable time and effort attempting to get as *far away* from Miami as I could, and now here I found myself within a fifteen-minute whisper-jet flight from home! Well, at least it wasn't Southeast Asia.

Chapter Three

From My First Assignment to a Near-Death Experience

My tour of duty on Eleuthera was normal except for two incidents (three if you want to count my rolling the Econoline pickup and shattering my wrist again).

The first was hurricane Betsy in September 1965. I spent the entire hurricane inside a metal electronics shelter that was anchored to the coral with chains and two-foot iron stakes I helped to drive with a sledgehammer. The shelter was located on top of a hill just north of Governor's Harbor. We were supposed to evacuate the site when the winds reached 80 MPH, but they went from gusts of around 65 up to 110 in a matter of minutes. So we were forced to stay put and ride it out.

It was a nasty storm, which did a lot of damage to the island. Braving the elements once, I was able to look toward the north end of the island and see huge breakers rolling across the entire island to the north. It was the only time I was outside, as the wind was picking up bits of rock and coral and pounding the side of the shelter with them. At the time it was quite scary, wondering whether or not the stakes and chains would hold, the rising water creeping in through the lower crack in the door, segments of plywood on the connecting shelter popping away into the wind, all in near total darkness, broken only by small candles. I shared the 5x10-foot shelter with one other man, a case of beer, and six tins of tuna.

We were able to maintain radio contact with the Florida coast through the passing of the eye and halfway through the hurricane's departure, but eventually we lost our whip antenna. I think soon after that the 30-kilowatt generators, one of the trucks, and most of the unattached items on the hill disappeared.

Before it ended, we were forced to lash the metal door shut with one-inch braided metal ground strapping, to keep the door from being sucked completely off the shelter. The wind meter sheared off the building after it jammed at a hundred and fifty knots. The hurricane sat on top of us, completely stalled, for about twelve hours, eventually moving north, dancing all along the coast of our island as it departed.

The others assigned to the site were ensconced in two locations. Half were socked in at our support base, an auxiliary Air Force base that was host to the downrange tracking facility that supported Cape Canaveral. The others were in a cavelike concrete bunker buried in the side of the hill facing the ocean, just below the trailer. Luckily, the waves didn't quite reach that point.

By the time the hurricane left, the windward side of the equipment shelter had most of the paint sand-blasted from it. It looked like highly polished stainless steel. It took almost a day for the main base to reach us with a bulldozer, plowing debris off the only road, which was pretty much scrubbed from the island.

It was kind of scary after we lost power, mostly because you couldn't see your hand in front of your face and the entire shelter was shaking violently. But the other man in the shelter and I did what we could to ensure survival of the very expensive and one-of-a-kind equipment. We were eventually forced to remove most of the electronics from the equipment racks and stack them near the roof of the shelter, where we eventually joined them. For my part in saving the equipment and some of the more sensitive gear, I later received a promotion to buck sergeant and an Army Commendation Medal, something everyone should have gotten.

The second event occurred sometime around midnight in the early part of 1966. We worked at a separate site, but we actually lived in apartments on an auxiliary Air Force base half way between our installation and Governor's Harbor. The base commander was the only Air Force officer on it. The rest of the inhabitants were employees of William Bendix Corporation, RCA Victor, and other subcontractors who operated the down-range telemetry gear for the

The Stargate Chronicles

Cape Canaveral rocket launches. (Eleuthera was one of a string of such bases that stretched all the way to the tip of South Africa.) On that particular night, Steve Roberts—the man I was working with at the time—and I went up the hill to the outdoor movie theater and club bar, where we attended a double-feature film and had a few drinks. It was a great way to spend an evening. The theater was in the open air so you could smoke and drink while watching the movies. If you wanted a drink, you only had to hold your hand in the air and yell, "Nurse!" and a young native girl would bring you what you wanted. While I know this seems to be an impossibly wonderful situation, it was a terribly boring assignment.

We finished the second feature around midnight and headed back down to our apartments. We left the ocean end of the club and were walking down toward our sleeping quarters, crossing behind the headquarters building on a row of sand dunes. The sky was totally clear with no moon, and the air was clear. It was one of those island nights where you can read a newspaper by starlight. A warm breeze was blowing east to west as normal, and it was absolutely quiet except for the breaking combers down along the shore a quarter mile away—when the whole area lit up like daylight. We found ourselves enveloped within a very bright cone of light, which was coming from the undercarriage of something hovering directly over us. The object appeared to be approximately fourteen hundred feet above the ground. It was making no noise. In fact, it was like standing inside a vacuum bottle: now we couldn't even hear the waves breaking on the beach to our immediate right. The object was elliptical in shape, and appeared to be quite large. The light was bright enough to make me want to protect my eyes from exposure. After a few seconds, the light winked off, and the object accelerated away, quickly disappearing from sight.

Steve and I were dumbfounded. We walked back to the club and asked if anyone else had seen it. No one else had seen it. At least no one would own up to it. The following morning we both were suffering from what appeared to be a severe sunburn. In fact, Steve's burns were serious enough to put him in a hospital back in Homestead, Florida, for a short period. He still wears the scars on his chest and is quite sensitive to direct sunlight. I was lucky, however. Since I spent a considerable amount of time in the water every day and was already cooked to a nice dark brown, I wasn't so affected by it. I am frequently asked about this event. While I can remember seeing what looked like panel lines and rivets in the underside of the object, as well as opaque ports that seemed to blend into the surrounding material, there isn't much else that I can say about it.

In the days that followed, I was able to determine from conversations with electrical engineers on base that much of the telemetry equipment had been overwhelmed with noise that washed out the scopes. Also, to this day, Steve has a memory of the light but not the immediate or subsequent actions. After that week, we never discussed it with anyone for fear of being reassigned—to someplace hotter and wetter. The peculiar part is that the military never seemed to show much interest in the event.

While the assignment was somewhat boring and repetitive, I enjoyed my eighteen months on Eleuthera. I spent at least half the time diving in dozens of coves on the ocean side of the island. On some of my days off, I entered the water at dawn and didn't leave it till early afternoon. Swimming is like walking for me. When I was little my grandfather used to say I had scales on my butt, then he would pretend to search my body looking for fins, tickling me all the while to make me laugh.

I departed Eleuthera in January 1967, and was reassigned to Homestead AFB, only a few miles south of my home. If I had been trying to stay close to home it probably never would have happened. The extra pay that came with the promotion to buck sergeant came at a time when Congress decided to boost military pay to a point that was reasonable. As a result, I began sending half of it home to my parents. When I joined the Army in 1964, my take-home pay after taxes was $52 a month. Granted, cigarettes were only $1.20 a carton, and a haircut only cost me 75 cents, but it was pretty low pay. After the government correction to military pay scales, my pay jumped to $282 a month. For me, it was an unbelievable sum, more than my father made after more than twenty years at the department store. When I got to Homestead, the colonel arranged for me to draw bachelor housing allowance and subsistence so that I could live at home. He knew I was giving it to my parents. So my pay increased to more than $450 a month.

The next four months I was assigned to work with the Navy on their "Bullseye" project, something the Navy was not very pleased about. Bullseye is the code name for the Navy's land-based High Frequency Direction Finding surveillance stations, in this case operating in the Caribbean Sea. I worked at the AN/FRD-10 antenna array at

Card Sound, Florida, just south of Homestead AFB. The interservice defensiveness about protecting knowledge about their individual collection systems back then was over the edge. Having an Army person behind their doors was like getting a sharp stick in the eye.

Even though I was being paid to live at home, only about an hour's drive away, I only visited my parents and sisters now and then, not as often as I could have. I had extracted myself from that situation and would not let myself be dragged back into it. Instead, I would park my new car on the point overlooking the bay on the back side of Homestead AFB, and would sleep in the backseat, fishing during my off-duty time. I took showers in the barracks and paid to eat at the military mess facility.

During this time I met and fell in love with my first wife, Sue. I met her at a party given by a friend. She was attending Notre Dame School for Girls, my old hangout. So, it wasn't long before I was back to meeting her on the same corner I hung out on back in high school, only now I was sometimes wearing a uniform, and either going to or coming from work. Sue was in her final year of high school. After dating for a few months, we became engaged. Things were really looking up, when the Army made me an offer I couldn't refuse.

If I would take what they called a short discharge and would reenlist for six more years, they would pay me a variable Category IV reenlistment bonus. Actually this equated to just a bit more than $11,000 cash. In 1967, it was too hard to pass up. I "kicked it" for six years and collected the money. I should have known they had something more up their sleeves. We were about to set the date for our wedding when orders came down from on high assigning me to the Republic of South Vietnam. Before I had kicked it for six, I didn't have enough time left in service to serve a full tour in Southeast Asia. That's why I had been approached for early reenlistment. That's why they had even waived what time I had to serve on my first enlistment so that I could reenlist. My whole focus had been on the money. See what I mean about being psychic about one's own self? It never works.

It was bound to happen eventually. I had watched my other friends pack off to that area of the world, so now it was my turn. To say it was difficult leaving home all over again would be an understatement. I was making good money, driving a brand-new Cobra that I had bought with a major part of my reenlistment bonus, and was engaged to a very lovely young woman. Having no choice, we postponed our wedding plans until I returned. And, of course, the unspoken thought was "*if* I returned." I once again said farewell to my parents and siblings, and to my fiancée and her family, and left for the West Coast. My journey, however, was not direct. The colonel, my battalion commander at the time, sent me via Fort Polk, Louisiana, where I attended jungle warfare school. I stopped off in New Orleans for ten days and took a Creole knife-fighting course as well. I figured, what could it hurt?

It would take an entire book to cover my experiences in Southeast Asia. Just as for most of the others assigned there, my tour was not pleasant. I came away convinced that all congressmen and senators should have their sons and daughters assigned to combat zones before being able to vote on commitment to war. Wars are evil. There is a lot more that I could say about it, but it will have to await some other manuscript. What is pertinent here is the effect on me as a psychic.

I was assigned to an Army intelligence company in support of MACV, the 4th Infantry Division, and 1st Armored Calvary, in the central highlands city of Pleiku. My tour included five major offensives, including the Tet offensive and mini-Tet offensive of 1968. It cranked up my psychic ability and increased my sensitivity to other forms of information transfer.

I had a profound experience almost immediately upon arrival. I was disembarking from the ramp of my C-130 aircraft. As my foot hit the pavement, I had a very clear vision of myself climbing aboard a bright yellow plane and waving good-bye to people standing next to the main air terminal building. It was so clear and startling that I made a point of describing it to the man standing next to me. He probably thought I was crazy. It was a recurring vision that I carried all through my tour there.

As an emitter location and identification specialist, I was expected to search out and locate enemy transmitters. With the equipment we had back then, it was not an easy job. Under wet jungle canopies, you had to be nearly standing on top of a radio to know where it was. For a while I worked out of a heavily fortified fixed site with fifteen other men. We were stuck way off on our own, away from anyone else, as too much wire or equipment would screw all our equipment up. These isolated sites were extremely vulnerable, but so heavily mined that you needed a good memory to walk across the compound to take a leak without blowing yourself up.

They kept us busy. When we weren't trying to make an antiquated piece of electronic equipment operate under impossible conditions, we were spending time protecting the other guys who were. I then spent time working with portable equipment they called "man packable." That meant it could be broken down and carried in backpacks or mounted on the rear of a Jeep. There were a number of things wrong with these types of equipment. The only human capable of ever packing them had to be the Jolly Green Giant. The other problem was that this equipment dealt with VHF, or line of sight, radio frequencies. This meant that you had to be close enough to see the enemy emitter for the equipment to be even halfway accurate. Obviously, if you were that close, you didn't really need the equipment to find the enemy, because you were more than likely already drawing heavy fire. Since it was a safe bet the enemy were the guys shooting at you, you didn't really need the equipment. But, in the wisdom of the United States Army, we proved that the equipment worked—sometimes.

After enjoying the glorious Tet holidays in Pleiku,[3] I spent some time working with experimental equipment mounted in a helicopter flying out of a place called "LZ Two Bits," in a place called Bong Song, north of Qui Nhon. The aircraft worked fine, but were overweight and unable to carry defensive armor or guns. Before long, the North Vietnamese figured out what our strange boxlike antennas mounted on the front were for. Since we always flew unarmed, we lost all the birds in a couple of months. Toward the end of my tour, while flying back into Pleiku on a Huey, we were suddenly converted from combat aircraft to a falling metal rock and crashed short of the runway. I woke up in the Army hospital with pins in my skull and sandbags hanging from my ankles. They offered to send me to a hospital close to my home, which I immediately refused. Had I accepted, I would have been flown back to the States short of a full tour and on recovery been sent right back again to serve my full twelve months in the green. (They weren't yet doing second tours.) Instead, I asked a medic for some painkillers and limped out of the hospital. I then

---

[3] As a result of these Tet holidays, I and others are still bolting awake in the early-morning hours more than thirty years later, with memories that would haunt Dante. Modern weapons of war do not simply punch holes in the human body, they shred them to pieces and strew them across open ground where they congeal and rot in the hot and humid air. The smell alone is sufficient to power nightmares for centuries after, never mind the visions seared across the backs of eyelids.

self-medicated my way to my normal rotation stateside, at the same time discovering that Jack Daniels is great for more than countering the effects of Benzedrine in getting to sleep, forgetting experiences impossible to describe, or just plain getting stinking drunk.

What is material about my time in Vietnam is how much I came to rely on my gut or intuitive nature. Many times I instinctively knew I wasn't safe, or that I was somehow exposed to danger. The small voice inside my gut became a lot louder and I listened. Inside and outside the base camp, I always listened to my inner voice, did whatever it suggested, and did it without question. If I felt an urge to get into a bunker, I did so immediately. If it was a gut feeling to zig rather than zag, then that's what I did. I once abandoned a Jeep and walked back to the base camp on advice of my internal voices. To the consternation of my first sergeant, the Jeep was never seen again.

While sitting in a listening post one night near a small unit outside of Tay Ninh, I had a terrible urge to move. The small voice in my gut was telling me to be anywhere but there. Movement was difficult because it was pitch black—the kind of dark where you can't see your hand right up in front of your face. I had to convince the two others who were there it was the right thing to do. It took almost an hour, but we shifted west of our original position by about sixty yards. Around 4:00 A.M. we heard a series of grenades going off in the area we had previously occupied.

During a firefight at LZ Two Bits, just north of Qui Nhon, I took up a gun position on top of a bunker facing the village just outside the wire. Within minutes my inner voices were screaming at me, "Be somewhere else!" I shifted to a firing slot inside the bunker. Seconds later the top of the bunker was racked with two direct hits from mortar rounds. My voices started yelling again, "Not enough! Get out!" So I quickly moved through the bunker entry, sliding sideways to a depression in the ground. I just cleared the bunker doorway when an RPG (a high-explosive rocket-propelled grenade) opened the bunker up like a banana hit with a sledgehammer. My voices kept me moving all night long.

My life was saved more than once by simply doing what my inner voices suggested, even if at the time it seemed foolish or stupid, or that I might embarrass myself. Some began to notice. Others began to do whatever I did, just from watching me. At one of the firebases, I noticed a young private lacing his boots the same way I did. I'm sure it wasn't because it looked cool.

When I left Vietnam, it was no surprise to me when the contracted flight back to America was an aircraft painted a light pastel yellow with the words "Freedom Bird" painted on the side. My vision was correct and the feedback obvious.

When I left Vietnam, I was a staff sergeant with nearly a year in grade carrying orders for southern Germany—a small place called Bad Aibling in southern Bavaria, south of Munich. I stopped long enough in America to be married, after which Sue and I spent a couple of weeks on our honeymoon, touring the East Coast.

My next three years were spent in different parts of Europe. I was originally assigned to the field unit at Bad Aibling. The base was unique, in that it was specially designed to give support to the U.S. Army in Europe, as well as the National Security Agency and other agencies that must remain unnamed. Inside the secured compound was a more classified or restricted area, and inside that was an even more classified and restricted facility. That was where I worked in support of one of those agencies.

Bad Aibling was also unique in that it happened to be the same location my mother's brother was held as a POW during WWII. I went to the approximate area of the airfield where he said his POW camp had been located, which was a huge grassy field approximately sixty acres. Intuitively searching it, I found an area with numerous belt-buckles and buttons from U.S. Army Air Forces uniforms buried in the dirt. He had told me about how bad the conditions had been in the camp toward the end of the war, about the starvation, and the cold. I can't imagine what it must have been like being trapped behind barbed wire for years, surrounded with what appear to be insurmountable mountain peaks, covered with year-round snow. He luckily didn't know that no one in the family knew that he was a POW. He had been reported missing in action, fate unknown. Over those years, my aunt never left her house, knowing that he was still alive, regardless of what anyone said to her. Maybe an intuitive nature is inherited?

For me, it was very comfortable living right on the edge of the Tyrolean Alps. So, I spent weekends climbing in the mountains, skiing the glaciers, hiking in the forests, and drinking a lot of beer. (My uncle did ask me to urinate in the Rhine for him, which I graciously did, and I sent him a picture, my back to the camera, a fine yellow stream arching into the water.)

After about a year, I walked into the border site commander's office and volunteered for border site duty. Eventually I was assigned as commander of a small border site near Passau, Germany, in Bavaria. There I managed a detachment of eighteen individuals doing classified border site work a hundred miles from the nearest American base. At the time, I was both the youngest and the least ranking border site commander in Europe. It was an awesome responsibility that I took very seriously.

The detachment sat on the outskirts of a village called Pocking, which lay due east of Munich along the Rott River and was predominantly a rural place of multicentury-old farms and stone buildings. It was a tough job for me, because I was younger than most of the personnel assigned, but outranked them. I was also the only person assigned who was married. There had been a great deal of reluctance to assign such a young man to this duty, but they felt that since I was married, it would probably balance out. As it turned out, this assignment was doubly tough on my newlywed wife. Aside from occasional detachment parties, there was not another English-speaking person around for a radius of a hundred miles. I was leaving Sue for extended periods of time alone in the apartment in town, where she had to fend for herself, a tough test of any marriage, never mind a new one.

Time we spent together was always with German nationals, or German senior noncommissioned officers and their wives. They were always very friendly and quite charming, opening their homes to us in friendship, but Sue was never comfortable. As a young wife who had trouble with the language, she appeared to become more and more shy about outside contact.

It was also hard being in charge of a remote detachment while having a family. All of the other men assigned were single, and my wife was a very beautiful young woman. So, attending the detachment parties was very stressful, especially for me. I understood my men, so it wasn't jealousy that made me wary. I also knew my wife was spending long hours alone, a serious situation under any circumstance.

It may sound as though I had very little time for my family life. Well . . . this is true. The demands of an active intelligence mission required days that sometimes exceeded eighteen hours, and there was always some form of crisis. The entire situation really sucked, and having done this sort of thing for twenty years, I can now understand why they've always said, "If the Army wanted you to have a wife, they would issue you one." Any man who has a career in the military

The Stargate Chronicles

and retires with the same woman he started out with should kneel before her feet and worship her forever, as she probably has more grit than he does.

While I was assigned to Pocking as the detachment commander in 1970, I experienced something that changed me profoundly and permanently. I had what can be called a classic Near Death Experience (NDE).

One Friday evening in July, I met my wife and another man from the detachment at a small gasthouse (a bed and breakfast, usually with a restaurant) across the Inn River in a town called Braunau am Inn. We were meeting for dinner. We ordered before-dinner drinks. After taking a couple of sips from my drink, I began to feel quite nauseated. Not wanting to be sick in the restaurant, I excused myself and tried to move outside. When I got to the front door and attempted to push it open, there was a sound like a pop and I found myself standing on the cobblestone road out front, watching with curiosity as the rain passed through my hands.[4]

Events then unfolded as though I were just outside the boundaries of reality. My initial fears departed and were quickly replaced with curiosity. I drifted over to see what the commotion by the door was all about and found myself staring down at my own body, lying half in and half out of the gutter. I watched as my friend pulled me up into his lap and attempted to put his finger down my throat. I had gone into convulsions and he was attempting to keep me from swallowing my tongue. I found out later that he was unsuccessful and I had bitten halfway through his finger. I watched them load my body into a car, and followed alongside the car as they drove back across the border to Germany, and a hospital located in Passau. Once at the hospital, I quickly grew bored with what the doctor and nurses were doing to try to revive me. I felt as though I began drifting upward toward the ceiling, then gently rolling over backward, where I suddenly found myself falling into a wide tunnel opening.

The emergency room receded, growing smaller and dimmer in the distance as I accelerated downward into the tunnel. As it faded from sight, I attempted to turn my attention to where I was falling. But I seemed to lose focus at that point. I was suddenly feeling very warm all over, especially across the back of my neck. A tingling sen-

---

[4]This NDE is covered in more detail in my book *Mind Trek*, Hampton Roads Publishing, 1993, Rev.1997.

sation washed over my entire being, almost like an electrical charge, but it wasn't at all unpleasant. The feelings kept growing inside me, until suddenly I entered a new space, which was filled with the whitest and brightest light I have ever experienced. I was overwhelmed with the sudden sense of joy, comfort, and love. I felt as though I had finally reached the ultimate destination, the one place where I could feel whole and complete, where I could simply be without any conditions, needs, or wants.

I then found myself reviewing my entire lifetime, good and bad. I saw all the ways in which I had failed myself or others. I experienced all the nonconstructive and noncreative aspects of my life up until that moment in time. It was just like reliving every single moment of my life up to that point, except that it went by incredibly fast. I became totally aware of all the feelings and intentions of all the people I had ever interacted with throughout my lifetime. When it was over, I was filled with the most incredible sorrow. Not so much sorrow for what I had missed or not done, but sorrow for all the times that I had misunderstood, thought wrongly or too quickly about someone, had not paid attention when they were needing something from me that I could have given. It was intensely painful, yet very cleansing. And then I had an intense feeling of forgiveness flood over me. It was a feeling of love that flooded inward, washing over my soul, flushing away the corruption, the guilt, and stupidity.

At that point a voice in my mind said that I could not stay, that I had to go back. It was not time for me to die. I tried to argue with it, but to no avail. There was a second sudden popping noise and I sat up on the hospital bed and looked around.

The Army moved very quickly. So quickly in fact, that the men who worked for me in the Detachment thought I was dead.[5] The next day, the military moved me to a private clinic in Munich and relocated my wife to military quarters on a base not far from there. I was forced to undergo numerous tests to determine how much damage had been done to my brain as a result of the event. I found out that after I had gone into convulsions and swallowed my tongue, I couldn't breathe, so it was not long after I stopped breathing that

---

[5] I was approached following a talk I gave on remote viewing in Lynchburg, Virginia, by one of the men who worked for me at the Pocking detachment. He said all those years past he was convinced that I was actually dead—a perception the U.S. Army never corrected.

my heart stopped. I had arrived at the hospital in Passau clinically dead.

Being in the Munich clinic was frightening. I was having numerous spontaneous Out of the Body Experiences (OBEs) over which I had no control. I also noticed that I could read the minds of those tending me. I wasn't actually hearing them thinking, nor was I reading their thoughts verbatim, but I was picking up on the general gist or subject matter contained within their thoughts. It was almost like seeing through an upper layer to another layer underneath.

At first I tried talking about what was going on with some of the doctors and nurses. It quickly became apparent that they didn't believe me. I was learning that if I ever intended to get out of the clinic, I was going to have to at least act normal. So, I made a decision to keep the experiences to myself.

The only problem with this decision is that once you have had an NDE, it is almost impossible to act normal again. It alters the very color of the light in which you see things. In addition, I lost my fear of death and began to dig much deeper into the metaphysical world—something I was neither familiar nor comfortable with doing.

I spent my free time searching out and reading some of the great philosophers' writings, and read copies of Judaism's Tanakh, Christianity's Apocrypha and New Testament, Islam's Qur'an, the Analects of Confucius, Hinduism's Rig Veda, and Buddhism's Dhammapada, which I admittedly gravitated toward the most. I even bought a set of the great books and started reading Homer, Plato, and Aristotle, picking my way through the 54 volumes. I found some of the writings of Madame Blavatsky, Jane Roberts (Seth), and Carlos Castaneda, although I had considerable difficulty assimilating all of the material into one naked ball of truth. Things that had previously been incredibly important to me became secondary or trivial. Parts of my character began to fade and be replaced with other elements that were totally strange to me. I began to actually look at reality in a totally different way. I used to pride myself on looking people directly in the eyes. But now, I was not only looking into their eyes, I was seeing through to their souls. Not in a judgmental way, but with a different kind of compassion. It was as though my inner sight had suddenly become crystal clear, no longer filtered through my greater burden of old history, but somewhat enlightened by my newfound sources of knowledge.

After I was released from the rest home and declared okay, I was given another job in the city of Munich, working for military intelligence, until I rotated to my next assignment.

In the meantime, within the newfound clarity of my paranormal mind, I was able to discover who had doctored my drink that night at the gasthouse. I know who they are. They should know that while it was my choice that they should go unpunished, they should never take this a sign of weakness on my part. I know who they are and where they live even today. It is my choice to let the matter rest and not theirs.

Chapter Four

Reaching the Top

Leaving Germany, I left my wife at her home in Miami, while attending an advanced school back in Area G, at Fort Devens. This was not by her choice or mine. I was authorized a single move from Europe to my next assignment, and rather than have her sitting and waiting for me at the new base, I felt being close to her home, parents, and friends might help defuse some of the difficulties she suffered for three years in Germany. I would later find that this, too, was a mistake, but hindsight is a cruel master.

The school I was attending was only for four months and I only took it because my career adviser at Department of the Army said it would keep me in the United States. What he didn't tell me was that with the additional school, I would be eligible to work as a noncommissioned officer in plans and operations. After four months in the snow and ice of Massachusetts, instead of permanent orders to an Army base, I was given temporary orders to Vint Hill Farms Station, Virginia, where I was assigned to work as a senior NCO on special projects for both the National Security Agency and the Central Intelligence Agency. The only redeeming value in being assigned there was that I was able to be close to my wife when our son, Scott, was born.

Back then, I was not allowed to stay in the room during the actual birth, but I did get to hold him within the hour of his delivery. It was absolutely breathtaking. In my memory it was like holding a small, warm star in my palms—a segment of the universal energy. He was absolutely beautiful. (I must admit to hoping the flat area on the back of his head would eventually fill out, however.) I spent the first months of his life watching him grow. I still have near-perfect memories of his little body falling asleep on my stomach, face down, drooling small stains into my dress green uniform. But I was living in constant fear of being sent back to Southeast Asia. It was 1972 and it didn't seem likely that the war would ever end. I had career friends who were returning for their third tours, so I knew it was only a question of time. I'd sit on the edge of my bed in the darkness of night in fear of what was to come. I was both shattered and relieved when orders arrived, assigning me to up-country Thailand. I didn't even know we had troops in extreme northern Thailand. While it wasn't Vietnam, leaving Scott and Sue was like cutting my heart out with my own bayonet.

From the latter part of 1971 through early 1975, Thailand was a hotspot for intelligence operations in support of the war that was winding down in Vietnam. I was assigned to a unit outside of Udon Thani City, Thailand. My old buddy Steve from the Bahamas was also in the country at the time, but he was down south near the Bangkok airport, instructing Thai soldiers in special intelligence technologies.

The time I spent in Thailand was good and bad. The times I spent working (which I'm not free to discuss) were terrible, but when I was not working I was able to spend time living in one of the local villages. The moments shared with the people of that northern region are still etched deeply within my mind and soul. Just across the Mekong River to the north of Vientiane in Laos, a secret war was being successfully waged against overwhelming odds. Had we used the same methods of warfare in the Republic of Vietnam, I cannot help but think things would have ended differently there.

My time in Thailand provided me with almost a natural backdrop to the pursuit of the metaphysical. The mountain people, whom I had the opportunity to live with off and on, were very much into the magical and mystical. The very way that birds would alight on trees told them stories about where they should hunt or when and where they should move.

My journey there opened new doors into an understanding of Buddhism, living myth, and the shaman rituals of animistic teaching. I learned there is real power to inscribing a prayer on your skin with a ballpoint pen, or tying a protective talisman made from bones and feathers, or even simple string, around your upper arm. I learned that the heart of any man is worth no more or no less than another, and that some hearts in the smallest bodies are greater than those in the largest.

The village I lived in for some time (whenever I was not working) had numerous young children running naked in the clearing. They used to point at me and call me names that roughly equated to specter or ghost, because my skin was not as dark as theirs. The kids used to try and rub through to the darker skin they were sure existed just beneath the surface layer. They would hold their breath when I bathed in the river, waiting to see the paleness slide off my body.

As a singular example of what a small world this really is that we all share, I'll jump ahead for a moment. In 1998, I underwent my second open-heart surgery. It was aggravated by a number of complications, so I spent a few extra days in the intensive care unit at the University of Virginia Hospital. One night, late, after shift change, the night nurse entered my unit to do her normal tasks. I recognized her as being Thai, so as best I could from a half-lying-down position, I raised my hands in a gesture of prayer above my forehead and bowed in formal greeting. "Sa'wa'dee Krop," I exclaimed.

She was very flattered that I recognized her as being Thai and responded in kind with a smile and a like greeting. I asked her from where in Thailand she had come and she told me it was a very small village, too small for anyone outside of northern Thailand to know of it. I pressed her anyway. To my total surprise, she said she was from the very village I lived in so many years before.

It was very endearing and quite emotional to know that one of those little kids who had once sat naked on my lap under jungle trees in northern Thailand was tending the high-tech equipment on which my life now depended.

I had my second near-death experience while assigned there. We had a field doctor whose automatic cure for almost anything was a shot of penicillin, usually nine million units, given in the buttocks with a 20-gauge needle. I woke up one morning running a slight fever and had the chills. I reported to him and received his normal cure. Over the next week I progressively got worse. I reached a point where I could no longer keep water down. My state of dehydration was so bad that I couldn't sit up in my cot. An Air America pilot friend with whom I had done some drinking rescued me, flying me to Bangkok in an antique DC-3. He had me delivered by ambulance to the American Tropical Disease Center, a converted four-star hotel. I was diagnosed with Hepatitis B. I spent almost three months flat on my back getting shots of an experimental drug under the skin or in opposite hands every morning. When I was discharged, they moved me to a Buddhist nunnery, where I recuperated. I had wasted away to about 129 pounds. The nuns fed me some of the rankest teas I've ever drunk, but eventually got me to a point where I could walk. When I returned to the unit, I was ordered to stay in the main base and only work half days. I also had to follow a very strict diet that lasted two years—no beer, tea, booze, or milk, and a severely reduced fat, meat, and oil intake. It was difficult.

During my tour in Thailand I was promoted to sergeant first class, after which I immediately applied for warrant officer. My application was turned down, because they said I was too young. I was 27 years of age, and had nine years of service, all (aside from my time in schools) spent overseas, a circumstance that was not about to change. After a couple of months pushing papers in the Mission Command and Control Management Office, I left Thailand.

I passed through Miami for thirty days en route back to Europe. At that point I had spent less than three months with either my son or my wife since his birth. It is difficult to explain how this affects someone. During my time in Thailand, I withdrew from everyone. The emotional pain that I was dealing with as a result of only having letter contact with my wife and seeing only pictures of my son was cutting to my core. I can only imagine what this must have been doing to them. I had an active and sometimes difficult mission to occupy my time, where they only had to wait. I knew by the tone of her letters that she was having a hard time. I was in agony over it. My increased sensitivity made it worse. I could feel her ache through the pages I held in my hand. When I finally returned home, what I found wasn't encouraging nor surprising. In my absence something had changed dramatically in our relationship.

It was obvious to me that she had been seeing someone else while I was away. Not only that, but she had also gotten involved with a group of people who were very much into free love, whirlwind parties, and smoking pot. Rather than losing it in anger, I wanted to hold on to what little I had: I chose to ignore the past and concentrate on the future. I thought that by moving her back to Europe with me, getting her away from the area, things would change. We arrived a month later at what was then the world's largest military intelligence collection site, Augsburg, Germany.

Because of my past experience in running isolated detachments, the border site commander called me in for an interview. He was the man in charge of a dozen or so remote intelligence collection sites along the borders to East Germany and other Eastern bloc countries. He desperately wanted me to take charge of a site that was giving him trouble. I politely refused. I knew that my marriage would not stand up to that kind of pressure, and I needed time to try and heal the problems in my relationship with my wife. He reluctantly agreed to my assignment elsewhere, which guaranteed a nearly normal home life.

I tried spending as much time as possible with both my son and my wife. I took him to the playground a lot, and we spent hours playing games on the floor of the apartment we had in on-post quarters.

Once again, just to demonstrate how little a psychic can pick up on when it's about them, it was a complete surprise when I returned home from work one day a month or so later to find my wife packed and going out the door with my son. I could not dissuade her from leaving. To say that it was a devastating blow would be an understatement. I knew instinctively that something was wrong, but never in a million years would I have thought that she would just up and leave me and take my son with her. I was absolutely shattered. And to make matters worse, one reason she said she couldn't be with me anymore was that I was spending more time with Scott than I was with her. There didn't seem to be any single answer for my situation, and I was almost incapable of rational thought.

The day she left, I went to my commander and asked for an emergency reassignment back to the States. This request was denied. He essentially said that my problems were not the Army's problems. His attitude was a total surprise to me. I had given everything but my life to the United States Army and when I asked for help received only a hostile attitude. What I was actually encountering was to be a common experience in the latter years of my service—it's called jealousy. My commander, like many others in the unit, had never been to Southeast Asia. For this reason, I was treated differently and it was obvious. I'm not really sure if it was a form of personal jealousy or just anger at not having served a tour himself, but it sure made a difference in how I and many other Southeast Asian veterans were treated. The war was winding down quickly. So, those who had not served seemed embarrassed by it.

Still hoping to find a way back to my wife and son, I went to the American Red Cross and asked for them to intercede on my behalf. They tried, but failed. In desperation I even tried going to the battalion sergeant major, but he wouldn't see me. His clerk told me that my situation had already been decided by my company commander so there was nothing else he could do. He wouldn't ask the battalion commander to intercede.

I remained in a sort of limbo state mentally and emotionally for nearly a month, with very little recall of what I was doing or where I was going on a day-to-day basis. I spent a great deal of time in the senior noncommissioned officers club.

Toward the end of the fifth week, there was a knock on my door. It was my mother-in-law and her sister. They had flown over to try and talk me into not filing for a divorce. They felt that with time, things could be healed. Unfortunately, I don't heal well when my son is separated from me by thousands of miles of ocean. I especially don't heal well when I know in my heart of hearts that there is another man who carries the interest of my wife. I was enraged and irrational, but was able to politely ask them both to leave. If my wife wanted to make a go of it, she would have to be the one to tell me. In my heart I hoped she would come and tell me this herself. I carried a hope that she would change her mind.

Little did I know that my mother-in-law was headed back to the States to give follow-on advice to my wife, "Dump the bum."

I received separation papers the following month from a Miami judge. I had no say in custody or anything else. I was actually billed for the proceedings and ordered by the court to pay $350 a month in child support, half my monthly income. I could have fought it under the Soldiers and Sailors Act, which would have dragged it out in courts for months, if not years. Instead, I simply paid it.

While a lot could be said about how it all happened, I never spoke to anyone about it. It is true that my wife chose to leave me, that she chose to take my son away from me, and that she sued for separation and divorce, as well as custody. But, it is also true that I put her in harm's way, expected her to take whatever I was taking, and filled her life with stress and difficulty. There probably should be a course for women who fall in love with soldiers, titled "Warning: This is what it's going to be like."

I've never said much about it to anyone. I guess in my heart, I can sense what it must have been like to a young girl from Miami, just graduated from high school, to be moved to a foreign country where she didn't know the language, etc. But as much as I missed her, it was my son whose innocence fed my heart. He was the tiny little fellow I most loved escaping to when I was home. I could spend hours with him and it never seemed enough. Since it seemed that I was never at home as much as I wanted to be, in the eyes of my wife it probably appeared a sort of competition. Feeling that she was not getting enough attention, along with the other challenges she faced, and the secret mail I wasn't supposed to know about from her boyfriend back in the States did not improve the situation. In later years, once the personalized pain had dulled, we both went on to live our own lives . . . but the real tragedy was the loss of my son. He truly was the light of my life, and I know he grew up far away from me apparently thinking or believing, despite the letters I initially wrote to him, which were returned unopened, that all the stories he was hearing were probably true. At the time it was all that I could do.

A few years later I actually spent a week in Miami on leave, parked in a rental car across the street from the home in which he was living. My ex-wife Sue had married her boyfriend and they all lived together in a duplex apartment in the Miami Shores area. I sat for hours watching him playing in the yard, observing his interaction with his stepfather (which appeared healthy and loving), all the while fighting the urge to make my presence known. I was at war with myself, wondering if suddenly reappearing in his life wouldn't undo all the stability that he now enjoyed. In the end, I drove away feeling as though I had been gutted hara-kiri style with a rusty knife and that somehow I deserved the pain I was feeling. I'd trashed Sue's life and my own; I felt I had no right to trash Scott's as well, at least any more than I had already.

I stayed in accompanied quarters because they had no room for me at the bachelor senior noncommissioned officers quarters, and spent almost eight months working at the huge field station building just outside of Augsburg. It was pleasant, because I was almost always drunk. I think it was one way of dealing (or not dealing) with the feelings that I needed to integrate. Since I was drunk so much of the time, I wasn't really working, either. This was an easy state to maintain in Germany, which is the land of liter-sized beer mugs. Also, the field station was so large and there were so many people, one could get lost in the crowd.

I was also obviously on the rebound, which has a tendency to draw lonely women to a man. I had a number of parties in my quarters that were greatly frowned on by the married couples and families living in the same stairwell. I would invite ten or more women to my party, leaving them with the impression that there would be a lot of guys present as well, but when they'd show up at the door they'd find out it was only me and them. Once they discovered I had no sexual goals in mind, we'd all have a great time, playing games like Monopoly and cards, while running the stereo at maximum bass, all the while putting a major dent in my liquor supply. I know my neighbors complained to the military police, but the problem was that most of the women I invited were MPs. Some mornings I'd find complete strangers sleeping in my bathtub, on the living room couch, or more than one sharing the guest room bed. In hindsight, I think I was trying to repair my personal image of my manhood, but without any form of commitment. Eventually, I burned myself out with the partying and began to dry out. I realized that I would either have to straighten out my life, or I'd end up one morning blowing my brains out on the golf course with my .45 automatic. I made a concerted effort to bring structure back into my life and carry out my duties as a noncommissioned officer.

After a few months, I met my second wife, Specialist Four Margaret Mary Murphy, while working a late-night shift. When I met her, she was actually called Murph by her workmates. Since I didn't know that we would eventually marry, we became very good friends. We would meet at the local *Gasthaus* (bar/restaurant) just off of Sheridan Kaserne, in Augsburg, after working a Mid shift (that's midnight to 8:00 A.M.). I actually liked working those late shifts because there were fewer people there, and they were of lesser rank, and they left you alone if you got the job done. When we met at the Gasthaus, we would consume scrambled eggs with ham, and drink a couple of liters of beer for breakfast, while writing letters home. She usually did the letter writing, and I did more of the drinking and watching. She took very good care of me. She always got me to my quarters when I was intoxicated and was able to keep me out of trouble with the locals.

The Oktoberfest that year got me off dead center. We all met at a friend's house where we warmed up on Harvey Wallbangers made in liter mugs. You know your drinking is out of control when you don't care how large the mug is they are mixing your drink in. I had two of those before we headed out for town and the beer fest. I drove, because I was the (comparatively) sober one in the crowd. We spent six hours at the beer fest, going from tent to tent, swilling beer out of more liter mugs, and chugging Steinhagger shots in between. At this point it gets sort of fuzzy for some reason. But, according to reports, I took everyone out to dinner at a very expensive nightspot on the top of a building in downtown Augsburg, one of those new rotating restaurants.

We had numerous bottles of wine with the meal, which everyone assures me were excellent. They also assured me that I was the soberest one of the bunch and was a perfect gentleman. The problem was that when the maid woke me up in a strange hotel room the following noon I couldn't remember where I was or where I had left my car. Actually, I couldn't remember much about what had happened after 7:00 P.M. On top of that, I knew that I had been robbed. I had started the previous evening with approximately $280 in my pocket, but now had a five and some change.

I found my car four days later, after spending a lot of time walking around Augsburg looking for it. I had spent all my money buying the dinner for which everyone was profusely thankful. But the whole experience scared the hell out of me. How could someone act perfectly normal, perfectly sober, act like a perfect gentleman, and have no memory of it? What if I had killed someone while my consciousness was out to lunch?

While this may be a somewhat foreign thought to most civilians, it is not for a soldier who has spent time in a combat zone. It sometimes doesn't take much to trigger the kind of reaction that results in a quick death, especially if you are not conscious of what you are doing or if your self-control has been altered by drinking. I could have ended up doing life in prison with absolutely no knowledge of having done the crime! A completely scary thought.

I immediately cut my drinking back to almost nothing, maybe a beer or glass of wine with dinner.

They say the best way to change something is to first alter the setting. So the following month, after thoroughly drying out and cleaning up my act, I requested a meeting with the border site commander and volunteered my services at a remote collection site. I was moved immediately to Schleswig am Zee, which back then was a small village up near the Danish border.

Schleswig was a damp and dreary place. In the winter there was very little sunlight, and everything was always covered in mist, fog, and rain. During the summer it was reversed, with darkness never quite descending over the land. It was the perfect little Viking village. It was a place on a deep fjord, where they still built magnificent boats for rich Europeans and Americans.

My tour there was fine initially. I was the detachment commander and made all the decisions. I had replaced a first lieutenant, who had "misplaced" a key component for an encryption system. (I later found it nailed over the door of the dump manager's shack. It still had the classified keys set on it.)

The only truly scary event was my own guard almost shooting me one night when I surprised him by walking into the operations building at 3:00 A.M. He had just reloaded his .45 automatic and had jacked a round in the chamber. When I suddenly opened the door and walked in, I startled him and the gun went off, burning a small scar across my left armpit. Good thing I had raised my arms while shouting at him. I think it scared him a lot more than it did me, if that's possible.

Eventually, the detachment became one of the best in Europe. It was so much in the limelight, in fact, that they eventually assigned a captain as the commander and my replacement. While there, I again applied for warrant officer, and again was turned down. They said I was needed where I was.

Not long after the captain arrived, a warrant supply officer was also assigned. Soon after that, a first lieutenant arrived, who became the operations officer. All of these people were doing the single job that I had been doing alone for nearly a year. It was clear to me that with the closing of all the other intelligence bases in Europe and consolidation at Augsburg, and the withdrawals of personnel from the Far East, they were running out of things for officers to do.

As a result however, I had lots of time at my disposal for goofing off. This allowed me to make a number of trips down to Augsburg over long weekends. I started seeing Murph again—now known to me as Peggy, as she had informed me her family addressed her as Peggy.

Eventually, Peggy finished her time in the Army and rather than reenlist, she quit. After a short visit to her home in St. Louis, she showed up at my apartment door in Schleswig. We lived together there until my divorce finally came through. In hindsight, marrying her was probably about the worst thing I could have done for her or me. But that's nevertheless what I did. I was still desperately in search of love, or at least what I understood it to be.

Immediately after the wedding, we both started trying very hard to change one another. Although we never did prior to the wedding, we started fighting with each other almost from that first day. We would have been better off if we had just stayed close friends. Repeating myself—being married to a husband assigned to a remote detachment is probably the most devastating thing that can happen to a military wife. And there I was, putting Peggy into the same circumstances that so aggravated my relationship with my first wife. Eventually, the marital stress got to me. I requested reassignment back to the Augsburg area. At least there, she would be among a lot more Americans, and I would no longer have to cater to what had grown to a handful of officers trying to manipulate their way to the top-dog position in the detachment.

A couple of days after my return to Augsburg, I was asked to drop in on the S-2, a Colonel David Schofield, who was the man in charge of physical and personnel security for the Augsburg field station. He said that he had followed my career at the detachments with great care and liked the way I handled security problems. Would I consider working for him? I agreed, even though I knew it would tick off the others in my MOS.

The single greatest insult to your comrades in arms is to abandon your primary MOS for another job, or so it would seem. But at the time, I really didn't care. I was burned out with all the emotional ups and downs with my second wife, and I just wanted a nice, stable job that wouldn't be too much trouble to my marriage. I was also fed up with those in charge within my MOS structure, because they had ignored my third request for warrant officer.

I must point out that applying for warrant officer is no easy task. It involves nearly three hundred pages of materials, including at minimum full-length photographs in dress uniform, medical papers, educational papers, test papers, and a few dozen specifically written recommendations from light colonels and up, as well as your entire military history, and supplemental forms for additional background security checks. If your application is accepted, you have to sit two boards, where you are grilled on your MOS, and you are competing with dozens of others of equal capability as yourself. One in a hundred applications eventually makes it. It was an exhaustive process that I'd already been through three times. This time I was not as well qualified as many others, although I had twice the field experience of anyone else applying. So, I decided to move to S-2. I accepted his offer.

Working in the S-2 was something entirely different. One of the older counterintelligence warrant officers spent a considerable amount of time teaching me what I needed to know from a counterintelligence standpoint. He also taught me how to cut and form my own lock-pick tools, and taught me how to use them. He taught me the differences between the high-security locking mechanisms of various countries. I learned what to look for as a security weakness and how such a weakness might be capitalized on or manipulated.

I was spending more and more time away from home, on one job or another, traveling from one site to another, visiting one border site region or city or another. So my home life was not improving. However, my mind was. There is nothing more intuitive in the intelligence business than physical security. You begin to develop a feel for something wrong long before you know what it is that actually tips you off. This is especially useful when you are looking for the guy faking it in a crowd of people. I became very good at the job and stayed with it until the latter part of the following year.

In the fall of 1977, I had once again applied for warrant officer—the fourth time. This time I had the added problem of my commander not wanting to sign off on it. Colonel Flynn had taken over as field station commander and his signature was required for my packet to go forward. But he refused to sign it. He said, "Because if I show you such favor, then I'll have to show the same for anyone else who wants to apply."

I suspect the real reason was because I embarrassed him during a personnel security inspection one morning during a shift change. I used a counterfeit badge with the picture of a large male chimpanzee on the front to walk right into his Secure Compartmented Information Facility (SCIF). I believe he felt the subsequent security report reflected badly on how he was running his field station. He failed to understand that we were paid to violate a SCIF in order to improve its defenses. In any event, it didn't matter. I was turned down a fourth time, this time for being way too old. With more than twelve years overseas fighting the good fight, I was now considered over the hill. I might mention they had promoted three others to warrant that I had trained.

In reality, the Army quickly recognizes people who always get the job done and done well. The problem is, in doing so, they make themselves too valuable to the job they are doing. Hence whenever someone who is doing a valuable job applies for a promotion, like an appointment to warrant officer, it means the Army will have to move you and at the same time release you from the valuable job you are already doing so well. In the intelligence business, a senior noncommissioned officer or officer will spend an average of five to six years overseas, at which point they are usually moved to stateside assignments, where they train other people. What I didn't know at the time was that my fieldwork was considered by many to be exceptional enough to keep me overseas doing it. I was more valuable in an active mission overseas than I would have been back in the States. So, they once again turned down my request for warrant.

I spent a year doing physical security and counterintelligence missions along the Eastern bloc border, and earned one of the first Meritorious Service Medals awarded at Field Station Augsburg. It was a new medal created in 1969 to acknowledge outstanding meritorious achievement or service in a noncombat situation. It ranks between the Defense Meritorious Service Medal and the Joint Service Commendation Medal as a noncombat award.[6] After more than twelve years overseas, I finally received my first orders reassigning me stateside—to a combat support unit located in Fort Bragg, North Carolina.

Anyone who has ever been in the Army will tell you that after more than twelve years overseas doing a real mission, such an assignment is the same thing as putting a gun to your head. I called the reassignments branch at Department of the Army to discuss it. It was patently clear that the assignment was in revenge for working out of my primary MOS.

I called everyone I could think of in the Washington, D.C., area to ask for help in averting the assignment, but no luck. I was going to Fort Bragg and nothing short of suicide was going to stop it from happening.

Once you've been in the Army long enough, you know that for every rule there is a counter rule, for every "no" there is a "yes" way of doing things. I took nearly a week off from work and spent the entire time trying to find a way out of going to Fort Bragg. Eventu-

---

[6] I actually earned two of these awards in Europe, as the Cold War was considered a noncombat zone. I also earned three Army Commendation Medals and three Meritorious Unit Citations while serving in Europe.

ally, I discovered an answer to my problems. I only needed to volunteer for something they couldn't afford to say no to.

The next business day, I sent a back-channel message to the Office of Personnel, Department of the Army, Washington, D.C., asking what specific language qualification the Department of Defense considered to be the greatest need. Their response was—Mandarin Chinese.

I checked with my education office and was informed that my language skills test (ALAT) was two points too low to qualify for Mandarin. So, I arranged to be retested the following afternoon. I scored one point off perfect with the DLAT (the ALAT re-test) and submitted my request for reassignment to the language school in Monterey California, to study Mandarin.

The following day, the personnel office in Augsburg, Germany, received a telexed cancellation of my orders to Fort Bragg and an amendment to them, which read assignment to Monterey, California, for Mandarin Chinese. With a long sigh, I figured at least I wouldn't be going to Fort Bragg. I was already beginning to plan my eventual assignment to the first military assistance group mission to Beijing, China, which was in the rumor mill. I figured three to six years in China would round out my career. I might even find a good job speaking Chinese somewhere after I left the service.

When I returned to the States a couple of months later, I spent leave time in St. Louis, near Peggy's family. I wanted her to stay in St. Louis while I was in Monterey because I figured it would be better for both of us. I'd be burning the midnight oil trying to learn a new language and she would only be bored. Besides, we were fighting like cats and dogs and it wouldn't have helped my studies.

About halfway through my leave in St. Louis, I got a phone call from the Intelligence and Security Command (INSCOM) headquarters in Arlington, Virginia. I recognized the voice. It belonged to the chief warrant officer in charge of my MOS, CW4 Richard Maher. He didn't beat around the bush. If they initiated the necessary paperwork to make me a warrant officer, would I give up my assignment to Monterey and accept a reassignment to headquarters? He was planning on retiring and they needed someone to take his place.

I didn't believe him, and told him so. I wanted confirmation from a higher authority. Moments later, I received a call from General Rolya, the commander of the INSCOM, who asked me if I would accept as a personal favor to him. Without hesitation I accepted, and two weeks later I was in Arlington looking for an apartment.

My new job was nearly overwhelming, nothing like anything I'd ever experienced. As a brand-new warrant officer, I was stepping into a job that had been filled for more than a decade by a very senior chief warrant. My new position was as the senior projects officer for the deputy chief of staff for Signals Intelligence and Electronic Warfare, INSCOM, and I was accepting responsibility for my MOS worldwide. I suddenly found myself buried in a mountain of paperwork. There were problems with training, equipment, and personnel that spanned the globe, and a number of multimillion-dollar research and development (R&D) programs already under way, and new ones in the works, and problems that hadn't yet been addressed.

Within a few months of my arrival at the headquarters, I found an apartment in Reston, about 25 miles from my work in Arlington, so Peggy was able to join me. I was fortunate, because they allowed dogs. I had brought my Dalmatian, Barney, from Germany with me. He had become one of my best friends, always at my side when I wasn't working. Unfortunately, none of us would be together very long.

Most of the R&D projects I found myself working on required an intimate knowledge of computers. So, I was sent to the advanced automated data processing (ADP) school in Fort Benjamin Harrison, Indiana.

Originally, the personnel office turned me down, because the primary prerequisite for attending the school was a degree in computer science, which I didn't have. But, buried within the fine print was an exception. They waved this requirement for chief warrant officers. Of course the Army never intended for that exception to apply to people who had been promoted to warrant outside of the ADP field. But, since it didn't say that specifically, I applied under the exception and was accepted.

I spent the next six months at Fort Benjamin Harrison being taught all I could learn about computers. When I first arrived, the assistant director of the school suggested I repack my bags and return to my unit. He told me that no one without a computer science degree had ever attended the school, and the chances of my being able to keep up with my class, having no background at all in computers, were remote. I rejected the idea outright and told him it would take a direct order. I think he let me stay to watch me fail. I put in seven-day weeks and sixteen-hour days, burning the candle at both ends. To everyone's surprise, including my own, I successfully graduated. When I returned to Arlington, I completely immersed myself in my job, which was building one-of-a-kind computer-driven black boxes and managing our numerous overseas sites and assets.

Almost a year after I had arrived at Arlington Hall Station, sometime during the month of October of 1978, my immediate supervisor, a GS-14, Ralph Maahs, handed me a rather cryptic note. The note asked me to report at one in the afternoon to an unused room on the third floor of the headquarters building. He said he had no idea what it was about, but the request had come from the deputy chief of staff.

When I reported to the room later that day, I met two military intelligence (MI) officers dressed in civilian clothing. The younger of the two introduced the older as Scotty Watt, then identified himself as Fred Atwater. (He now goes by "Skip," and is my neighbor.) Fred asked me if I knew why I was there, and of course I said no.

They opened a briefcase and dumped a number of classified and unclassified documents out onto the desktop, and asked me to look them over, which I did. There were numerous documents addressing psychic programs in other countries and newspaper clippings containing some of the same subject matter. I took my time looking the material over. When I was through, they asked me what I thought about the material. How did I feel? Did I think it was bogus?

At the time, I was almost positive that I was being set up. I had a strange gut reaction to the material on the table, as well as a large "caution" feeling regarding the two men standing in front of me. It made me feel very wary, and on my guard. So, when I responded, I did so with something like, "I'm not sure I believe any of this, but if it is only half true, then it should be looked into." They then asked me where I worked, which I told them, then they cautioned me not to discuss the subject matter with anyone else, even my immediate supervisor, to which I agreed. Mr. Maahs later asked me what the meeting was all about, and I simply told him that it was a survey the operations security people were running. That seemed to satisfy him.

A number of weeks went by during which I heard nothing. Then one afternoon while I was working out some developmental scheduling, I got a phone call from Scotty Watt. He told me straight out that I had given all the right answers and they now wanted me to attend a larger meeting. I would be advised as to where and when that would take place. When I asked him what the meeting was intended for, he responded that he couldn't discuss it over the phone; I would have to come to the meeting to find out. He told me to tell Mr.

Maahs that my attendance at the meeting was on the instructions of the chief of staff. I could tell by Ralph's reaction when I told him that he was getting peeved with my being called away to clandestine meetings he didn't know the reason for. I really couldn't blame him, as we were buried in enough work to keep half a dozen people inordinately busy.

It was the beginning of my second year of assignment at the headquarters of INSCOM. The new commander, Major General Freeze, had just promoted me from warrant to chief warrant officer, and I was beginning my second year in what was considered the top job within my military occupational specialty.

To demonstrate the width and breath of the job without violating any subject matter classification, let's equate my job to something in the civilian world. In terms of responsibility, I was something akin to the director of product development for a major manufacturer. While such an example might seem at face value inappropriate, it demonstrates the level of technical and operational responsibility commensurate with my job.

To put it into an appropriate perspective, you need to understand that I shared that responsibility with a man named Ralph Maahs, a senior government civilian. Ostensibly, the reason for having a senior civilian within a military office, especially a headquarters, is to ensure continuity between people like me and people who replaced people like me. Since I was an Army officer, and Army officers are generally moved from station to station on a rotational basis, assigning a senior government civilian is a way of ensuring the wheel doesn't get reinvented. (However, I have to add, this may or may not be true with regard to my particular office, because the chief warrant officer I actually replaced held the job for a period exceeding fifteen years. It should also be noted that Ralph was also a retired chief warrant officer who held that same job before being hired as the senior civilian.) Therefore, while on the surface I may appear to be far more important than I actually was to the process, in my office there was continuity and experience going back probably to the date of Adam's original sin and we were all warrant officers originating from the same rib. This also meant that I was being groomed, which would have a major impact on my relationships there later, as a result of my involvement with the remote viewing project.

In any event, Ralph and I ran the MOS worldwide. This means we were responsible for everything that happened operationally or technically—present or future. To equate it to the manufacturing example, this means we were responsible for all the items being manufactured, why they looked and operated the way they did, where they would be sold or used, how people were trained to use them, who would use them, and what they could or might be capable of doing—manned or unmanned, local or remote.

We were responsible for coming up with the designs and capabilities for the vehicles that might replace and/or carry the items, how and where they would be manufactured, what their ultimate distribution would be, and how new models would be paid for or by whom. In addition to the above, we were responsible for coordinating all in-house and out-of-house manufacturing, funding, and production. We directly interacted with and coordinated agreements with other parts/subsegment manufacturing companies (in this case other services with like MOSs), deciding which markets would be addressed, when they would be addressed, and how they would be addressed.

Imagine all the people, funding, software, hardware, and training it takes to do all of that, and you have covered approximately half the job description, the technical side. Balancing this out was the operational side. When you think of the operational, all I can suggest is that you start with the following two words—*threat* and *world*. This gives you some kind of idea of what my job was like.

Now why is this important? Well, I want to make a very specific point. Within my MOS, or group of peers, I was sitting in the catbird seat. There just weren't any jobs really that were better, more demanding, or more respected than the one I was sitting in. I was working right next to the flagpole, putting in ten- to twelve-hour days with lots of weekend overtime, dealing with unbelievable challenges, and loving every minute of it. No one else in my field had access to this exposure and experience.

But, I gave it all up.

In one brilliant flash of insight, I said what I said and changed my life forever. In that one small instant in time, I let a little voice from somewhere deep inside my head tell me what to do. Would the director of product development for General Motors do that? He probably wouldn't. Well then, why did I?

In hindsight, I think it had to do with a process of self-selection. The way I was approached, the material I was shown, and the almost derisive context in which it was presented did everything possible to ensure that I was completely turned off regarding any interest in the paranormal. In subsequent discussions the two men in suits—Skip and Scotty—implied that it was all part of an elaborate scheme they had for locating and recruiting sensitive (psychic) people, but I did not buy it. In reading further you will understand why.

Chapter Five

The Special Project

So, who were these two men? And, how did I end up sitting in a chair in a sterile room at the headquarters of U.S. Army INSCOM? Their story began some years earlier with a report floating throughout the intelligence community that was written by a CIA analyst named Dr. Kenneth Kress in the winter 1977 issue of *Studies in Intelligence,* an internal newsletter published within the Central Intelligence Agency (see appendix A). In this report, Dr. Kress talked about experiments in something called remote viewing, which had been ongoing at Stanford Research Institute (known now as SRI-International) since the 1972 time period. In these experiments, a man by the name of Pat Price, a retired police officer, was reputed to be describing the inside of controlled NSA operational sites, as well as providing information regarding code word materials stored within files located at those sites. An example of one of Pat's drawings, a crane, is included at the end of appendix A, and referenced within the Ken Kress document. The crane was part of a Soviet nuclear test site for which Pat also provided drawings of underground devices that were not known to exist at the time of his remote viewing.

It has subsequently come to be known that Mr. Ingo Swann was providing remote viewing support in that same time period. Swann is a psychic now residing in New York. He is also the author of numerous books of note in the paranormal field, both fictional and nonfictional. He is an exceptional artist and has produced paintings as well as prints coveted by people the world over. He is also a master at many other skills too numerous to list. While we've had our arguments and disagreements, I like to think of him as also a friend. He is certainly an exceptional remote viewer, and probably knows more about human superskills than any other man alive today. He is also a brother in arms—having served in the Army when his country called.

In the Army, many may have read this report, but only one individual truly understood its importance. That was First Lieutenant Frederick Atwater, now known to his friends as Skip. He clearly understood the potential this document represented, as well as the possible threat to national security. At the time, Lt. Atwater was a counterintelligence officer working for the 902nd Military Intelligence Group, located at Fort George G. Meade, Maryland. The other man in the interview room with me on that day was Major Watt, known to his friends as Scotty. Because he had been passed over twice for promotion, the powers to be felt he couldn't be damaged by association with such a project. So he was assigned as a volunteer supervisor.

What I didn't know at the time, but would later find out, was that their original assigned task was to locate and recruit potential remote viewers to test the degree to which remote viewing could be taught, organized, and utilized for intelligence collection purposes. In my opinion, based on my very early interactions, Scotty and Skip were pretty much split as to whether or not they believed remote viewing would be effective. It was clear to me that Skip came from a background where the possibility of psychic functioning was very real, and while Scotty was not closed to the possibility, I believe he considered its eventual verification as somewhat remote or even dubious.

The fact that these two very professional intelligence officers could differ so radically on the subject but be open enough to attempt its verification is a testament to the ingenuity and skill of those recruited to do the job of defending the nation. I'm not sure I would have had the same courage in like circumstances.

Despite the above, one should not automatically assume that the United States Army was encouraging such exploration, because—as time would tell—it was not. From the outset, great care was taken to keep the effort as quiet as possible. This was done not only for the normal security considerations, but also to ensure that the automatic ridicule that is nearly always generated by the subject matter did not kill the effort in its premature stages.

Initially no one actually knew how to recruit a psychic. No documents or studies outlined what you needed to look for in a psychic. About the only way to really tell was to directly test someone—an expensive proposition, even back then, but especially when you begin hiring scientists working in the San Francisco Bay area.

Skip was able to find a document that provided some insight about general traits alluded to be found in people who were thought to be psychic. This is provided as appendix B. Generally, it suggested people who were well liked, who tended to seek answers to problems outside the norm, who were seemingly successful in their careers, and were self-starters. The backgrounds of successful intelligence officers might on its own generate even more problems in narrowing down the pack. Usually if an intelligence officer survives a career, that alone speaks to his or her ability. But, it was at least a starting point.

Over a considerable period of time, they picked through the records and narrowed the possibilities to those recommended by senior supervisors within the headquarters. One of those supervisors was my own, Ralph Maahs. I remember the day very well. I arrived at work very early, as was my custom, made the first pot of coffee and started working my way down through the foot-high stack of new work jammed into my in box. Ralph came into my office and told me that a couple of "spooks" wanted to meet me the following afternoon in an empty office at the end of the hall. I asked him why, and he only said they were interested in interviewing me. I pressed him, asking what the interview was for, and he reiterated that he didn't have a clue. I was to find out later that in actuality he didn't know at the time, though he was informed indirectly by the commander, General Freeze, at a later date that it had something to do with the paranormal. I only came to know this at all because some months later Ralph pulled me aside and warned me that my involvement with such craziness was putting my soul as well as my career in great jeopardy—a somewhat scary but typical reaction to what we were attempting to do in the Star Gate project.

I approached the interview warily. Generally, someone was called to such an interview with a couple of suits for one of only a handful of reasons. First, it was almost always in conjunction with a background investigation on a coworker who might be in jeopardy of losing his or her clearance because of some action or inaction they thought you might have witnessed or had informative access to. No one likes to be put in the position of having to report on someone, especially when you already know there is nothing overt enough to have created any kind of a warning blip on your own radar screen. Second, it could have a direct relationship to some action or inaction of your own. An even scarier thought since I could not recall anything that I might have done to warrant an investigation.

Most people do not realize that people within military service and the intelligence branches can be, and are, frequently targeted to do nefarious work for enemy intelligence services, or sometimes their own people.

Peter Grose wrote a book called *Operation Rollback: America's Secret War Behind the Iron Curtain* (Houghton Mifflin Co., 2000). From it I quote a Communist counterintelligence agent of some note, Samuel Ginsberg, a.k.a. Walter G. Krivitsky, reporting to the House Committee on UnAmerican Activities about inappropriate activities of members of the Communist Party. "It very often happens that a member of the party furnishes information . . . to individuals whose identity he does not know, without realizing that he is thereby engaged in espionage," which means people can be enticed into doing things they believe to be right which are ultimately wrong.

And third, the system has discovered some way they can use you for which you would never volunteer your services—something that had occurred on numerous occasions when I was stationed overseas, and something that was almost always terribly unpleasant in its outcome.

So, to say that I entered the interview nervously would be an understatement.

As I've already noted, I did follow the small voice in the back of my mind, and at the time responded in what I believed to be as truthful a way possible. I honestly felt that should psychic functioning be real, it would pose a very severe threat to our nation's security and we should know as much about it as could possibly be understood. My responses were about as perfect as one could hope for, falling about midway between Skip and Scotty's position on the matter, thus assuring me a second interview.

I walked away from the first interview wondering more about the strangeness of our counterintelligence division than about their long-term intentions. Had they told me that they were planning to actually investigate the use of psychic functioning as a collection tool, I probably would have done what most others still do, and resorted to some form of ridicule, followed by laughing my way out of the office. Instead, I left as mystified as when I entered. When I got back to my office, I went back to the more mundane issues of my job, like figuring out how to wisely spend a couple hundred million dollars of taxpayer's money. Little did I know there would be a lot more happening a lot sooner than I expected.

If I had been asked in 1978 where I would be in 2002, or what I might have done in the interim, I would surely not have responded accurately. Psychic or not, there was absolutely no hint of the circumstances that drove me down the path I ultimately pursued.

(In fact, just to demonstrate the depth of this mystery, the old Soviet system has collapsed, and I am sitting in a hotel in Moscow working on this very paragraph—something that would not have even been a remote possibility in 1978. Never mind the fact that I've just given a paper on the paranormal at the University of Moscow, which was crowded beyond belief.)

The second contact occurred approximately two weeks later. I received a call from Scotty asking me if I would please travel to Fort Meade to attend a meeting with some others in reference to the discussion we had previously had. He stated that I should not talk about the subject matter, as it was sensitive, and if I required someone to speak to my boss, it could be arranged. I explained that it was difficult for me to take time out from my job without an exceptional reason, so someone would have to at least speak with Ralph for me. Less than an hour later, Ralph was called to the chief of staff's office where he told me that the chief of staff wanted me to attend a meeting to be held at the 902nd MI Group's conference room the end of the week. I asked him what it was in reference to, and he said that he didn't know, but the chief of staff had made it very clear that I was to attend and that it was important to the commanding general. The chief of staff never looked up from his desk.

Impressed by the amount of pull Scotty apparently had within the command, I decided to go. A couple of days later I drove early one morning to Fort Meade to see what the meeting was all about.

I arrived about fifteen minutes early, and was ushered into the 902nd MI Group conference room—an impressive place, with heavy wood paneling, and appropriate "war room" accouterments, buried deep inside an older brick building and layers of security doors. I was surprised to find about eighteen other people present as well. A few of them I remembered seeing in the halls of the headquarters building, none of whom I knew personally. Some were in civilian clothing and some were even wearing Navy uniforms. I was somewhat disappointed because it made me feel vulnerable to some extent. If Scotty intended to talk about the subject matter we had previously discussed, I certainly wasn't going to be comfortable doing so in front of a room full of strangers.

But, maybe that was part of the plan—make everyone feel as uncomfortable as possible and see who sticks it out. Of course those thoughts were anything but clear at the time.

To complicate matters, when Scotty and Skip entered the room they carried numerous classified documents, which they scattered across the tabletop. These addressed specific threat assessments concerning other countries' efforts in the paranormal, something that came as a total surprise to me. Having been initially reticent about discussing the subject matter, I quickly became curious as to what these other countries were doing and how they were doing it. As can be imagined, the information was quite sketchy and not very detailed, based mostly on rumor or innuendo cooked from second-hand or tertiary reporting, attributed to both reliable and unreliable sources. But, it would be fair to say that it was very interesting. In any event it certainly piqued my curiosity as I moved in for a closer look.

I suppose part of the plan was to allow us to read and discuss the information to see what our reaction would be. The little voice in the back of my mind was talking to me very softly once again, and it was saying,

This is a part of the test. Be careful here. Don't believe everything you are being shown. Be careful here.

As a result I was cautious about what I would say or not say to others within the room. I neither trusted nor distrusted those present. I adopted a "let's wait and see" attitude.

After about an hour, Scotty and Skip returned to the room with a Major Keenan, who I was later to learn was the officer who, along with Skip, had actually initiated the proactive investigation into psychic functioning. He announced that since we had had a chance to read over some of the material and discuss it among ourselves, we should be able to respond to his first question. I can only paraphrase his first question, which went something like the following, "Do any of you feel uncomfortable about the subject matter?"

Clearly, it would have been a huge understatement to say no. A large number of hands went up. This sort of surprised me I think, as I was not particularly made uncomfortable by the material itself. What made me more uncomfortable was the fact there might be some serious threat posed by such a possibility. In my discussions with some of the others present, I gravitated toward two individuals—a man by the name of Kenneth Bell (Ken), and a Melvin Riley (Mel); both seemed to be not only comfortable with the material, but they were even down-to-earth about it. Their matter-of-fact attitude was more of an encouragement to me than not. It helped to keep things in perspective. The little voice inside my head said,

Be cool. Hang in there for a bit longer and see where this is going.

So I sat comfortably in the back of the room with the idea that I would eventually see where all of this was going. (Or, another way of looking at it, just how far was this going to take me?)

Major Keenan then said, "Those who are uncomfortable can leave. I caution you that you should not discuss anything that you might have seen here today. Those of you who stay will be asked to sign agreements to protect what you are about to find, hear, or see."

I stayed.

What is interesting to me in recall is the number of things I noticed back then but never really thought about until now. There were interesting observations that may or may not be important, but probably should be noted, simply because they happened.

1.) There was a preponderance of men. Out of approximately eighteen people present, only two were women. I don't know statistically if this was about the same male/female mix as existed in the headquarters at the time. While this is possible, the little voice in the back of my head tells me that it is probably not correct. From the outset, I had a sense that there was a negative reaction to women within the project, and this has never left me. It was further evidenced by actions that occurred that I'll discuss later. In any event, the two women present chose to stay, and for all intents and purposes appeared to be just as critical in their thinking, and just as cautious as any of the males.

2.) Everyone present was being cautious. It was clear that the subject matter was disturbing to many, not so much from what it actually was, as what it represented. If we were somehow vulnerable to psychic functioning, then there were no safes or locks sufficient to block access to our most treasured secrets. In fact, that meant that we were all vulnerable to exposure, no matter what our jobs or responsibilities were. Somewhere out there was someone possibly accessing our very thoughts. This was serious enough a threat to make one's blood run cold at the thought, and it was a thought that I'm sure most of those present actively resisted. Instead, it was my desire and hope that what we would eventually find out was that none of it was real, none of it really worked, and we could all sleep happily and comfortably in our beds at night, convinced of our invulnerability. But, the little voice in the back of my head, while not content with that, was at least not pushing it any further.

3.) As I said earlier, it is nearly impossible to know who is psychic and who is not without a direct test. This was certainly the case back then, and to my knowledge is still the case today. I've heard others claim to be able to tell, but I've never seen that demonstrated. It is one reason why later on in the project we ended up with people involved who were not so much psychic as crazy. As with being psychic, many believe they can tell if someone is crazy or not. But if anyone thinks that by looking at someone they can tell whether or not they are insane, I've got news for them. Someone does not have to be staring off into space and drooling out of the corner of his or her mouth to demonstrate insanity. (In fact, I've done just that many times myself, after spending weeks in the field under a blazing sun in 100 percent humidity, then simply having an ice-cold beer set down in front of me.) So, testing is an accepted necessity—and back then, it was even more so.

In hindsight, I would also suggest that those of us who decided to stay that day were in actuality going through a very clear and systematic self-selection process. Again, I would like to credit Major Keenan, Scotty, or Skip with that complex a thought process, but I can't. I believe it was more synchronistic than not.

In any event, those who did stay opened themselves to the next level of investiture—a direct interview with the people from SRI-International—who, up until that moment had been kept secretly hidden out of sight.

Dr. Hal Puthoff and Russell Targ were waiting in the wings to present our first exposure to remote viewing, which was a movie of a retired police officer, Mr. Pat Price, doing a typical "outbounder" remote viewing session. An outbounder was someone who actually traveled to a randomly chosen site and interacted with it. In this case, the target was the courtyard of the Stanford Medical Center.

With no one in the room having ever seen a remote viewing before, to say that it created quite a sensation would be an understatement. Pat Price was taken to a sealed room on the top floor of the Stanford Research Institute's Radio Physics Laboratory, where he was kept for approximately half an hour, while Hal Puthoff randomly selected a sealed opaque envelope from a safe drawer. Puthoff carried the envelope out to the parking lot and climbed into a car with the cameraman. After driving around in traffic for a bit of time, he pulled over to the edge of the road, opened the envelope, and read the directions inside, which instructed him to drive to the Stanford Medical Center, and walk around the inside courtyard. The inside courtyard has a very distinctive pattern to it, and some interesting patterns on the walls.

Back in the windowless room a few miles away, Pat Price was sitting with Russell Targ in front of a camera, as Russell asked him to draw his perceptions about where Hal might be standing.

The film showed Price drawing an enclosed courtyard, with similar patterns to those found within the Medical Center courtyard. Even the layout was presented with a very clear approximation of size relationships between objects and distances within the courtyard. Unbelievable! One could assume that if you were familiar with the area—which I was not at the time—it would be no trouble to determine where Hal was actually standing, no matter how large the search area might be.

Such a demonstrated potential was both mind-boggling and frightening. It left me feeling that a new door to reality had just opened. At the same time, I could feel the flow of ice water across the underside of my arms. From a spying standpoint, we were obviously vulnerable in the extreme. How much detail could someone like Price provide on a specific target location? Were there others like Price? My head was suddenly filling with questions and possibilities. And the greatest question of all—what was I doing in the room and how would I be involved in this strange new world of remote viewing?

After the film had ended, we were asked to continue reviewing the materials that had been provided, as each of us would be individually interviewed. I remember sitting down at the conference table across from a Capt. Kenneth Bell, then a counterintelligence officer.

There was another gentleman I met at the time, whose name I would also later come to know well, Melvin Riley. He was a staff sergeant and photographic interpreter. We talked in very low voices about the apparent possibilities we had just been introduced to. I remember we were all somewhat in disbelief about what we had seen. We were of the same mind, in that while we were willing to be open, we reserved judgment about the subject matter or its veracity based on what other proof might be proffered to us at a later time. Eventually, it became my turn for the interview.

When I first entered the room, I was surprised to see only Hal present. I thought that both would be doing the interview. As I later found out, they were surprised at the number of people who had been located and who had decided to stay and be interviewed. I think they were not used to finding so many with open minds in one location, or at least not so many potential remote viewers. They had had to split up the group to do the interviews.

Hal asked me a little bit about my background, which I openly shared. I did not feel that I was any more open about the subject matter than anyone else might be. In fact, I probably would have responded that I felt myself a little bit more in disbelief. When you are faced with the possibility of paranormal functioning, your natural inclination is to "not believe." What I had kept well hidden of course was the fact that I had had a near-death experience seven years earlier in Europe. I had learned very quickly that most within the United States Army had very little openness to such an experience and, for all I knew, these scientists would be even less inclined to believe my experiences.

Hal had obviously been shown an information sheet about me and began his discussion with some general questions about my background. Where did I grow up? What kind of general background did I have? What were my overall feelings about the possibilities I had been shown within the Price film? I remember my answers were all very cautious. I allowed him to know that I was very curious about what I had seen, and at the same time not quite sure I believed it. I tried to walk the razor's edge, so to speak, never really giving any information that might demonstrate how it had profoundly affected me, nor what I might actually believe about it. I stayed as neutral as I could be.

After about fifteen minutes of what I would call general banter, Hal looked me directly in the eye and asked, "Have you ever experienced anything that might be equated to a paranormal event?"

My first inclination was to lie and respond in the negative. But the little voice down deep inside me would not allow me that protection. It was saying,

Now is not the time to be timid. Answer the man.

So I did.

"Well, actually, I've had like experiences in my life. Ever since I had an NDE back in 1970."

I could actually see the light in Hal's eyes immediately brighten. He did not seem to be shocked by the response at all, but sort of seemed to expect it. I then gave him a very brief summation of my experience, and alluded to the fact that ever since, I sometimes seemed to sense things, or know things, either just before they happened or about events that I could not have access to in a normal sense. He asked me if I would be willing to be tested by them at their lab in California.

Again, that little voice jumped to the fore and responded in my stead.

Say yes, damn it!

"Yes, of course."

Hal was pleased and said that we would talk again. I returned to the conference room.

Once everyone in the room had been interviewed, a process that took nearly two hours, Scotty Watt returned and informed us that we had all been very supportive to the process. We were told that some of us might be contacted in the future and some might not be. We should return to our units and our jobs and not discuss anything that had occurred. I bid farewell to those I had met and returned to Arlington Hall Station, where I finished the day heavily distracted by what I had been exposed to. Little did I know at the time that events were going into motion that would forever change my life. I could not know at the time that these changes would ultimately call for the destruction of my career, a divorce from my second wife, and another complete change in my perceptions about reality.

These changes would bring me a great deal of exposure within nearly all of the major intelligence agencies of our government, would thrust me into the halls of both the Senate and House of our government and eventually result in my appearance on all the national networks, as well as major networks in numerous other countries. Had I actually known at the time the extent to which I would be affected, I am sure that I would have chosen another course of action.

One of the most troubling aspects of remote viewing is the need people feel to take a position on it. These positions are inevitably extreme. When first exposed to scientifically demonstrated RV, people usually either react with disbelief and automatically resort to ridicule, or the opposite occurs, and their curiosity is sparked.

In the first case, this results in what are usually vicious and personalized attacks on the remote viewer's integrity, reputation, or history. In the second, the viewer is overwhelmed with requests for personalized proof: "Okay, show me! I want to see it for myself." Even though there is sufficient extant scientific evidence to fill a room, they either want to destroy the possibility (viewer) or demand that it be demonstrated. This puts a huge and unfair burden on the subject or viewer, resulting in a great deal of stress.

In my own case, because of my reputation within many of the agencies I supported, the history of the project and my contributions to it, and the history of my participating within the research, this has become almost unendurable. The demands that have been made on me have now gone way beyond reasonable.

I am constantly being placed between a rock and a hard place. If I do not acquiesce to the demands for proof through a live demonstration, I am accused of being a fraud, or worse, accused of having cheated in my previous work. If I do the demonstration and it fails (which it is apt to do a percentage of the time), then I'm also accused of fraud or the skill is put down as "he made a great guess before" or "it must have been luck." If I succeed, in many cases the person walks away and refuses to talk to me again, as I must be doing the work of the devil, or it quite frankly scares the shit out of them and they are unable to cope with it.

Only a small percentage has taken the healthy, or middle, road, and agreed that quite possibly there is something going on that can't yet be understood and that it requires further study, or care in its use or application.

When you've dealt with these conditions for 23 years, it begins to wear you down. Add to this the fact that in many cases, my public demonstrations are usurped by others and used as proof for their own capabilities when they could not remote view their way out of a wet paper bag, and you begin to understand why, if I had had a clear view then of where I am now, I might not have even entered the program in the first place. The frustration these experiences present at times is almost overwhelming. It is not my place to make everyone who comes into contact with remote viewing comfortable with it, nor do I have to prove it to anyone but myself.

When it comes to understanding the kind of differences that lay within the past of someone who believes in the paranormal and someone who doesn't, almost always people point to my NDE as the probable event affecting my belief, perhaps the key reason why I am open to the paranormal, and perhaps the reason why my informational boundaries are somewhat different from the norm.

But I vehemently disagree with such a perception. It takes a lot more than a single experience to build the philosophic and spiritual structure of an individual. Certainly, an NDE has a great deal of impact, but it is more the straw that breaks the camel's back than a single transformational event. In my own case, I've gone back over my life numerous times to try and pin down what makes things different for me when it comes to the paranormal. I just can't seem to find any angle that has that specific an impact.

In any event, a number of weeks went by and the memory of the events of that day faded. The conditions at home were not improving in my relationship with my wife, so I buried myself deeper into my work. She countered this by looking for and finding work with a newspaper publishing company in the Reston area.

Chapter Six

A New Remote Viewer

I received a phone call many weeks later from Scotty Watt. He said, "Well, you've said all the right things." I wasn't sure what he meant by that at the time, but later he told me that people who appeared to be too eager to join the unit were discarded out of fear that their eagerness might hide an underlying instability that would cause trouble later on. Whether this is true or not, I've never been sure, and I don't think they were either. He asked me if I could come to the office at the 902nd, and I agreed, not really having any idea why.

The following Monday when I visited the office, I was told that arrangements were being made to send me out to California to visit with Dr. Puthoff and Russell Targ. My boss, Ralph, would be given an appropriate cover story. The trip would be for a period of two weeks—an exceptionally long time given the amount of work and commitments I had at the time. This worried me considerably, because I wasn't sure they'd be able to actually do what they said.

One comical aside to the trip was that I was supposed to sign into the lab at SRI-International as Scotty Watt, "to protect my identity." The problem was, SRI had only one receptionist, and she had no difficulty in determining that the five individuals who followed me later on, one of whom was a woman, were surely not all named Scotty Watt. I had been overseas working a live mission for so many years. It bothered me a lot that a more serious attitude was not in place.

Leaving my boss thinking that I was going out to California to test some equipment at the Electronic Signals Laboratory for the chief of staff, I arrived early on a Monday morning at the receptionist's desk of the radio physics lab, at SRI-International. Signing in as Scotty Watt, I waited for only a few minutes before being greeted by Dr. Puthoff, who then gave me a tour of the lab facilities. Mostly it consisted of offices for research personnel on one floor and an actual windowless remote-viewing room on an upper floor. Their entire area was sealed off from the rest of the building by a security lock. I spent the entire first day becoming acquainted with the facilities and generally talking about remote viewing and ideas about how they felt it might work.

While it was clear that everyone felt remote viewing worked, there was no clear idea of how or why. This actually increased my curiosity. I had heard many stories about Pat Price and Ingo Swann that were fascinating, but didn't give me any further clues to how I might be able to do my own remote viewing. I spent the rest of the afternoon lounging in a pool at the Mermaid Inn a few blocks from the lab facility. (Everything was within walking distance, which was nice.)

The following morning I reported at 8:00 A.M. to do my first remote viewing scheduled for 9:30. This was the first fact I actually learned about remote viewing—the importance of what they called "rise-time." As it was explained to me back then, rise-time meant scheduling a specific time for the actual RV so that you had plenty of time to spend clearing your mind and adopting an appropriate attitude focused toward success, or at least an expectation of success.

In my career, there had never been any latitude for rise-time or an attitude adjustment in preparation for an event. In my world events just happened, usually with very little warning. They could be and usually were serious crises, and you were trained to deal with them in that fashion. If failure followed, you would quickly find yourself doing something less demanding. So, to be honest, I thought the idea of rise-time was quaint, and I didn't buy it outright. It sounded like what we would call "fluff"—extra chrome to make something look pretty . . . but when in Rome—so I arrived at 8:00 A.M. sharp.

I was taken directly to the third-floor RV room, where I made myself comfortable with Russell Targ. He locked the door, lowered the lights, and asked me what I thought of remote viewing or the paranormal world in general. I sensed that he was sort of setting the scene and attempting to make me comfortable. Unfortunately, I was beginning to feel performance anxiety creep in the back of my mind. So far, no one had told me any of the secrets that were supposed to enable me to do the RV. Surely, you'd get a hint or something? In any event, I played along.

At precisely 9:30 A.M., Russell said the outbounder was probably at the target site and we could begin. The outbounder was supposed to be a person on whom I would mentally focus, in the hope that accurate information would then be passed. Back then I was led to believe that no one was sure if another human at the site wasn't needed for passing information. In actuality, they already knew that wasn't necessary, but they also knew having an outbounder at the site was more conducive to helping me to believe in what I was about to do. They were attempting to help me convince myself that it was possible to do RV. They knew it was possible, but at the time, I didn't. My first target outbounder was Hal Puthoff.

A detailed description of my first target, which was the Stanford University Art Museum, can be found in *Mind Trek* (McMoneagle 1997). There is no reason to go into a lot of detail about it, other than to say that what I was able to imagine turned out to be sufficiently accurate to achieve a first-place match (the highest category match.[7]

We skipped a day between each RV, allowing me enough time to process the results and discuss them with whoever happened to be involved in the experiments. Over the two-week period, I was never able to go beyond a belief that I was inventing the information, or simply looking into my imagination and reporting whatever I was finding there. At the end of my stay they did an independent judging of all six sessions combined and told me that I had five first-place matches and a second-place match, one of the best series results they had ever seen. I was now officially a remote viewer. I returned to my job at the headquarters more confused than not.

A week later, I was asked to report to the RV project office at Fort Meade on Wednesday afternoon of that same week. Ralph was testy about it, but since the directive came from the chief of staff, there really wasn't much he could say about it. I reported in at Fort Meade and found out that one of the original six individuals was already out at SRI enjoying the swimming pool at the Mermaid Inn.

---

[7]Targets were independently judged by someone using the remote viewing results to select the best match to a possible five target sites. A first-place match meant there was sufficiently detailed information to permit picking the actual target from a pool containing the target and four controls.

Capt. Ken Bell was already there when I arrived. He had not been out to SRI yet, so he said they had asked him to help out with the practice sessions we were going to run. Using the same protocol that had been used at SRI, a sealed envelope held in a safe was chosen by tossing a pair of dice, and an outbounder—in this case Scotty Watt—departed for a secret location. In this case, there was no risetime, and no special facility. We made do with what was at hand. We locked the door and I stretched out on the old leather couch!

Fred Atwater acted as the monitor, and Ken Bell observed. I stretched out on the couch and closed my eyes, trying to shut out my surroundings as well as the distractions. This was very difficult to do. I could hear the muffled voices of people through the interior walls, as well as footsteps on the bare floor just outside the door. Birds were chirping in the bushes outside the window and there was almost no air circulation in the tiny room. There was even the sound of commodes being flushed in the bathrooms overhead. But I did the best I could. At the time I didn't feel I should complain; it was either going to work or it wasn't.

After about twenty minutes, Fred informed me that Scotty was now at whatever location he was supposed to be at, and I should try to describe it. We had a small recorder going and some blank sheets of paper to draw on. I opened my mind to whatever my imagination had to offer and got exactly nothing—my mind was blank, zip, nada, zilch! After about five minutes of silence I made stuff up. It was about as general as I could come up with—large building nearby, grass, sidewalks, streets, telephone poles, etc. After sweating along for fifteen minutes, I admitted that I didn't have a lot but what I had given was about it.

Fred never flinched. He thanked me for the information and asked me to draw some of my perceptions. We terminated the session.

After Scotty returned, we all went out and piled into the government car and drove across post to the front of the post exchange facility. It was a relatively new building, stretching out across the face of a very large parking lot. But, there was absolutely nothing relating to it in my session. I was totally bummed out.

A lot of doubt then entered my mind—had my time in California been rigged? Had they looked at my results and taken me to some place that seemed to match? My memory said no. None of my material had been shown to the outbounder until after I had been taken

The Stargate Chronicles

to the targeted site then returned to the building. Could it be the absence of a rise-time? Maybe. I had an urge to make some very general correlations to my RV information—I said large building, and there it was, wasn't it? Well . . . sort of. I let it go. It was a total failure and nothing like the results I had out on the West Coast. I was very disappointed and confused by the entire experience. I felt like I had wasted everyone's time as well as my own.

When we returned to the office we talked about it. Scotty was matter of fact about it. I sensed that his attitude was that it probably wasn't really going to work and he had been proven correct. He didn't actually say that, but I could sense he was somewhat unsurprised by it all. Fred, on the other hand, was very supportive. He told me that I gave it a good try and that we could expect failure at times and not to worry about it. I'd nail the next one. We called it a day and everyone went home.

Well—Fred was wrong. As the weeks passed and the other five individuals finished their times out at SRI, I continued to report on Wednesday afternoons and we would run through practice sessions. Usually two of us reported on the same day. On Wednesdays it was usually Ken Bell and me, but sometimes a retired Navy petty officer, Hartleigh Trent, would be there.

Ken and I hit it off from the outset. He was a very serious-minded counterintelligence officer who approached everything very logically, and it was easy to see that he took this very seriously. It took a long while, however, for him to open up and talk to me about his own experiences beyond those we shared in the group sessions. He was one of the best people I've known in developing his ability to meditate. He carries that ability into his martial arts and it makes a lethal combination. Eventually, we became very close friends and still are today. Ken lived in base quarters at Fort Meade, and could almost walk to work.

Hartleigh was a large man with a very dry sense of humor who loved collecting original hand-painted bird prints, and viewed himself as a sort of inventor. He worked as a government civilian at the NPIC (National Photographic Interpretation Center.) The *Encyclopedia of the U.S. Military* in 1990 described the center as a facility operated by the Central Intelligence Agency, charged with imagery analysis of satellite reconnaissance. We also became very close friends as the project progressed.

On one of my trips to his Maryland house, I left my wife, Peggy, drinking tea with his wife while he took me down the hill in the backyard to show me his new queen bee and her colony. We were standing there totally unprotected as he gently lifted the top from the hive and extracted the centerboard, where her nest was situated. Her soldiers were somewhat excited and were swarming all over us both, landing on our faces, exploring the insides of our ears and noses. He calmly pointed to her with his finger and explained that as long as you projected gentle and protective waves to her, the others would leave you alone. I found that he was correct. As he began to slide her back into the hive, however, Peggy appeared at the top of the hill and, seeing us completely covered with bees, let out a yell, "Oh my God!" By the time we had re-covered the hive and extricated ourselves, my eyes and nose were swollen to twice their natural size. We then sat on the back veranda while his Italian wife showed me how to make a home remedy for bee stings. That's the way Hartleigh was, larger than life, and always exploring it.

Over the course of a couple of months, I did 24 practice sessions, none of which exceeded the quality of my first attempt. It was very depressing. I could see some of the others having minor successes in their efforts, but for me there was only failure.

On my 25th attempt, something happened. I remember sitting in the small room trying to shut out the surrounding noise, concentrating on trying to imagine what the target could be, when I was suddenly disturbed by what felt like some kind of strange noise that wasn't in the room. I thought, "Could that be in my head?" I mentioned it. It was in some way connected with an open-faced building with some kind of funny lemon-green metal objects. It all seemed quite bizarre, but I dutifully reported everything anyway. At the end of the session I did some drawings that seemed to make some kind of sense to me, but really didn't depict anything that I was familiar with. The outbounder returned and we all loaded into the car to travel to the target site. I expected nothing more than another failure. When we pulled up in front of the base fire department, I could suddenly see all the fragments of my session falling into place. It was like suddenly seeing new information and recalling it, all at the same time. It wasn't perfect, but I knew that I had made significant contact with the target. Fred looked at me and said, "Now I guess we know what you were telling us about." And smiled.

In a very strange way, I suddenly felt as though everything I had experienced out in California had come all the way around the barn and landed in my lap again. Suddenly everything was connected in my head. It was as though I suddenly knew there was a special switch up there in my mind somewhere, and while I wasn't exactly sure how to throw it, I knew I could find it again. From that point on, I began to improve remarkably from practice session to practice session.

The weeks continued to pass and everyone was improving incrementally. No one person was pulling out ahead of the other, but we were all finding our special skill and honing it in slightly different ways. Eventually I was able to meet the rest of the crew as well.

Staff Sergeant Mel Riley was our only enlisted man. He was a photo interpreter who did a job similar to Hartleigh's, but worked in a building on Fort Meade. His job there was primarily operational security.[8] From the outset I could tell that there was friction between him and Scotty. I was never sure if it was personality-generated or based on the fact the Mel was enlisted. In any event, it went on the entire time Mel was with the unit and Scotty was present. What I liked about Mel was the fact that he had spent time in Europe flying covert collection missions through East Germany. I had been aboard a few of those aircraft and personally preferred to keep my feet on the ground. I knew that he had been shot at more than a few times. He knew what it meant to put it on the line, which wasn't something everyone had the opportunity to do while serving the country.

The other participants who had gone through introductions to RV at SRI were two civilians. Since they prefer to keep their names private, I will refer to them as Frank and Nancy. Frank was a counterintelligence agent who worked out of the headquarters at Arlington Hall Station and Nancy worked in the same facility as Hartleigh, as a photo interpreter over in the Naval Yard in Washington, D.C. Besides these original six, there were four other participants, two of them civilian employees of the government and two intelligence officers. Due to their sensitivity about possible exposure, these participants will remain unidentified.

Early in the project we encountered a major glitch. An officer working in the Office of the Army Assistant Chief of Staff for Intelligence advised the assistant chief of staff for intelligence, Maj. Gen. Ed Thompson, that we were probably operating not in compliance with the directives regarding human use. Since the CIA's involvement

---

[8]Measures designed to protect information concerning plans and operations (past, present, and future) against unauthorized disclosure.

in the early fifties with LSD experiments and mind control, all programs using people were sensitive to meeting certain human use requirements, and ensuring that all participants gave informed consent regarding their participation. We all had to fill out a pile of forms, which were forwarded, along with a classified request, to operate the project up through the system to the Army's surgeon general. Many felt that the requirement was stupid and time-consuming, but I didn't. It was clear to me from the problems that I was having in adjusting to some of the experiences that someone less stable might slip over the edge. So we stopped practicing for almost two months while they processed the paperwork. I found out much later that the science side of the project actually took it a lot more seriously out at SRI. They would actually establish a human use oversight committee to maintain vigilance over their experiments and methods—something never done on the military side.

Before, there had been some hilarious events during our practice trials at Fort Meade. Acting as an outbounder for one of the other viewers, I drew as a target a small tourist gift shop on one of the main highways leading into Washington, D.C. When I got there, the instructions said to spend fifteen to twenty minutes looking at the gifts and then report back, which I did. I did not know that the owner, who was sitting in a rear office, had been watching me on a security monitor system. When I got back, Fred, the viewer, and I loaded into the car for our return visit, which was the feedback portion of the remote viewing exercise. We all descended on the gift shop, moving among the aisles examining things, but of course not buying. The owner, still in his office, noticed that I had returned and this time had brought friends. Feeling that his place was being "cased or targeted," he called the local police. When the police car pulled up outside, the remote viewer and monitor immediately left the store without notifying me. I was "apprehended" and questioned.

"What are you doing? Where are your buddies? Why are you casing this store?"

I had to think fast.

I laughed and said that I was a consultant working for a production unit out of Los Angeles. They used me to search out possible shooting locations for scripts they were considering.

The owner beamed at the possibility that his store might be considered for a scene in a movie. He quickly dismissed the police, saying that he had made a mistake. I spent nearly an hour in the owner's office drinking coffee with him and talking about the script and what might be needed. I left him with a promise to send him my card and information on the movie should they decide to shoot it in the Maryland area.

When I got back to the office, everyone laughed about what happened. In truth, it was a difficult situation, and one that I might not have been able to talk my way out of.

On another occasion, the outbounder for one of the military viewers was a woman. The specific target selected was a restaurant with a peculiar façade. What we didn't know, but probably should have, was that it was also well known to the police as a location where prostitutes sold their wares. After standing on the corner for approximately twenty minutes, she was "apprehended" and hassled by a couple of officers doing their duty. She returned to the office absolutely mortified. Needless to say, there was no direct feedback for that viewer.

During this stand-down period, I stuck to Arlington Hall Station and worked full-time in my office there. I remember being concerned, while we all waited for approval from the surgeon general, that the project wouldn't continue. It seemed inconceivable that it wouldn't, given we had the full support of our own commander at INSCOM, Brig. Gen. William Rolya; Army Chief of Staff General Meyer; and Secretary of the Army Clifford Alexander. In fact, I was somewhat amazed at the level of exposure such a small project got. Access to the project was not only controlled by level of clearance, but it was designated an "access by name only" operation. This is not a matter of trust, but of controlling access only to those who have a direct need to know. This is usually reserved for the most sensitive kinds of projects, where life and death matters are always at hand or operatives are in deep cover and at great risk. We knew the Russians were working with psychics. I suppose others were concerned that if the Russians got wind of what we were doing, they might take action to neutralize our facility in some way. This was a major stretch of the imagination for most, but a very real possibility in the minds of others. I suppose it depended on just how real one felt the project was.[9]

Originally I was told that the project, first named "Gondola

---

[9] Many felt, and still do, that the close-hold secrecy was to protect the participants from ridicule. But, if this were truly the case, the project would never have been approved in the first place. Some later commented on a fear of Senator Proxmire's Golden Fleece Award, but that was long after the project had proven itself under fire.

Wish," was approved to operate for three years, primarily as an OPSEC function. The first year was to be used for training, the second for collecting information by targeting U.S. intelligence operations for which ground truth was known, and the third year to be spent analyzing the results and evaluating the potential threat. I was told that I would only participate when needed, and at most two afternoons a week. This was sufficient to piss off my boss, who was ordered to allow my absence by the chief of staff, and could do nothing about it. While this was in essence true—he actually couldn't do anything about it officially, except live with it—I could see the issue beginning to appear in my in basket, with small notes that said things like, "I need you to do (whatever it might be at the time), if you aren't too busy hanging out with the chief of staff." Normally, I'd pitch the notes, but they started to appear more frequently. What I didn't know at the time was that Ralph was already considering his retirement in three or four years and I was possibly one of the warrant officers being groomed to take his place. One of the reasons for bringing me into the office was to train me for the day that I would retire from the Army, at which time I would be an eligible and long-term replacement.

I wasn't cooperating and I was afraid that it was going to start showing up in my annual officer's evaluation statement. I vacillated for many months, trying to decide whether or not I should continue with the special project, at risk to my career. A number of events made the decision a lot easier than I thought it would be.

Eight months into the project, the accuracy of our viewing against ground truth targets was beginning to be noticed in the Office of the Assistant Chief of Staff for Intelligence. Some details we were able to provide about ongoing U.S. intelligence operations were, to be frank, scary. At the same time, we began to notice an unusual level of interest being shown toward our office by others within the building. We were the only locked and sealed special-access room inside a locked and special-access-controlled building. People with the highest-level clearances were not allowed behind our green door, but the rank of those who were was not going unnoticed. A decision was made that to maintain the integrity of the operation we would have to find another place from which to operate.

At the time, Fort Meade was already overstaffed and space was at a minimum. There were no standalone buildings anywhere on the post that anyone knew about. After a visit to the base engineering

The Stargate Chronicles

office however, we discovered some buildings that had been condemned and were scheduled for imminent destruction. This was an old cook's school that existed back during the war—the big one—WWII. The old school consisted of six two-floor barracks buildings, a single-level administration building, and an Army mess facility. It was empty and had not been occupied for probably fifteen years. It took going to the post commander, but we succeeded in getting a freeze put on destruction, and moved in. The site was excellent, sitting under a grove of huge live oaks in a large field directly across from Kimbrough Army Hospital.

Building 2561 was the old mess facility (Army dining hall), and was essentially one long, open room. The first thing we did was to remove the numbers from the buildings. When you entered, the first third was red clay tiles, one foot square, which were actually black from years of grease and dirt. There was a raised area in the tiles where the huge ovens and stoves had once set, and a giant overhead steel hood for removing the fumes. Against the wall was a very large quarter-inch-thick iron plate that was originally a heat shield for the ovens. It was about six feet high beginning at the floor and stretched about twelve feet along the wall across from the entry door. The place was filthy, with holes in the plaster, and we couldn't tell what color the actual floor covering was. It reminded me of the old mess halls at Fort Jackson that were being torn down when I attended basic training back in 1964. We spent an entire weekend cleaning the floors and repairing the walls. We also had to repatch some of the heating pipes that ran along the wall, which were covered with a wrapping that looked suspiciously like asbestos. Most of the red tile had to be scraped clean, using paint scrapers, (down on all fours), then rescrubbing with steel wool. All in all, it was a very nasty business. I think most would have been surprised to see so much rank doing the grunt work.

We used the raised tile areas to support our long row of steel safes; the garbage area was used for storage; the single bathroom got a unisex label (probably the first on Fort Meade); and the old storeroom became Scotty Watt's new office. The rear wall behind his desk was a loading ramp with double steel doors, so we had to hang a curtain to cut the draft across his backside during the winter. Over time we continued to add to the building, a wall here, temporary office dividers there, nicer furniture, desks, chairs, tables, etc. But initially it was pretty Spartan.

Across the small road was building 2560. It had a front entry room; three RV rooms; an observation room, from which someone could monitor a session using audio only; and a break room, which we filled with more comfortable furniture and all-frequency lamps. Fred eventually turned it into a small greenhouse with more than a few dozen plants. We went to great lengths to ensure that very few visitors ever got to see that specific building. It was where the viewing took place and we didn't want our feelings about the place disturbed. Eventually, the front room became the operations officer's and Mel's office area.

All the work we did was on off-duty time and weekends. This meant a two-and-a-half-hour commute each way for me, and more impact at home. I wasn't totally open about what I was doing with Peggy, which only caused more problems between us. But the difference in the RV atmosphere between the new building and the old was like midnight and high noon. For all intents and purposes, we dropped off the face of the planet.

The only outward appearances that changed were the doors and windows. Security cages were installed across the windows and painted to blend in, and the mostly wooden doors were replaced with steel ones and high-grade security padlocks. There were never more than three or four civilian cars parked out front, and everyone wore civilian clothing, so we generated very little curiosity. Without building numbers, we seldom had visitors who didn't belong there.

At the end of 1978, our project underwent a major change. Up until that point we were only evaluating the effectiveness of RV against known targets. Some of our reports were being passed around areas of the Pentagon and were being viewed with great interest. Our accuracy against many of these targets was even more astounding since only the people in the Pentagon who identified the targets with coordinates knew what was actually located in those positions. Some of the targets were even deliberately skewed to see what would happen.

As an example, I was handed an overhead photograph of an aircraft hangar surrounded with planes and told there was something inside the building that was of interest. My job was to target the building and tell them what it was.

At first I was angered by the request. Doing a remote viewing without any front-loading at all is difficult enough, but now they were showing me pictures of the buildings I was targeting, which caused me a tremendous problem with overlay. Nevertheless I relaxed back onto the worn leather couch and prepared by closing my eyes and trying to relax, emptying my mind. I'd come a long way in just seven months and I would do what I could. I tried to forget about the building completely and challenged myself with opening only to the target of interest. That's all they really wanted to know about, I kept telling myself, so that's all that I would concern myself with.

After twenty minutes or so, I brought myself out of a deep place of meditation and slowly opened my mind. The first thing I saw in my mind's eye was what looked like a short stubby periscope-type device with some form of optical view-port. I began to sketch and describe it in as much detail as possible. Soon what looked liked two layers of a vehicle interior appeared with what appeared to be armored seats. There was some kind of a hardened military-type computer built in with a modified keyboard, which I also tried to draw. Eventually I began to have images of what appeared to be very large bullets or shells lying on their sides (indicative of an automatic loader), all following some kind of a curved track. They disappeared to the rear of the seats. I continued drawing what I was seeing in my head, one element sort of leading to the next, not really knowing exactly what it was that I was presenting. Eventually the information signal line dried up and I had to quit. I sort of sat there in a daze, feeling completely drained of energy.

I looked at my drawing and laughed out loud. "That sure doesn't look like any airplane I've ever seen," I remarked. Fred agreed but didn't seem disappointed with me. By this time, he was becoming a pretty good judge of when I was in contact with a target location and when I wasn't.

Many weeks later I found what had gone on. The Army was getting ready to field its new heavy tank, the Abrams XM-1. Back then, there were only prototypes in existence and few were allowed access to them. They had parked one inside an aircraft hangar and surrounded the hangar with airplanes as a test to see how much of an effect front-loading might have on a remote viewer.

Another problem with moving into operational targets was their time requirement. They'd always come with a drop-dead date or time. As in most operations, we'd usually be the last people notified, and there would be very little time in which to respond. So the stress was terrific, especially on the viewers. I was beginning to carry that stress back to my apartment with me and my relationship with Peggy was getting worse. We almost never talked about anything. I was cut off from the outside world of news, so current topics were out, and we shared zero friends. Most of her friends didn't have a clue about the military, never mind intelligence, and probably would have totally lost it if they had known what I was doing. My friends, of course, were limited to Ken, Mel, Fred, Scotty, and Hartleigh. Beyond that, there were only a few of the part-timers who would drop in once in a while for a cup of coffee, or to work a specific target, and those visits were becoming less and less frequent.

During this same period, we got word that sometime in the next year the American Skylab was expected to fall from orbit and break up. Just to get a break from some of the more serious targeting we were doing, I took it on as a personal project. In a conversation I had with Hal Puthoff while I was out in California, he had said one of the best ways to prove RV would be to do a target for which there was not yet an answer. In this case, no one on the planet knew where or when it was going to drop out of orbit and hit the Earth.

I wrote out on a small card, which I slipped under the glass of my desk, "When and where is the American Skylab going to reenter the atmosphere?" It seemed an impossible task.

Scotty thought that it was a target that couldn't be answered, because it had not yet happened. I took it on anyway.

After working on the problem at my desk for a couple of days, I decided the issue was more complex than it appeared. It wasn't a simple answer like, here and when. But, eventually I produced a map that I gave to Scotty and also forwarded to Hal Puthoff at SRI. I had selected a spot in Australia about two-thirds of the way west, across from the easternmost coast and about a third of the way up from the southern coast, and drew in a pear-shaped area running from the narrow end westward to a much larger end. I darkened in the narrow end and said that was where the primary craft pieces would impact, with the larger end area being the debris field that would be spread over about 1500 miles of area some sixty miles wide. It was the latter part of 1978. I predicted that reentry would occur around the 5th of July, 1979.

Skylab reentered from Earth orbit on the 11th of July 1979. I missed the primary impact area by approximately sixty kilometers, as the area I selected was a bit farther to the north. I also missed the reentry date by six days and a few hours and minutes. The other strange thing was my debris trail. For some reason I had flipped it over 180 degrees out of proper orientation. This was something I was beginning to notice in some of my drawings. It happened so frequently I decided that it must have something to do with the physical layout of my brain. Rather than try to figure out why it was happening, I just started correcting for it by drawing everything backward and upside down. I was disappointed that my results were almost ignored. Scotty never said a word to me about it. But, the next time I saw Hal, a few years later, he said that it was one of the most impressive predictions he had ever seen. I think the problem within the unit was that we had so much operational tasking to worry about they did whatever they could to discourage us from freelance-type viewing. I could understand that, but still, it would have been nice to have someone notice that my Skylab stuff had been both precognitive and accurate.

At the same time, I didn't know it but my XM-1 tank was added to a growing list of mind-blowing targets that were accumulating in a briefing book that was being passed around at the highest level. More than just the Army began to notice. As a result, a decision was made by the ACSI, General Thompson, to begin allowing other agencies to task our unit, operationally that is, for other purposes of collection than just OPSEC. Putting money behind his decision, he assigned three permanent personnel slots to the unit and increased the funding. The project name was changed to Grill Flame. This resulted in other changes as well. The work being done at SRI-International was combined with our collection project, which essentially doubled the remote viewing assets and enabled us to obtain research support as well. Mel Riley, Ken Bell, and I were asked to move to the project full time. So this became a pivotal moment of truth for me. I now had to decide if I wanted to continue with the project or resign from it.

For nearly a week I vacillated over the decision. I had no one with whom I could discuss it. Part of me was committed to the Army and what I had originally been trained to do. I knew that my office in the headquarters needed me and needed me badly, but at the same time, I knew this new form of intelligence collection was proving to be more than anyone ever thought it could be. Eventually my choice boiled down to which decision would do the least amount of damage and what was the highest probability of damage that might occur as a result of whatever decision I made. Whatever I decided to do, there would be no turning back.

In my MOS, 29 other warrants were considered as qualified as I was. In my own mind I was not irreplaceable. It might cause some problems, but eventually they would find the means to replace me. I knew it would cause a great deal of anger, though at the time I didn't actually realize how much. On the other hand, if we were doing as well as we were with the remote viewing, then the Eastern bloc countries might be doing at least as well. This meant that we needed to put on the afterburners and see if we could at least discover a defense against it. I knew by experience that it wasn't easy finding someone in the Army with the kind of talent needed to do remote viewing. I also knew, based on what I had already observed, that even when they did, it was going to be more difficult getting them to commit to participate even on a part-time basis, never mind full time. If I walked away from the project now, it could take months to replace me and perhaps I could not be replaced.

After anguishing over it for days, I finally knew that I would have to just suffer the heat and make the change in assignments. I had no idea how much angst it would cause among so many of my career-long friends.

After a long weekend, I went directly to the chief of staff's office and told him what my decision was going to be. I think he was surprised. He advised me to reconsider, and told me that if I did this, I would be doing irreparable damage to my career. I told him that, given the circumstances, I couldn't not do it. He said he would bring my boss in and tell him that they were reassigning me to a black project of national import.

My boss did exactly as I thought he would—he just stopped talking to me. You could almost feel the heat radiating from his body when he'd enter the office. I silently cleaned out my desk and packed my carryall. As I headed out the door, he stopped me and asked if I was absolutely sure this is what I wanted. I told him that it really wasn't what I wanted, but it was something that needed doing, and I was in a position to do it. He turned his back on me and never said good-bye.

What needs to be understood is the fierce intraservice competition that exists when it comes to certain issues pertaining to personnel. In my own case, the field in which I worked contained very few officers—all of whom were warrants. It took an average of nine to twelve years of experience to produce someone who could fill one of our warrant officer positions, and then only one in twelve who applied were ever selected. This was because of the extensive knowledge of technology required to fulfill the job requirements. We had recently entered the computer age and most of our electronic equipment was rapidly contracting from truck-mounted, half-ton van-sized shelters filled with electronic racks, to suitcases. Understanding the developmental mechanics and software, mission integration, support, repair, and training requirements was pushing the intellectual envelope of most of the people involved to the limit. Having a warrant officer who understood the intricate details across the board, able to fulfill that role, only to have him walk out to do someone else's project was viewed as the worst possible sin. I was a traitor in the eyes of those I left behind and treated accordingly.

Maybe they didn't know the reasons I felt I had to go, or maybe they didn't understand what I had come to understand about the threat. It didn't matter. It's just the way it was.

It really hurt leaving my old office. I was altering what had essentially driven me for more than 13 years. But I did what I had always done with things that were distasteful, ugly, or painful—I buried it somewhere inside my head. My whole focus had to be on the new problems I'd be challenged with. That's what soldiers do.

Chapter Seven

A Crisis

The Grill Flame project office was now staffed with Scotty (the boss), Fred (the operations officer), Mel, Ken, and myself as viewers, and a secretary. The secretary was a young and very beautiful young lady who was very competent in her office skills and could translate the tapes from the sessions, as well as do the normal office paperwork. Scotty and Fred actually shared duties in each other's areas of responsibility, so were interchangeable if one was not there and a decision had to be made. While Fred and the rest of us were convinced through experience that RV was a unique collection device and that it worked, at least most of the time to a usable degree, Scotty was the hardcore skeptic in the house.

As we progressed against unknown targets, he was constantly trying to test us in some way to try to prove to himself that this was actually happening and that we were not cheating as a group and trying to fool everyone. While that was a possibility, one only had to observe two or three remote viewing efforts to see that there wasn't enough information available to anyone that would permit guessing a right answer, never mind producing the kinds of details that we were producing. Scotty was constantly coming to my desk and challenging me with things he would cook up on his own.

One day he came to my desk and carefully unwrapped a deck of playing cards, shaking them out into his hands. He then pulled the

The Stargate Chronicles

jokers and direction card from the pack and began to shuffle the deck. All the while he was watching me very carefully.

I watched him shuffle the deck eight or nine times, then set it on the edge of my desk. "Cut it," he said, which I did, four times across outside to inside. We both stared at it for a few seconds. He then said, "If you're really psychic you should be able to sort them face down by color." I don't know why, but this really pissed me off. So, I picked up the deck and quickly dealt the cards into two piles. I pointed to the left pile and said, "These are the red ones." The only black card on the left side was the ace of spades. The only red card on the right side was the ace of hearts.

"Oops," I said. Picking up the deck and reshuffling it six more times, I then had him cut it, and redealt them into two piles. This time all the reds were on the left and all the blacks were on the right.

Scotty didn't say a word. He just picked up the cards and returned to his office. Ken Bell looked across from his desk and, with incredulity in his voice, asked, "How in the hell did you do that?"

"Beats the hell out of me," I responded.

I honestly didn't know. I sat at home later that night sorting cards for an hour and the best that I could do was about 75 percent on any given run.

A year later Scotty called me into his office, along with the rest of the shop. He had discovered a new kind of game. It looked a lot like a cribbage board, with five holes across and a line of rows perhaps thirty in length. It came with eight different color pins that fit into the holes. The first row had a dark black cover, which would hide the first row of pins. The idea of the game was to put in the starter row and not tell anyone what it was. It could be any combination of pin colors, or even all one color, whatever you wanted to put there. Once it was set up, the opponent would guess the colors of the pins. For example if the first row was

RED GREEN BLACK YELLOW WHITE

And the person guessed

RED BLACK YELLOW GREEN WHITE

The person controlling the game would then put in a white pin where they were correct, and black pins where they were wrong. So, the player would see

WHITE BLACK BLACK BLACK WHITE

This would tell them that their guess for the first pin and last pin was correct, and they would continue to guess until they could name them all in appropriate order.

Scotty had already set up the game and had it sitting in the middle of his desk. He announced that he had played it with his wife for a couple of hours the night before and the absolutely best game was three moves. He said according to the book three moves was exceptional. He looked over at me and asked me to give him the colors in proper order and we would see how good I was.

Initially, I was angry with him, because it was obviously meant to put me in my place, or otherwise prove that I was only lucky. The fact that he had invited everyone who was there inside to watch was adding to the insult.

"Go ahead, Joe, do it." Ken poked me on the shoulder.

He was actually giving me support, because we had become very close friends and he had a lot of faith in me.

So, I closed my eyes and let my breath out in a long, slow exhale. My mind became totally blank. I relaxed into it and began shutting out the rest of the world.

After about five minutes of total silence with me sitting there, eyes shut and meditating, Scotty said, "Well, are you going to do this, or aren't you?"

I opened my eyes and very calmly said, "I'm waiting for you to pass the answer to me." Which wasn't completely honest, but I knew it would make him uncomfortable.

He kind of chuckled at that but closed his eyes for a second, then quickly opened them. "Okay. I've passed it over, what's the combination?"

Without hesitating a second I gave him the five colors in order, got up, and walked out of his office. I didn't even wait for a response. There was silence in the office as he slowly raised the black-plastic cover. By the time I reached my desk I could hear a soft, "Holy shit, he did it!" Which kind of drifted across the room. Ken came out of the room smiling ear-to-ear. That was the last time Scotty tested me.

I liked Scotty a lot. I liked him because he was one hard-assed skeptic, which was exactly what the project needed. If we could do the kind of viewing we were doing under his guidance and using the SRI designed protocols, then there was very definitely something going on. It's hard to believe, but today I find myself asking the kinds of questions that Scotty was always asking back then; where's the hole, where's the leak, how can we make this tighter, how can we prove this stuff doesn't work? It would certainly make for a far less complicated world if it didn't.

The targeting was done in a sort of stepped, or progressive, fashion. It took a bit longer, but in the end, it was the best way to do it, because it provided us with checkpoints and incremental verifications along the way.

A target would be delivered to the unit and passed only to Scotty Watt. It might contain a picture of a building. Accompanying the picture might be a series of questions or directives: Describe the interior. What's being constructed there? What's the most vulnerable entry/exit?

Scotty would set up the remote viewing by placing the photograph (or sometimes a portion of the photograph he would scissor out). Sometimes the photograph had stuff on it that might give clues, or ideas about the structure he wouldn't want us to know. He never quite trusted anyone who held the envelope, even his operations officer. The questions would be on a piece of paper and both photo and questions would be sandwiched between two thick sheets of cardboard, black on each side.

Once Fred and I (or another viewer) were in the room, Fred would pull the envelope from a briefcase and lay it on the table between us, and say something like, "This is your target. Tell me what I need to know."

If I was on target, I would describe the building in general and its surroundings. I might even talk a little bit about the interior or what was going on inside. If I wasn't on target, I might describe an aircraft, or an event taking place in a subway. The beauty of this totally blind targeting system was that you could instantly tell if the remote viewer had acquired the right target by the first session. If I talked about the subway event, obviously I wasn't on target and would have to go through the same process again later. The next time the target package might be renumbered or reidentified in some way to encourage me as though I was going after a new target. If I gave a good description of the exterior of the building, then Scotty would restructure the targeting by asking specific questions based on my own transcript.

For instance, if I had described the building correctly, and had mentioned a room where something was being constructed. I would be shown the same envelope and the conversation would be something like this:

Fred: "Remember this target?"

Joe: "Yes."

Fred: "We're interested in the room in which you said something was going on."

I'd then retarget the room and try to describe with better accuracy what I had seen going on in the first targeting.

This material would be summed up in a report and passed back to the office requesting support. Since they were the only ones who knew or suspected what was going on in the building, it would then be compared to other information they possessed and deemed either supportive or nonsupportive. In any event, it would be used to generate newly formed leads for more traditional methods of collection, but it was never used as material that stood alone, nor was it material that was fed in to the viewer with a specific expectation or preconceived notion of any sort. Multiple remote viewers might revisit the target a dozen times before a final summary or report was issued. In some cases, it was so overwhelmingly clear what the viewer saw, it was reported immediately.

Working at Fort Meade instead of Arlington Hall Station created a huge increase in personal discomfort for me. The closest place I could afford to live on my salary as a chief warrant officer while working at Arlington Hall Station was Reston, Virginia. Commuting to the office from home was, depending on traffic, a minimum of an hour and thirty minutes one way. Sometimes I would leave for work in Arlington at 5:30 A.M. just so I could shave twenty minutes off the trip and have a leisurely cup of coffee before all hell broke loose when the general got to work at 7:30 A.M. Changing work locations to Fort Meade more than doubled the driving distance in traffic and put me on the Beltway, which as everyone who works in the D.C. area knows is a moving deathtrap. You can almost hone your psychic abilities just driving on it every day.

To get to the Fort Meade office by 7:30 A.M., especially in the winter, I was sometimes forced to depart Reston at 4:30 A.M. If it snowed while I was at work, I could look forward to not having dinner at home until sometime around 10:00 P.M. One miserable night in the middle of winter in 1979, it took me two hours just to get through one traffic light between the off ramp from the Beltway and Rt. 7, the main thoroughfare to Reston. The road had iced over and, because most people who drive in the D.C. area have not heard of snow tires with chains, or spikes, I burned a quarter tank of gas in my little Fiat 124 watching them run up and slide backward, down the slight rise in the road in front of the light, one after another. As crazy as it sounds, the only place you could pull off the road was into the huge shopping mall at Tysons Corner.

Sometimes I tried hanging around the office to wait out the worst part of the traffic, but this could be very unhealthy. By the time you got onto the road it had become what I called the "witching hour." All the people who hung out in the watering holes and taverns decided to hit the road after waiting out the same period sipping on double vodka martinis or gin and tonics. The traffic was lighter, but the people in adjacent cars were either a lot more aggressive or stupid.

Leaving for work every day a couple of hours before my wife got up, and getting home about the time my wife wanted to go to bed really had a tendency to trash the relationship. Since ours was fast-tracking it to the disposal anyway, it actually seemed to help. It saved us from a lot of fighting that would have otherwise been going on had we spent more time together.

This really ground on me a lot. Peggy was a beautiful woman who really cared about me and I was doing to her exactly what I had done to my first wife—putting job before everything else. My heart would ache sometimes, when I would get up to leave or come in so late she was already in bed asleep. I'd look down at her lying there so peacefully, and hate myself to the very core. But there didn't seem to be any way for me to extricate myself from the situation. I thought about moving a lot closer to Fort Meade, which would have actually been a lot cheaper and less expensive for us, but I couldn't get more than a year-to-year commitment out of anyone with regard to how long the project would last.

This was a problem inherent within the project all along. We were essentially allowed to exist and operate as a result of the degree of competency we displayed in our work. If the remote viewing efforts weren't good to excellent, we would not survive. If it was, then we were approved on a year-to-year basis and re-funded accordingly. That may be the proper way to run an iffy program, but it was not very supportive to making personal decisions. I was the only one not living in on-post quarters at Fort Meade, or in a house within a few miles of there. The round trips were very trying on me, and my psyche.

I raised the issue about this with Scotty and the man who replaced him, but was told that since they couldn't guarantee continuance of the program, they couldn't justify moving me into on-post quarters.

During this same time period, I received a call from "Branch" at the Department of the Army, the senior chief warrant officer who managed all the chief warrant officers in intelligence. The Military Personnel Center office or the specific management office at Department of Army headquarters in Washington, D.C., had a specific "Branch" that maintained my personnel records and was responsible for the management of my career as a warrant officer in the Army. He—or sometimes she, depending on the year—was responsible for guaranteeing equity in assignments and equal operational exposure for all warrant officers in the intelligence business. Without this kind of management, warrants requiring special schools or experience would probably never get it, and those working as the liaison officer to the military assistance group in Tahiti would never rotate out of their jobs. Those who were really good in combat situations of course would end up only in combat until their number ran out or they could find a volunteer to take their place, whichever came first.

Anyway, he called me and asked me to send him a job description for my new assignment, because it was a special slot, called a 99 position. The space I filled had to be a 99 position, because there were no military occupational specialties that called specifically for "chief warrant officer psychic spy." But my being carried in a 99 position meant that INSCOM headquarters was officially listing me as "being in excess." This had two immediate effects.

First: A very complex cover story had to be written for what my daily duties were and why I was doing them, all of which had absolutely nothing to do with my primary or any of my secondary MOSs—not something that would slip by Branch.

Second: Because I was being carried as excess, I was automatically moved to the top of the list by the system for reassignment. It was just the kind of thing the people at Branch were always looking for. They were always in need of a warm body to replace someone overseas; or in a hardship tour, an unaccompanied tour of twelve to eighteen months, where you spent the time without your family; or in a job that was usually undermanned by 20 percent or more, ensuring fifteen- to eighteen-hour days.

So, a special envoy from the Office of the Army Chief of Staff for Intelligence (ACSI), General Thompson's office, made a trip over to Branch and had a chat with the senior chief warrant who managed my file, and took a copy of my new job description with him.

Unfortunately, this made matters even worse. As was quickly pointed out to the envoy, I was one of (then) only 23 warrant officers in my specific MOS (they had lost six through attrition in two years—a result of being overworked) in an MOS that historically never exceeded 75 percent fill worldwide. They said I was desperately needed to fill a slot—one of those suggested places, of course, being the place I had vacated at Arlington Hall Station. Because of the immense workload the job carried and the intensity of the mission, it was historically avoided like the plague. The only way they got me in the first place at Arlington Hall was to bribe me with the warrant commission and a shortened period to promotion to chief warrant officer.

The senior warrant officer manager was promptly put in his place with a direct order from the ACSI office (to which he owed his own job) to cease and desist pursuit of the matter and pretend that I just didn't exist, which he promptly did, and I became a nonentity.

The problem with being a nonentity is that you no longer have someone looking out for your welfare within your MOS structure, so where you may fit in the promotion line is then conveniently misplaced. When annual officer evaluations that attest to your ability to do your job become due, and they aren't filed, no one cares. When too many evaluations go missing, there is no hope of ever seeing a promotion.

The storm abated and I accepted total banishment to the nether world of the special program, figuring my career was now dead, which it most assuredly was.

Chapter Eight

Fighting the System

In the early part of November 1979, I received a call at 4:00 A.M. asking me to report directly to the office; at the same time I was ordered not to listen to any radios, watch any television, or read any current news reports en route. As strange as that sounded, I followed my orders and traveled to the office at Meade. So, I arrived not knowing that the American Embassy located in Tehran, Iran, had been invaded by Iranian revolutionaries.

It was still dark when all six permanent and part-time remote viewers joined the operations officer, Fred, in the office. He said it was going to sound like a strange request, but that a number of Americans had been taken hostage in a location overseas, and they needed our help in identifying them. He then threw a pile of a more than a hundred photographs onto the tabletop—tell us which are the hostages and which are not. He left the room and left us to the problem. This began a yearlong problem involving hundreds of individual remote viewings trying just about everyone's patience.

It is almost impossible to describe how difficult it is to target the same thing over and over, day in and day out for months on end. The front-loading problem, born out of repetitive targeting on the same people, buildings, and areas, becomes overwhelming. You quickly become quite confused about what is real and what isn't, and what you imagined the day or week before and what is real in your remote viewing of today. The amount of tasking that was coming out of the National Security Council, the CIA, and other agencies with respect to the same target also had to be kept separate, as well as the results. Eventually, that issue was transferred to a higher echelon at the Pentagon.

What was targeted? Everything! Every building, every room, every person in each of those rooms, what everyone was doing, what they were wearing, what they were carrying, what they were eating, what their health was like, what the furniture looked like, what kind of paint or pictures were on the wall. How long the grass was in the quadrangles between buildings. Essentially, they wanted to know just about whatever one could ask about everything five cubic blocks of space had in it, within a city thousands of miles away, on a day-to-day basis. What they got was more than they expected.

They got a separate location for hostages who really weren't hostages and a different embassy where they were being held (the Canadian Embassy, where they were actually being protected). They got descriptions of three individuals who were not in the original pack of pictures, and a description of a separate building they were being held captive in (our agents who were picked up and held in a separate location.) The descriptions of the floor layouts and rooms were accurate enough to amaze people brought in who had just left the country and who had previously worked in them. The actual physical locations of each of the hostages was reported, specifically where they were being held, and how they were being treated, to the point that when one of the hostages was released early because of medical reasons, and shown the information we had accumulated, he was enraged. In his mind, the only way we could have possibly had such accurate information, would be to have someone inside the embassy with the hostages, all the time they were being held, and if that was the case then why were they still being held? He was not allowed to know.

While all of this was going on, we viewers were keeping to our word by continuing to avoid listening to radios, not watching news programs or special bulletins on TV, and avoiding newspapers and news magazines. The impact on us was that our social world collapsed. It was like being inside our own kind of self-designed jail.

Throughout the Iranian affair, we continued to do OPSEC missions, as well as other operational collection missions in support of other agencies, primarily the Central Intelligence Agency (CIA), the

National Security Council (NSC), the Defense Intelligence Agency (DIA), and most branches of the Department of Defense (DoD). The workload just continued to grow exponentially.

In the early part of 1980, we began to pick up on other things. We were picking up on U.S. military exercises, which at least to our psychic minds seemed related to the situation there. Other things were happening in and around Tehran that were quite sensitive and seemingly mysterious or out of place, involving other Americans or at least people allied to the American cause. When we began reporting these mysterious observations, we were almost shut down. We had stumbled quite blindly onto the preparations for the rescue attempt being planned. Rather than turn off the spigot of information that was flowing in, they suggested that we focus on this as well, thus performing an OPSEC mission as well as continuing to focus on filling the more conventional intelligence requirements.

When the rescue operations finally occurred, we were all moved to a single floor of an inn located in Laurel, Maryland, where we did round-the-clock remote viewing, providing a minute-by-minute description of the operation.

One of the women viewers who worked part-time was actually remote viewing at the time of the explosion at Desert One. She broke down into tears, reporting a huge fire, which she couldn't understand the reason for. Minutes later the telephone rang and Scotty informed us that Desert One was terminated for lack of surviving resources.

Upset at the sudden turn of events, the viewers as a group left the motel and went looking for a way to relieve the pressure that had been building for many months. We decided to blow off steam together in the motel, so we bought a few bottles of self-medication and brought them back to one of the rooms, where we all began to get politely obliterated.

Scotty found four of us still drinking sometime well after midnight, and one thing was quite clear, we were feeling absolutely no pain. The problem was that this included an enlisted man, and one of the three officers was a woman—all drinking and socializing, all drunk together. I guess this was more than he could take. He ordered us to go to our respective rooms and to go to bed. The following day he chose to call onto the carpet only the enlisted man (Mel) and the woman. He read them the riot act for what he believed was conduct unbecoming. In my opinion, this was totally incorrect and uncalled for. We were all workmates and close friends and we were only blowing off steam, and shaking off the result of being driven like psychic slaves for so many months.

Mel relocated himself permanently to the smaller building opposite the one Scotty resided in at work and refused to leave it. The woman, on the other hand, let Scotty know what she thought of him, firing back with as good as she got. She was an officer in the United States Army, and she had every right to be anywhere any male officer wanted to be, and do any damn thing any male officer wanted to do. She had behaved well within the expectations of proper conduct, and besides we were her friends and damned if anyone was going to tell her how to be with her friends. She scorched the walls of Scotty's office and walked out of the building never to return. It did not go unnoticed by the rest of us, that he never mentioned a thing about it to any of the rest of us. This underscored the differences in how the Army was run back then, and how it is run today. I hope the women in today's Army continue to fight for their equality, at least in regard to treatment and respect.

A few weeks later, one of the other part-time viewers quit. He said he was burned out and fed up, and would never do any more remote viewing. We were down to four. The demands for RV increased. The Iranians had moved the hostages to other sites located throughout Tehran, and we needed to relocate them all and begin from ground zero helping to prepare for a second hostage rescue attempt—only now we were operating with a 35 percent reduction in collection personnel.

About the middle of 1980, Jackie Keith came by the unit—just to visit, he said. Actually, he was supposed to be on a plane traveling to a meet with another agent. When he entered the building, I met him and said hello. His response was strangely phrased and he said he was feeling, well . . . sort of funny and very tired. This was unlike him. He was usually a ball of nervous, kinetic energy. I suggested he get a cup of coffee and go over to the RV building and take a nap on the couch there. A few minutes later Fred came in yelling for someone to call 911.

I rushed across the street and found Mel rolling Jackie over and checking him for a pulse. There was none. Mel immediately began CPR, pausing every sixth push so that I could give him mouth-to-mouth air. Many in the military are trained for it, but up until this point I had never been in a position to have to do it. No one had warned me that someone getting CPR will sometimes begin puking into your mouth. When that began happening, neither Mel nor I hesitated. I'd stop to spit to the side and Mel would use the break to give him CPR. I guess we were in a zone, because when the medics arrived with the ambulance, it seemed like only a few minutes had passed, but it had actually been almost a half an hour. We were located directly across the street from the hospital, but the only available ambulance was all the way across the base. When the medics took over, I also noticed that Mel and I were alone. I guess the sight was too much for the others. They called Mel and me over to the hospital later that afternoon, where we sat down with the coronary specialist in the emergency room who said our CPR had been impressive and we should not feel like we failed our friend. He said that Jackie's blood gasses were about as good as any he had ever seen, but his heart had been seriously damaged from the kind of heart attack he had suffered. There was nothing anyone could have done better. I'm not sure, but I think Jackie was 29 years old when he died. A gray cloud the size of Minnesota hung over the unit for quite some time. We might have done all we could have, but it hurt deep inside, losing Jackie. I dealt with it the way I'd always dealt with loss over the years. I buried it and carried on.

At the very end of 1980 we had a major security leak, which occurred as a result of a press conference given by President Carter. When he appeared on national television to talk about the ongoing Iran hostage problem, he was photographed holding a folder labeled Grill Flame. This increased the curiosity of some of the reporters who watched the program. Knowing it must be directly connected in some way with the Iran Hostage problem, many began probing for connections to Grill Flame and what it might represent. Access to the project was tightened even further when ACSI General Thompson was replaced by then Maj. Gen. William E. Odom. He had actually taken over the reigns of ACSI in the previous year, but was becoming more and more negative about the Army's use of psychics—at least that was the general scuttlebutt. In reality, it was one of those "if it's working, don't mess with it" kind of things the Army is famous for.

The commanding general of INSCOM, General Rolya, had also been replaced by Brigadier General Flynn, the ex-commander of Field Station Augsburg who had refused to sign my fourth application for warrant officer. He came out to the Grill Flame project for his

The Stargate Chronicles

introductory briefing and probably felt as though he was stepping off into Dorothy's territory in the *Wizard of Oz*. I knew that he was a very religious man and I expected (prematurely and incorrectly) that he would have severe personal problems with what we were doing. It was not unusual for people to personalize their acceptance of what we were doing, regardless of extant proof. Rank also did not matter in that consideration or reaction—good or bad.

On the day of his visit, I stayed across the street, watching through a window as he was brought into the main building. After a thorough briefing with newly promoted Lt Col. Scotty Watt, he came into our building to meet the rest of the players. When he came in, he took one look at me and froze. A small grin crossed his face and he said, "Well . . . I might have known you would be involved with this unit." From that point on, we were friends, as if all of our differences just faded into the past. Flynn didn't stay long, but it was evident from the briefing that he was pleased with what we were doing and our progress. He encouraged us to continue, but to make sure we closely monitored the protocols.

The continuing Iran hostage problem weighed heavily on us and we continued to pump out the remote viewing in support of NSC requirements. We were also tasked with other problems of an operational nature and national import—one of which was later discussed openly by President Carter. During a presentation to a group of college students in 1995, he talked about a missing Soviet aircraft that had gone down over the central African Congo, Zaire. The Soviet bomber was thought to be carrying nuclear weapons or other technology, which would prove beneficial to anyone who could locate it—not only U.S. and other country's intelligence agencies, but terrorist organizations as well. So, there were a lot of people looking for this aircraft for some period of time.

Given the square miles involved, and the difficulty of the terrain, it was difficult finding the aircraft even with the aid of overhead surveillance and photography. Search after search failed. It was brought to the Grill Flame project as a target.

This would be the perfect test. If no one else could find it, it would take some extraordinary means to locate the remains of the wreckage.

Mel, Ken, and I placed the aircraft in a specific area of Zaire, our three locations overlapping a thirteen-kilometer circle. A location given by one of the remote viewers from SRI also put it within that circle. Search teams were sent into the area and the plane was located within a kilometer of the location given by the SRI remote viewer. All locations were within eight kilometers of the crash site. Search teams on the ground said as soon as they entered the circled area on the map they began encountering natives on the trail carrying pieces of the wreck to use in the construction or reinforcement of their village huts.

This one case was publicly known to have reached at least a presidential level of interest. It also belies later CIA claims that remote viewing information was never used as standalone information, or used at national levels of intelligence importance.

On the 18th of December, 1981, still reveling in no longer having to do Iranian RV targets and actually beginning to relax with a much slower pace, I entered the office and was immediately grabbed by Scotty and led into his office. He said he wanted me to just sit there and not speak with anyone, because a problem had just been brought in and he didn't want me to know specifics. I sat for some time and waited.

Eventually, Fred came and got me and we moved over to the RV building. After my cool-down period, when I said I was ready to proceed, he handed me a picture of a man and said that his name was Brigadier General Dozier. He told me that the general was taken by force from his apartment in Verona, Italy, and he asked me to tell him where he was located.

In actuality the general had been taken the day before and it was just beginning to hit the news in the United States. Dozier was kidnapped from his home at 5:30 P.M. on December 17th by Marxist terrorists known to be members of the Red Brigades, who were posing as plumbers. Dozier was the senior United States officer at the NATO Southern European Ground Forces base, in Verona, Italy. He was also deputy chief of staff for logistics and administration.

One of the kidnappers hit Dozier over the head with his pistol butt and forced him into a trunk, which they half carried and dragged to a waiting van. The van was a rented blue Fiat. Dozier's wife, Judith was bound hands and feet with chains, and her mouth and eyes were taped shut. The group searched the apartment, presumably for guns and documents. Later, police said that there were four who actually carried out the kidnapping, and at least four, including a woman, who acted as lookouts. On the day of my viewing, a Red Brigades terrorist called and said that the kidnapping was organized by the

Venetian Column and branches of the Milan, Naples, and Rome brigade elements had participated. They referred to Dozier as the "hangman." This was the first action by the Red Brigades against a military officer and an American (Mickolus, Sandler, and Murdock 1989).

My first RV was not very good. I was getting a way too general area to be any good for locating a missing person. I had a sense that it was a place located between a very large city with a harbor and the place from which he had been taken, which was Verona. But where I had said that he had been fooled into opening the door to his home by these terrorists because they had been posing as some sort of repairmen, in fact the general and his wife had been preparing to attend a community event when his doorbell rang. They were the only two Americans living in the apartment building, so seeing a couple of plumbers at the door would not have been a surprise. The plumbers said they were there to fix a leak.

According to a later assessment, the Doziers had ignored two important tip-offs that something wasn't right. Normally, the downstairs doorbell rings before the one at their door, and the landlord would have warned them that they would receive a visit from plumbers.

I had also said that the event took place in the kitchen, but was wrong about only the general being in there at the time.

When a leak couldn't be found, everyone went back into the kitchen where his wife, Judy, was preparing dinner. As soon as the general turned away from the men, they pulled guns and jumped him.

I did not report a struggle in my RV, but later when he was asked the general stated that he did struggle, but when he saw his wife down on her knees with a gun pointed at her head, he immediately ceased. That is when they hit him on the head, handcuffed, blindfolded, and gagged him and his wife. Leaving his wife behind, they loaded him into a trunk about the size of a small refrigerator and moved him to an apartment in another town.

I didn't know at the time of my first RV that Hartleigh and Ken were giving approximately the same version of the kidnapping.

Over a number of days we were asked to target the general and try to develop enough information to aid in his being located. Because the general's wife had been bound and gagged, it was some hours before the authorities were made aware that the general had been taken. By then, the terrorists had nearly a six-hour head start. Using the Italian Autostrada, which was much like the Autobahn in

Germany, with no speed limit, they could have moved the general almost anywhere in that area of Europe, including Eastern bloc countries. It was a huge search area, and a very difficult problem.

We also didn't know at the time that the Italian police were being inundated with information from psychics—information from both inside and outside their country. At first they were open to using the more credible-sounding material in their search. However, after surrounding a number of remote villas and raiding them, only to find an important diplomat or other government official enjoying the attention of someone other than his wife, they ceased paying attention to any of the material of psychic origin—which included the Grill Flame information.

On December 20, United States Department of Defense (DoD) antiterrorist specialists joined the Italian forces in the nationwide manhunt for Dozier. Given the previous experiences of the Italians, they also ignored any suggestion that our information might be different from the normal psychic fare.

On December 22, a caller speaking perfect Arabic told the Italian ANSA news agency in Beirut "the Red Brigades of the Baader-Meinhof claim responsibility for the death sentence and execution of the American general, James Dozier, found guilty by the people's tribunal. The corpse of the American pig is in a country village and the police will find it after 8:00 P.M."

But two days earlier, Hartleigh, Ken, and I had all agreed that we were sensing the general being held alive in the same place and he wasn't being moved around.

During that same time period, Hartleigh stated that he felt as though the general were being held inside something that was located inside something, that this was something cloth, and very much like a tent. Ken reported the general as being secured by a sort of handcuff and long chain, which was connected to some pipes. We all reported him alive and having his eyes and mouth taped shut, with a set of earphones taped over his ears, as if he were being forced to listen to music he didn't like.

After his rescue it was determined that he was actually chained to a cot (the long edges of the cot would look like pipes because they were constructed from pipes.) The cot was located inside a tent, which had been set up inside the apartment. We reported that he was not in danger and that he was being treated if not well, adequately, which was true.

The Stargate Chronicles

On Christmas Eve, I got angry over the whole situation. The thought that a fellow soldier could be held somewhere against his will during Christmas, and the fear that I sensed his wife was feeling, really got me stoked. I went into another session with only one goal in mind. To bring him home before the new year—alive.

During that RV session, I felt as though everything came together. I felt like I was locked solidly into my groove and whatever I was getting was pure signal line, as we sometimes referred to the source of all information we received that we felt was accurate. I started the session with an almost perfect image of a coastline, the right-hand side of Italy toward the north. I then got a vivid image of mountains to the north and northwest. I began to feel as though I was actually floating over the area and could see as far or as much of what I wanted to see. The city along the coast looked somewhat familiar to me; I knew that I had been there.

I followed my instinct and began moving away from the coastal city due west along the main road, toward what I sensed was the town from which he had been taken. I felt like I was actually following the track his kidnappers had originally taken; I was coming in on his location by following in their footsteps.

I suddenly found myself hovering directly over a fairly large town not far from the coast and just south and southeast of a very large mountain range. I moved closer to the ground and began to pick out roadways and buildings. I followed the roads and eventually found myself near a small central plaza, across from some kind of a fountain, and picked up the smells of a butcher shop, and the faint hint of a place where they did some kind of tanning, or worked with hides. I got an image of a very large apartment building and settled in on the second floor. I came out of the session knowing that I could pretty much replicate the images and streets that I had seen.

Fred asked me to draw my visions and recollections, which I did. I produced an overall map depicting the location of the city, seemingly specific enough to say that the city was Padua (the older name for Padova, located just inland from Venice). My familiarity with the coastal city then made sense, as I had visited Venice numerous times and have always loved the city and the people. It is my favorite city in Italy.

Fred asked me why I had used the older name Padua and not Padova. I commented that it must mean the older area of the city was more important than the newer area. I then sketched as best I could the city street map that I had seen, drawing the streets closely to scale, as best I could. I pointed out the location of the apartment house on the street map, and said that the apartment he was being held in was on the second floor.

After spending so much time with each viewer, Fred could tell the difference between when we were doing a so-so target and when we were really cooking. He knew from observation that my session was about as good as it gets. He quickly arranged to have the materials passed to U.S. representatives on the ground in Italy.

The Army INSCOM was not the major player in the operation to find and free Dozier. So, there were a number of other players involved. One of those was a man by the name of Dale Graff. He had recently moved from an Air Force assignment to the Defense Intelligence Agency. The nice thing was that he was familiar with remote viewing and how the information was collected, as well as how it could be used.

Just prior to the general's kidnapping, Dale had received information from a remote viewer at SRI that a senior American official would be taken in the near future. The viewer also said he would be removed with the use of a blue van with white markings by people with Mediterranean features. This viewer had gotten the information while doing a predictive/preemptive RV in support of a search for another suspected terrorist at large at the time, the infamous Carlos the Jackal.

Other information the SRI remote viewer provided proved to be equally accurate, but was somewhat ignored by the administration. The problem was, so many psychics were forwarding information, it was beginning to be difficult to tell the wheat from the chaff.

One person at DIA, seeing how effective the Grill Flame material had been on other targets, decided to fly his own psychic into Italy and manage him on site. This only resulted in embarrassing the Italian counterterrorist teams when they raided innocent civilian's houses. That specific psychic also made a lot of special demands regarding his treatment, which made him a further pain in the ass, souring people on-site even worse.

Because Dale had a long association with our material and was handling the RV information coming into DIA, and because he already knew the local authorities in Italy would probably not use it unless it was damned accurate, he picked through the material very carefully. In doing so, he found my most recent viewing, with the accompanying drawings and sketches of the streets near the apartment building I described. Surprisingly, it was an almost exact overlay for the search maps the Italian police were using to search the Padua area. He began making arrangements to hand-carry the remote viewing drawings and materials to Italy himself. Dale was thwarted in this effort by U.S. officials on-site in Italy, who had now become weary with all the previous psychic intervention and wanted no more of it. So, my information was never forwarded to Italy, although I was led to believe until recently that it had been.

About 42 days after he had been taken, General Dozier was freed from his captives unharmed in Padua, Italy. All of my drawings were accurate and would have contributed significantly to finding the building and floor within which he was being held. When General Dozier was later shown our materials, he stated that, in his opinion and with regard to his own memory, the material was significantly accurate and the more personal "thought-content" stunningly so. His only suggestion to our project manager at the time was to think about designing a short class where high-ranking U.S. military and civilians could be trained on how to think and what to think, while being held captive.

It was clear from his comments that information in our reports had originated within his own thoughts while he was being held—blindfolded, tape across his mouth, being forced to listen to hard rock, heavy-metal music through headsets thousands of miles from our small RV rooms under the oaks at Fort Meade, Maryland.

Prior to 1981, I participated in another project that at least in some small degree ended up adding to the project's avowed enemies.

One of the first operational targets brought to the program around September of 1979 originated within the National Security Council. A naval lieutenant commander assigned to the council who had seen some of the previous OPSEC reports was enthusiastic about using RV for offensive intelligence-gathering purposes. He brought a photograph of a large building that was obviously an industrial type of building for targeting and development. The building was seen to be near a large body of water, but that was all one could tell about it. Materials were stacked on the exterior of the building, but they were general in nature and did not add clues about what might be going on inside the building. The building was huge, labeled as building number 402, and was located somewhere in Russia. (We were to find out much later that the facility was located at the port of Severodvinsk, on the White Sea, very near the Arctic Circle.) The NSC was very interested in knowing specifically what was going on inside.

In my first session against the building, I was given a set of geographic coordinates, clearly somewhere in the north, probably in the Finland or Eastern bloc region.

I began the session by reporting that it was a very cold wasteland. But within it was a very large industrial-type building with huge smokestacks, and not too far in the distance was a sea covered with a thick cap of ice.

Since I clearly was in the right place and on the right target, Fred showed me the picture of the building, which looked to me like a very large storage shed, an extensive, unremarkable flat-roofed building. Fred asked me what I thought might be going on inside it.

I spent some time relaxing and emptying my mind. Then, with my eyes closed, I imagined myself drifting down into the building, passing downward through its roof. What I found was mind-blowing. The building was easily the size of two or three huge shopping centers, all under a single roof. In fact, it was so huge I was only able to see one or two walls that ran lengthwise down the center as support walls. Even these were open in segments along their length. I felt as though I were standing inside the building and able to actually see vividly what was going on. This rarely occurs in remote viewing, but for some reason it was happening on this target.

In giant bays between the walls were what looked like cigars of different sizes, sitting in gigantic racks. One seemed older and I felt as though it were under repair, but the other was absolutely huge, beyond anything I could ever have imagined. Thick mazes of scaffolding and interlocking steel pipes were everywhere. Within these were what appeared to be two huge cylinders being welded side to side, and I had an overwhelming sense that this was a submarine, a really big one, with twin hulls. The entire area was filled with a cacophony of sounds and loud machining noises. The air was filled with smoke from dozens of very bright arcs of light emitting brilliant blue flashes. There was so much input, it was difficult to even begin to report on what I was seeing. I did some very poor general drawings of segments of features I perceived inside and said that I thought there was a ship or something, possibly a submarine, under construction inside the building.

Two or three days later, Fred asked me to visit the building again.

What I didn't know was that my session was reported back to the NSC and created some dissension. The almost unanimous belief at the time, by all the intelligence collection agencies operating against the building, was that the Soviets were constructing a brand-new type of assault ship—a troop carrier, and possibly one with helicopter capability. A submarine was out of the question.

On my second visit, I got up very close to the larger vessel and was amazed at its size and height. Hovering beside it, I guessed it to be about twice the length of an American football field and nearly seventy feet in width, and at least six or seven floors high (if it were sitting next to a standard apartment building.) It was clearly constructed of two huge elongated tubes run side-by-side for almost their entire length. (I didn't think this was possible with submarines.) There seemed to be other separate tubes or compartments as well. Its primary drives were completely shrouded and looked quite different from normal. I moved up over the deck and was surprised to see that it had canted missile tubes running side by side. This was critically important because this indicated that it had the capacity to fire while on the move rather than having to stand still in the water, which made it a very dangerous type of submarine. It was so huge and the hulls were so thick, it was evident that they were using some new form of plasma welders to blend the steel plates together.

After the session, I did a very detailed drawing of the submarine, adding dimensions, as well as noting the slanted tubes, indicating eighteen to twenty in all. This material, along with the typed transcript of my session, and additional validating RV material that had been produced by Hartleigh, was forwarded to the naval lieutenant commander at the NSC.

(We were told that the material we provided was actually rejected out of hand by the others working at the NSC. It is critical to note here that one of those "others" working in the NSC at the time and participating in the collection of material relevant to this specific problem was Robert Gates. Gates one day became a deputy director of the CIA. Later he sat in front of cameras on Ted Koppel's *Nightline* in 1995, when the Star Gate project was openly and deliberately exposed to the public and systematically ridiculed, and said that no remote viewing had ever been done that was "critical to national interests," and "at no time had remote viewing material ever been used as standalone material.")

We soon received a follow-on request from the Naval lieutenant commander to return to the target and to try to provide an estimated time of completion for the larger submarine. It was clear that one of the problems dealt with the fact that the building in which the megasub was being constructed was actually situated some distance from water.

I revisited the site and, based on the speed of construction and the differences in the condition of the submarine from one session to the next, I guessed that it would be ready for launch about four months later—that would be sometime in the month of January—a singularly crazy time of year to launch a submarine from a building not connected to water, near a sea frozen over with ice yards thick. (I reported that very soon a crew of bulldozers and other types of heavy equipment would arrive to cut a channel leading to the sea.) The folks at the NSC had a lot of fun poking at the psychic intelligence.

Satellite photographs taken of the facility in mid-January of 1980 showed a new canal running alongside the building and out to the sea. Standing at the dockside was the new and huge boomer, which had never been seen before. Tied up alongside it rested the now somewhat dwarfed Oscar Class attack sub, which had been in for repairs in the other bay. Clear in the photographs were twenty canted missile tubes. The completely new submarine was named the Typhoon Class, a tribute to the amount of water it displaced.

We now know that the Typhoon submarine is the largest submarine ever built by anyone. Built in the Severodvinsk Shipyard on the White Sea near Archangel, the first moved out into the water for sea trials in early 1980, and was commissioned as TK208 in 1981. It was followed by TK202 in 1983, TK12 in 1984, TK13 in 1985, TK17 in 1987, and TK20 in 1989. They were all stationed in the Russian Northern Fleet at Litsa Guba. The sub is now known to be multi-hulled, consisting of five inner hull segments constructed within a superstructure consisting of two parallel main hulls. The inside is coated with sound-absorbent tiles, and in all there are nineteen separate watertight compartments. The submarine carries twenty RSM-52 intercontinental three-stage solid-propellant ballistic missiles situated in two rows of launch tubes in front of the main sail between the two hull sections. Each missile consists of ten independently targeted multiple reentry vehicles, or MIRVs, each having a 100 kiloton nuclear warhead (or city buster)—ranges of 8,300 kilometers

The Stargate Chronicles

(5,000 miles) and accuracy of 500 meters (a couple of city blocks). The submarine is 172 meters long and 23.3 meters wide (or about 1.75 times the size of an American football field in length, and about 70 feet tall, or close to six and a half stories.)

This new submarine constituted a fairly large and distinctive new threat to our national security. It could target 200 American cities in an arch that covered most of the continent. Six of them could stand off shore and pretty much decimate 1,200 of our major cities with absolutely no lead time or warning.

Any hopes that remote viewing might be viewed by the NSC as valuable were severely damaged when we later heard that some thought my material was just a "lucky guess." Perhaps that was the viewpoint of a CIA Russian analyst on loan to the NSC at the time, who would later ridicule the project as useless, as never producing anything of national significance. Could it be embarrassment that someone sitting in a small room in a condemned building somewhere on Fort Meade could invade what all of modern intelligence technology could not? Could that be threatening to billion-dollar budgets for newer forms of technology? I've thought many years about the matter. My conclusion is that it really had to do with nothing more than stepping on the toes of a few egotistical individuals, who at the time were highly exposed at a significant governmental level, and couldn't get beyond hypothetical troop carriers without the assistance of remote viewing. Simply put, we produced information of national-level interest at a time when it was unavailable from any other source, something that some people said then—and still say today—that a good remote viewer can't do.

Chapter Nine

Downward Spiral

The rest of 1981 was filled with a growing list of both clients and targets. My own health began to give me growing problems as a result of both increasing stress and lack of exercise. Up until about mid-1980, I spent a considerable amount of time in the gym at Fort Meade, usually working out during my lunch hour. I found that hard exercise of any kind was an excellent counterpoint to lying on my back. Scotty, Fred, and I sometimes played three games of what we called "combat racquetball" during our lunch hour. That's where it's always two against the guy with the next shot at the ball. Full-body blocking is appropriate, and body slams against the wall, as in ice hockey, while frowned upon, were usually employed with great effectiveness. Given that Scotty was bigger than I was, and Fred was actually the smallest of us three, I admired Fred's game. Fred really had game! Scotty could make a falling upper-corner three-wall shot with his body parallel to the floor with ease. On the other hand, my backhands were blazing arcs of blurred metallic blue metal (the color of my racquet). The number-one rule in combat racquetball is—never—never—*never* turn around to see where the ball is. Sometimes the next player on the ball would drop back and wait for the ball to come off the rear wall, just to break the stride of the other players. The "stride" was born of the average time it took to return the ball to the wall, while a shorter and shorter stride became the norm as a result of better play—you got to recognize it like a heartbeat. So, when the beat suddenly stopped and nothing seemed to happen, the next player waiting for his turn to hit the ball had a natural tendency to turn to see what happened to the last player—presuming he missed it, or that he perhaps collapsed somewhere on the court from exhaustion. In any event—the number-one rule and perhaps the only inviolate rule was that you never turned around to look.

One day our play was the best I'd ever seen. People were watching from the upstairs peanut gallery. We were on a roll, with recovery after recovery and I sensed a beat was developing—probably two-thirds of a second between shots—the ball hitting maybe 175 MPH. When it came around to me again I let it go by, intending to take it off the wall, breaking the beat. Turning to catch it when it did, I had my back to the rest of the court. The ball came hard off the back wall and I hooked it with my blazing backhand, which Fred (who had turned to see what was going on) stepped directly into. Since I always twist my racquet a full 90 to 120 degrees to put downward spin on the ball, my racquet face was parallel to the floor when the edge of it caught Fred across the face, just over his eye. What a great shot—and what a lot of blood. Fred just sort of stood there a few seconds; his eyes looked very strange, then he just kind of sat down. I thought I had killed him.

It turned out to be a sizable cut that looked a lot worse than it actually was. He had caught the extreme edge of my racquet. Had he caught it full-faced, he probably would have needed a few weeks of microsurgery to remove the waffle marks. He wasn't mad, but I was absolutely horrified. I stopped playing racquetball. It was becoming harder and harder to get time for anything anyway.

But now I was no longer exercising, I was spending hours stressed out at work, and hours stressed out in traffic, and—given the hours I was leaving and arriving—my diet was long since shot to hell. I began to gain weight, and a disc injury I had suffered in Vietnam back in 1968 began to resurface. I had suffered severe disc problems as a result of the sudden decompression in a helicopter crash. Some of my vertebrae were crushed and fractured through and through, most of my separator discs were either already in pieces or decaying, and a vertebra between the C7 and C8 disc space was rotated more than 30 degrees out of alignment. My lower back was beginning to give me fits—from the stress and driving I'm sure. The pressure from these disc problems began to produce significant numbness in my left leg, hip, and thigh, as well as tingling and numbness in both of my hands, arms, and portions of my face. A significant amount of pain accompanied this—especially on cold or wet days.

Hartleigh began to suffer a sharp pain in his left hip. We would sometimes sit and talk with each other about how bad it felt. I started gaining even more weight as a result of the steroid shots they began giving me over at Kimbrough Army Hospital.

It wasn't long before the command began climbing up my backside about my weight and conditioning. I almost stopped eating, because that was about the only way that I could keep my weight down under the military maximum. This further added to my physical condition by making me extraordinarily tired all the time. Meanwhile, Hartleigh got worse.

Eventually the doctor at Kimbrough called my commander and told him that I was going to be put on probation for both my weight and my medical problems. They couldn't seem to find a solution for fixing my trashed back. On the other hand, I was learning to do my remote viewing in spite of the pain. That's when I noticed something. If I could learn to do my RV in spite of mind-numbing pain, then I should be able to do remote viewing in spite of almost anything.

(For a long time I was bothered by the excesses which everyone seemed to be going to in order to improve their remote viewing capability. First we blocked up the windows in the viewing room so we couldn't hear the birds chirping in the trees outside. Then we reduced the light to a level you almost couldn't walk through the room with. We kept adding to a long list, much of what was based on recommendations being made by the SRI lab. We removed everything from the room but a table on which to do the drawings, and a dental chair, which we bought at auction. The chair was kind of cool, actually. You could lean way back in it; it was semimolded to your body; and it was really very comfortable. They even painted everything in the room gray—the walls, ceiling, and table. The chair was already gray. We even had a rug installed that was close to the same shade of gray. Walking into the room under low light would give you vertigo if you weren't careful. In any event, I began to resent it. I began to view the long lists of "must dos" as simply a preloaded list for failure. When you screwed up a remote viewing, you could always find a reason on the list for why it failed. I began cranking up the light, sitting at the table, and even doing some of my preliminary work before ever getting the target while sitting at my desk across the street. It was clear to me that if you couldn't do this thing called remote viewing under any conditions, it was going to prove of little value on the street or in a war zone. The funny thing was, my viewing improved somewhat. I eventually got to the point where I could RV almost anywhere at any time under any conditions. Once I reached that point, it was more a matter of simply paying attention to the job and getting it done.)

After a few months of arguing, the doctor at Kimbrough Hospital called me over one day and told me that he was going to officially recommend a medical discharge for the good of the service. It was clear that because of my back, I was incapable of doing my duties as a soldier. He so advised Branch.

This created a major personal problem for me. Branch was obviously going to support him because they wanted my warrant officer space back where it belonged in my primary MOS area. What most people don't know, however, is that this is sometimes a move the military makes as a form of indirect punishment. I had obviously pissed off the doctor at Kimbrough by never getting better, no matter what he did, which was a reflection on his own officer's evaluation form and has a direct effect on his own promotion and ego placement within the scheme of things.

The reason it's viewed as an indirect punishment?

a.) If I retired (at that time I would have been eligible to retire within two years and three months), I would have received a full retirement as a chief warrant officer.

b.) If I was medically retired before I reached my eighteenth year, then I would not be eligible for that retirement check should my situation later change medically.

c.) Once medically discharged with less than eighteen years' service, I would have gotten a rating of something less than 40 percent disability for my back problems, which would have been about a third of my possible retirement salary (win one for the Army system).

d.) If, after I was medically retired, my medical problem was eventually fixed—in other words, in their opinion made less of a problem through the application of heavy-duty drugs—my disability rating would be reduced to less than 20 percent, possibly to 10 percent—now equating to less than a tenth of my possible retirement salary (a second win in the Army column.)

e.) If they made the problem go away altogether, I would have no disability pay at all and no retirement, because I would not have made it to my eighteenth year (win three for the Army accountants.)

f.) Applying for reinstatement at that time to complete my military career would then have been denied because I would have been too old (win four, trump, and checkmate).

As impossible as this may sound to many, it has been done to hundreds of military veterans, officers and enlisted alike, over the years—but it wasn't going to happen to me.

I challenged the doctor with the regulations, which simply stated that if I could pass the annual physical training test for my age group, the Army considers me healthy enough to serve. Back then this test required running a number of obstacle courses in minimal times, doing a minimum of overhead parallel bars, a minimum of pushups, and finishing a two-mile run within a specific time wearing the utility uniform (fatigues) and combat boots. Although at the time I was using a cane and couldn't get in and out of a car without help, I figured I could do almost anything to get through a single day of pain.

I took the day off prior to the physical testing day and saw a private doctor who prescribed pain medication. The following day I showed up and took the tests. I can honestly say that the only thing that got me through the day was what I had learned about meditation through remote viewing. I put myself in a mental state that completely disassociated me from where I was and what I was doing. It was the two-mile run that did my lower back in. I actually finished it within the allotted time, but when I sat down in the grass my left leg wouldn't stop running, I was also on the verge of passing out from the pain. Ken saw what was going on and came over and sat on my left leg till it eventually ran out of steam, all the while talking to me like nothing was going on, the whole while my eyes were rolled up in the back of my head and I was barely conscious of what was going on around me. After a short time, Ken carried my card over and turned it in for me, then after most of the people left, helped me work my way over to my car. I called Scotty the next morning, took four days' emergency leave for personal business, and signed myself into a private clinic for pain control. The doctor at Kimbrough gave up, but the folks at Branch reaffirmed their desire to make me disappear from their rolls.

While at the clinic, someone recommended that I might want to check out the pain clinic at Walter Reed Army Medical Center—which no one in the Army seemed to know existed. I did this in the following weeks and was treated there by a Chinese doctor using acupuncture. He couldn't correct all the problems I was having, but he reduced my back pain to a level that was manageable without drugs. This was important, because it allowed me to continue clear-headed with my RV in the unit.

Hartleigh fared much worse than I, because the subsequent testing of his leg pain proved to be a result of cancer that had developed in the muscle mass and bones of his hip. When he first started going to Walter Reed Medical Center, they believed he was suffering with essentially what I was dealing with, disc problems. After numerous treatments, they decided to operate to correct the problem. When they opened him up they found no problems with his disc. After the operation he continued running a low-grade fever and they eventually discovered the mass in his upper leg and diagnosed him as having Hodgkin's disease. We got to be even closer friends. He went through all the radiation and chemotherapy treatments, but to no avail. His remote viewing quickly petered out to none, but we continued to spend a great deal of time together. He'd come into the office and we'd talk philosophically. Ken would join in on the conversations as well. As Hartleigh got worse, he could no longer sit up for long periods, so Ken and I would entertain him while he would lie on the couch in one of the apartments he owned and we repainted the ceiling and walls. On one Saturday afternoon, Ken and I repainted the same room three times, two different colors—color a, then color b, then back to color a. He never noticed, or did and enjoyed watching us do it. Hartleigh was a good man, a good sailor, a close friend, and one hell of a great remote viewer. When people denigrate remote viewing through ridicule or misrepresentation, I think about Jackie Keith and Hartleigh Trent and it angers me.

When Hartleigh finally died, I was standing beside his bed with his wife, in the hospital near where he lived in Maryland. He had been delirious, and in and out of consciousness for more than a day. When his end was near, his eyes suddenly popped open and he smiled at us. "It's really quite beautiful where I'm going," he said. Then he commented about how full the room was with all of his friends (only his wife and I were standing there. It was clear to me that a lot of people he knew had come to see him off or were there to greet him when he passed over. It seemed a happy day for him. No more pain. For me, there was only a very large hole in my spirit it would take a long time to get used to.)

One of the facts of military life is loss. The rate of divorce is three times higher than in the civilian world. It comes from being in a job that involves life-and-death decision making—sometimes on a daily basis or sometimes with long periods of mind-numbing boredom and frustration in between. The effects of divorce means separation from the rest of the family—your children. If you somehow survive the threat of divorce, you will spend years away from those you love, in places no one should have to talk about, never mind endure. And then there is the loss of friends. Twenty to thirty years in the military kills people. If you don't see your friends shredded on a battlefield, many will die along the way from stress, wounds, and complications, usually the result of exposure to rare diseases, chemical agents, biological contaminants, and things like "Agent Orange." In most cases, a soldier has no time for grief. The mission has to be finished, if for no other reason than to honor those who've already died trying to get it done.

What happens to all this grief? You put it away somewhere in the back of your mind, bury it under layers of callused scarring from years of accumulated experiences. Before being crushed by it, a soldier learns to use his or her grief as a motivator. He or she uses it to produce anger or rage to compensate for the repetitive frustration and bitter feelings that eventually develop from the experience. But, one thing soldiers never do. They never take the time to process the loss. They suck it up and move on, putting one foot in front of the other. Over time, the grief they've accumulated and buried becomes so great it can never be processed. Opening the door to those feelings would be like splitting the face of a dam. Once the water started to flow, there would be no way to stop it.

I put Hartleigh and the way I felt about him with my other friends and moved on, putting one foot in front of the other. The way to honor him was to keep remote viewing.

In a very short time, Scotty Watt, who had earned a promotion to lieutenant colonel as a direct result of managing the project, retired. He was replaced by another lieutenant colonel, whom I will call Bob. The rest of us had hit our three-year rotation dates, which

The Stargate Chronicles

meant that everyone in the unit except the civilian secretary and the new boss would soon be receiving orders for a reassignment. This would shut the project down completely. The crap hit the fan.

It was about this same time that INSCOM Commander Flynn was replaced by Maj. Gen. Burt Stubblebine. We heard that Stubblebine was generally positive about what we were doing, but we weren't sure if he could shield us against the growing resentment being generated by the new ACSI, General Odom. Odom obviously viewed us as a personal liability regardless of how well we might or might not be doing operationally. The phrase "no one wants to be caught dead standing next to a psychic" was beginning to spread. It actually didn't matter at the time, because by then we had major clients throughout the intelligence community. We were providing support to the Central Intelligence Agency (CIA), the Defense Intelligence Agency (DIA), the Secret Service (SS), the Air Force Intelligence Agency (AFIA), the Naval Intelligence Command (NIC), the Naval Investigative Service Command (NISC), the National Security Agency (NSA), the Army Intelligence and Security Command (INSCOM), the National Security Council (NSC), the Federal Bureau of Investigation (FBI), the United States Coast Guard (USCG) (at least two districts), the Drug Enforcement Agency (DEA), internal elements of the State Department, the Bureau of Alcohol, Tobacco, and Firearms (ATF), and other more specific agencies or departments that still cannot be mentioned.

Attempts were made to negotiate with Branch to extend my assignment as excess (99) in the Washington, D.C., area, but they would have none of it. I received alert orders for Korea that were immediately canceled by General Stubblebine. Within a week I received new alert orders for Fort Bragg, N.C. The general canceled these as well and actually sent his chief of staff over to Branch to discuss my situation with them. According to the general, I was "his people" and he could do whatever he wanted with his people.

Ken was able to manage a one-year extension on his three-year tour at Meade. Actually, by the time he got it approved he was already three months into the year. Fred received orders to attend the advanced intelligence course in Arizona, which he accepted, with the understanding that he would be reassigned back to the unit. As a result, Fred left rather abruptly for six months. Fred actually was able to return in five, because he amassed sufficient credits to pass the course and departed before graduation, something most career officers would not have attempted.

Mel received alert orders sending him back to his old unit in Germany, only this time as a sergeant first class. He was finally promoted in spite of his working in the project, a promotion that was probably way overdue anyway.

My own situation was eventually settled at the major general level. Evidently, an agreement was struck. They simply made me disappear from the Army system completely. The Army would forget where I was until I decided to retire. The only problem with this agreement was any hope of further promotion in my case ceased to exist. I was a permanent-grade chief warrant officer and since I wore civilian clothes, most weren't even aware of that. I decided to grow a beard to protest and most didn't notice that either.

Toward the middle of 1982, the only ones doing RV within the unit were Ken and myself. Our new boss, Bob, was learning how to run sessions coming out of the starting gate, and Fred was out in Arizona learning everything he could about what wouldn't be applicable to what we were doing. (Fred returned at the end of 1982.)

My recollection of the times between the beginning of 1982 and the early part of 1984 are almost completely clouded in a mist of pain, stress, and exhaustion. Because Ken and I were the only two now doing the remote viewing, we were completely buried with work. Much of the tasking that was brought to us from the multitude of agencies involved was related directly or indirectly to terrorist activities, which seemed to be growing exponentially.

Between Christmas Day of 1981 and February of 1984, I participated in 168 separate intelligence problems addressing terrorism (11 incidents in Africa, 29 in Europe, 36 in South America, 31 in the Middle East, and 61 on United States soil). This total was not the total amount of terrorists' actions by a long shot; it was hardly a percentile of the total. This was in addition to other forms of tasking. By the time I reached my own retirement date in September of 1984, I had participated in addressing well over 1,500 individual intelligence problems. Ken worked at least as hard as I did up until the day before his rotation, at the end of 1982. In my heart, his departure was another mark in my loss column.

One serious problem with the project was the need for new and talented viewers and sufficient overlap time for them to learn the business. This need was never addressed, or at least not until the very last minute. Nearly all the original selection criteria and methodologies for selecting remote viewer personnel had been abandoned as both too time-consuming and too expensive. Our tasking was increasing approximately ten percent per month, while our funding and personnel were *decreasing* at four times that rate. The solution was to get someone trained and trained fast. This made me very uncomfortable. I could remember all the time and discomfort I had in learning about RV and convincing myself that it was real. Now they were expecting someone to adjust without any time at all. Not good.

Fred returned to the unit just as our boss Bob was being replaced by a new boss, whom I will call Lieutenant Colonel Franks. I think Franks recognized the shortage of viewers as his most serious problem and took it more seriously than anyone had. Fred advised him of two people in another class out in Arizona who showed some promise, and he and Franks flew out there to recruit them.

Robert Cowart and Tom McNear came directly to the unit from the Army's advanced intelligence course at Fort Huachuca, Arizona. I believe their selection and subsequent assignment to the unit happened mostly because it was easier to arrange an assignment for someone coming out of a school. After hearing what we were into, they had volunteered. This was actually a very large plus. By this time, no one in his right mind would risk his career being devoured by our very bizarre unit. But both of these new people knew Fred, and I think he felt that given our dire situation, if they weren't terribly psychic, they could by God learn, or at least make great RV monitors, helping to alleviate the strain on himself. (By this time of course, Fred was fully capable of intuitively selecting someone that he felt was more psychic than not.)

Also, by then a belief was blossoming (out of the ethers) that remote viewers could be trained simply through repetitive and controlled experiences, and that talent wasn't necessarily that important—something that actually flew in the face of what had thus far been demonstrated both at Fort Meade and SRI.

Ingo Swann, the top remote viewer at SRI and one of the founding members of remote viewing development there, sensed that RV skills might be trainable, but he was only beginning his look into it and wasn't yet sure. The system he was developing was under construction and was not thoroughly tested. (His method at the time consisted of a planned six stages, of which only the first two or three actually existed in an outline format.) Someone at the project decided that it would have to do, and at the end of 1982 they began sending Robert and Tom out to SRI every two weeks. They would train there for two weeks, then return to the unit and practice on their own until they could complete the new training program.

A few months prior to 1983, Ken departed for his next assignment. He was rightfully concerned that if he stayed any longer his military career could be damaged. I was pleased to hear many years later that he achieved the rank of lieutenant colonel just before he retired.

Just prior to his departure, I came very close to dying in an accident on the Beltway. (It was actually the sixth accident that I had been able to avoid.) I was on the inner loop heading North approaching the Cabin John Bridge in heavy traffic, at that time in the morning when the light is just beginning to build, and the rods and cones in your eyes can't make up their mind if it's still dark or light.

The inner loop lanes narrow by one just as you enter the bridge. A tractor-trailer was clipped by a Mercedes and lost control. The trailer actually separated from the tractor and spun sideways before doing a side-over-side roll. Instantly more than a hundred cars were locking their brakes and changing lanes involuntarily. My whole front view filled with light blue smoke from tires being fried to their rims—then the air was filled with the sounds of tearing metal. I could see hubcaps beginning to bounce high into the air. It suddenly became slow motion in front of me, with all the cars in my lane and the surrounding lanes beginning to slide sideways and bounce one off the other. Since everyone was doing more than 70 MPH, what looked like the gentle brushing of fender to fender was actually the crushing of metal like tinfoil. I had just enough time to mumble "holy shit" and brought both arms up across my face, bracing my body for impact. I knew there was absolutely nothing that I could do to avoid being buried in the landslide of vehicles piling up on the road at the far end of the bridge.

But after what seemed an eternity, nothing happened. I opened my eyes, and the entire five lanes in front of me were clear of cars or trucks. I quickly looked into the rearview mirror and I could see the small tunnel opening I had passed through squeezing shut behind me. I coasted to a stop and got out of my car and looked back at the destruction behind me. There had to be fifty cars crushed into a parking lot the size of a basketball court. I couldn't stop my hands from shaking.

When I finally arrived at Fort Meade, I calmly walked into Franks's office and said that unless I was moved to Fort Meade, I quit. I couldn't take it any more. His only comment was "took you long enough to ask." Within the week, I was in officer's quarters less than half a mile from the office.

Peggy had a total meltdown. She was now faced with a choice of either commuting the opposite direction to her work with the publisher in Reston or quitting. She chose to continue working, which lasted only a few weeks. This of course was my fault. The larger problem was the loss of her income. (It was somewhat ameliorated by no longer having to pay rent in Reston. The Army's housing allowance to defray the costs of living in Reston was never enough.) So, it cost us money to move into on-post housing. The greater effect was that she now was cut off from all of her workmates and friends. Making friends in the on-post quarters wasn't easy for her. She couldn't talk about anything I was doing because she didn't know much about what I was doing. Our immediate neighbors on either side were wonderful people, but they had their own schedules to keep. The man to our left was a chief warrant officer in supply, so we had absolutely nothing in common. His wife and family were really nice people, which only made Peggy angrier for some reason. In retrospect, I think she thought his wife was hitting on me. The couple to our right was a newly married second lieutenant. At least they had a dog and their dog really liked our dog. My Dalmatian, Barney, really liked the move, because he got to spend a lot more time with me. Because Peggy's and my relationship was in tatters, I spent an increasingly longer time walking Barney all over the golf course that backed onto our quarters. He and I would spend long hours out there walking and sometimes when no one was looking, I'd release him from his leash on the fourth green and let him run the length of the fairway, a special treat he came to expect.

At work, things began to get somewhat nasty. Robert started telling me about the training system at SRI. The way he explained it to me, he would sit across the table from his trainer and in a very rigid and specific manner, write down what came into his mind about the target. He had to do this according to a very well-defined framework that identified elements and conditions at the target. When he was right, the monitor told him he was by saying "correct." When he was wrong, he received no feedback at all. He said that through this rote repetition he was learning to open the contact between his subconscious and conscious minds where the information was probably being generated. I could understand this as a method for learning, but was having difficulty understanding how the leap would be made from learning to remote viewing targets for which the monitor had no knowledge. Or, if the monitor did have knowledge, I couldn't understand how they would prevent steering the viewer to whatever they assumed was accurate about the target. Clearly, there was a long-range plan, but that had not been revealed yet.

I made the mistake of discussing this with him. It was apparent from the outset that the monitor would have to know the answers or what the target was in order for this to take place in the manner he described. If that were the case, then wasn't this just an extension of the old colored-pins game that Scotty had whipped on me? By deduction, anyone could eventually be guided by the monitor, by omission, to the target. He said it wasn't like that. So, we began to get into philosophic discussions about what was going on. This wasn't something new; it was something we had all done together since inception of the project. We believed that by arguing about things you would always eventually reach truth. This had the added benefit of preventing any one of us from drifting off in some way, or deluding ourselves into believing something that wasn't real. But, in this case, it hit a major nerve.

After a short time I was called into Franks's office and asked to refrain from discussing their training methods with them. I argued with him. If they really wanted to learn what's going on inside their minds, they needed to discuss it openly with others of like mind and within the safety of the office.

But, this wasn't the way it was being looked at now. The method of instruction they were receiving was in effect indoctrinating them to believe there was only one way to evaluate what their minds were telling them and that was the severely structured format they were currently learning at SRI.

I pulled away from both Robert and Tom for a bit, thinking that I would wait and see how well this new training system worked. In the meantime, I continued being the only person in the office doing the RV. After a bit, the project secretary showed me some of the practice sessions that Robert and Tom were doing when they were at Fort Meade. I did not seek them out. She brought them to me because she said she was having a difficult time interpreting what they were actually doing. What I saw astounded me. After nearly ten months of training, all either of them was doing was drawing simple lines or scribbles down the side of a page and writing in a few accompanying words of description. Some of the words were pertinent to the targets they were working, but many of them were pertinent to almost anything else in the target files. I knew I was missing something.

I carried one of the folders to the boss and asked him what exactly was going on. I told him that I was concerned that maybe this wasn't the appropriate approach to teaching someone remote viewing. A person with talent should have been able to draw at least fragments and segments of a targeted site by now. He explained to me that they were being taught by rote, incrementally, how to build the picture of a target step by step. I complained that I wasn't sure that was the case at all. In my observation, they were being incrementally led to the appropriate answer by the monitor who was training them. A simple comparison between teaching targets and actual targets displayed that. The examples from their instructional classes were tenfold better than the ones they were attempting blind for practice.

Franks ordered me to go back to my cubical and to not speak with either Robert or Tom again. I was ordered to not leave my cubical unless I was remote viewing, and to otherwise mind my own business. He would not have me screw up the only training system they had for teaching new viewers. I did as I was told. But it sure got lonely in the huge room within which my desk sat. I was hidden behind a large section of wall dividers from those around me—now wrapped in an imposed cone of silence.

I stopped communicating with either of them. I stopped communicating with anyone but the unit secretary. It was her encouragement that kept me from quitting the unit altogether. In the meantime, I continued to do the viewing, averaging two or three operational targets a day.

Chapter Ten

The Army and Bob Monroe

In 1983, Fred suggested I accompany him to a place called The Monroe Institute (TMI). He said the man who owned and ran the place could do out-of-body travel—astral projection—at will. He wanted me to meet him and thought there might be something there that could help me be even better with my viewing. I knew they wanted me preoccupied with something else. Or maybe I was becoming paranoid and just thought that. In any event, I went down to visit with Mr. Monroe around the middle of 1983.

When I first met with Robert Monroe, he and his wife and stepson lived in an apartment directly over the office of the Institute. His wife struck me as a wonderful sort of old-fashioned Southern lady, the kind of person who always makes sure the company feels at ease and at rest in her home. The fact that they lived over the store seemed to bother her terribly, but in my mind, her home was just that, a beautiful home and something to be happy about. Monroe had just returned from the hospital, after having had work done on his cardiovascular system—specifically repair to the major leg arteries just below the bifurcation valve in the lower groin area. He was still in considerable pain and was not a happy man. (He struck me as someone who didn't deal with pain very well.) But he was very courteous and friendly with me. It was obvious that he already knew Fred.

While talking with Bob, his large cat, "Blackie," climbed up into my lap and began to purr. So I started stroking her. Bob warned me not to do that because he said that Blackie got unusually excited by that and would probably bite me. I smiled and ignored him. When Bob looked away to pick up his cigarette and coffee cup, Blackie bit all the way through my left thumbnail, burying her fang in bone. I pried her tooth out of my nail and dumped her to the floor while crossing my left index finger over my thumb to stop the bleeding. Bob looked around lighting his cigarette and smiled. I smiled back, while shoving my left hand in my pocket as though nothing had happened. He didn't notice.

After our meeting, Fred took me up to the main building to give me a tour. On the way, I had to wring the blood from my pocket liner. Good thing I was wearing dark blue slacks.

What I didn't know was that Fred had suggested to Bob that he work with me to help me develop control of the spontaneous out-of-body experiences I'd been having since my near-death experience in Austria in 1970.

While touring the Center building, I bumped into Ms. Nancy Honeycutt, Bob's stepdaughter, who had just returned from the West Coast, where she had been working for a major textbook publisher. She was now working for one in the Virginia, North Carolina, and Tennessee area, selling textbooks to colleges in the region. We sat and talked on the rear deck for about 45 minutes. She tried various questions in an attempt to learn who I was and where I was from, which I avoided answering in any specific sense. While the conversation was pleasant we eventually shook hands and I left to look for Fred and Bob. Many years later, Nancy said that it was the longest "noninformation meeting" with someone she had ever experienced. She knew exactly the same amount of information about me when I left as when we met—zero. She also says that it made me even more mysterious than I otherwise would have appeared to be. She had a sense that I was military, but beyond that, nothing.

On returning to Fort Meade, Fred asked me to write up a justification for attending the Gateway Seminar at TMI, and we'd see how that would affect me, or my viewing. This I did, and received orders to attend within the month.

The Gateway Seminar was and still is the backbone of The Monroe Institute. Back when I attended, there were only a handful of trainers, and my group's trainers were Melissa Jager and Fowler

Jones, a psychologist. The seminar began at noon on Saturday and ended the following Friday morning. We spent all day listening to the Institute's Hemi-Sync™ patterned tapes, which are designed to encourage the brain to develop a frequency following response. These specific frequency mixes are designed to assist someone in a course of self-discovery. In my case it was meant to improve my remote viewing, or at least that was the thought.

My wife didn't like the idea of my attending the seminar. For her, it was a far-out kind of woo-woo thing. (As if remote viewing wasn't!) More and more of my paranormal beliefs were coming up in conversation and I think this was frightening and unsettling for her. I think many of the things I was doing were beginning to put a lot of pressure on her religious convictions as well. While I could tell that she was upset with me, she wouldn't sit down and discuss what was bothering her. When I would bring it up, she didn't want to talk about it.

When I returned from the Institute, I felt somewhat different, obviously a direct effect of the tapes and sounds I'd been exposed to. In hindsight, I would say that all of these effects by their nature felt positive. At least, I could determine no negative effect. I was able to sleep better than I had been, was able to deal a lot better with the day-to-day stress, and I was able to focus my mind more clearly, which had an immediate payoff in the viewing room. So, I would have to say that my viewing did improve a bit, at least in the sense that I could relax and better focus on the targets, which increased the amount of accurate information I was able to produce in any given session.

Right after I returned from the Gateway Seminar, I received word that my mother had passed. Peggy and I drove down to Miami to help Dad make arrangements for her funeral. I and my sisters—all but my twin, Margaret, who was having difficulties of her own trying to remain mentally stabilized—agreed to split all of the expenses. Besides, Margaret actually hated Mom with a passion that cannot be expressed with words—ever since my parents forcibly took her child from her. Margaret and Mom never spoke to one another when together around other people or when forced to be in the same room together.

It was a surprise that Mother, who was only in her late fifties when she went, had died from a previous heart condition. This was something she had never shared with any of us. Sitting with my father after the funeral, he told me that she knew she had a severe problem but had made him swear on his own grave not to tell any of us. I'd always suspected that she had liver problems from drinking and the terrible way she'd massacre a dinner, but to suddenly lose her was a terrific surprise.

It turned out that she had had a major heart attack almost a year earlier and, because she couldn't afford to pay for an ambulance, she had caught a bus and ridden it for more than an hour, making two connections, to reach the hospital emergency room. He said when she arrived they asked what her specific problem was and asked how she had gotten there. On hearing that she had ridden the bus they assumed that she was having a problem with gastritis or something of that nature and had her wait for nearly five hours before treating her. I asked my dad what kind of treatment she had gotten and he said they had kept her overnight and then, when her pain was gone, had given her a bottle of pills and had told her that she would have to take it easy once she got back home.

Of course I was enraged with a system that could have done more but chose not to, because she couldn't pay. I almost couldn't believe my ears, sitting there listening to him tell the story. But it was difficult to know if it actually happened exactly that way, or maybe my dad was telling it to me this way, so that I wouldn't know that he and she, or she alone, had made a decision to not pursue a more aggressive medical solution. In any event, I let it go, trying more to console my dad in his grief.

Throughout their lives they had fought like cats and dogs, but they were so wedded to each other, it was as if a huge wound had been opened in his side and he was slowly leaking out of it. Almost nothing I could do would console him. My sisters, Peggy, and I buried Mom in a grave in a small out-of-the-way burial ground located in the northern area of the city. It was a plot my grandmother (Dad's mom) had reserved and bought for herself.

While we were spending the short time with my dad, I noticed he had a constant need to clear his throat, and a somewhat dry cough. I don't think my sisters noticed, or if they did, they said nothing about it. When my dad and I were alone, I asked him what was wrong. He just stared at me for a long time and finally said that he had esophageal cancer. He said it matter-of-factly, as though if he treated it with normality it would disappear.

I asked him to come back to Fort Meade and live with us. Because he was indigent and elderly, we could claim him as a dependent and he could move in with us. As a dependent, he would receive the best medical support money could buy, through the Army hospital system. I knew that a lot could be done for him at Walter Reed Medical Center. He said no. He also made me swear that I would not say one word about our conversation to anyone else, even my sisters. When I asked him why he wanted it that way, he said it was because he was tired of living anyway, and didn't want to be here any longer since Mom was gone. He said he'd rather be where she was. I have to say, that if I had not been all those years in the Grill Flame project, and had not attended the Gateway Seminar, and had not grown in personal enlightenment during that time, I probably would have forced him to move to Fort Meade. But it was as if I could look deeply into his heart and soul. I knew that he was right. He had every right to decide the issue for himself, and I told him that I would honor his decision. When I left Miami, I knew I probably would not be seeing him again, at least physically. (Since then, I sometimes get a whiff of his aftershave lotion. So I know that he visits now and then, at least in spirit, or in my mind.)

By the time Peggy and I returned to Fort Meade, I was close to burnout. For long periods of time, all I could do was sit in the easy chair by the sliding door and stare off into nothingness. I was now traveling to Walter Reed Medical Center every Friday evening for acupuncture at the chronic pain clinic. They also started giving me pain medication to take when I couldn't lie flat or sleep. In the middle of all this, I was continuing to do all of the remote viewing at the office.

During this same time period we were beginning to have funding difficulties with the unit. General Stubblebine was straying further and further afield in his quest to learn as much as he could about altered states of mind and how he might be able to apply them within his command to meet the mission goals. I had some talks at the time with a new colonel on the block named John Alexander. The general was using John to chase down a lot of his information for him. I liked John a lot for a number of reasons. He was a solid kind of guy who had spent time in Southeast Asia and was not shy about putting his own butt in the wringer if he felt it could be for the good of the service. In shorter, more military terms, he had balls. But, the general had put us between a rock and a hard place. By virtue of who we were supporting and the sensitivity of what we were doing, we were given direct orders not to exchange information about the project with anyone who was not cleared by name first either by the chief of staff, the ACSI, or by the general himself. Hence I was not allowed to speak about Grill Flame with John, and he couldn't speak with me about whatever he was into. We were compartmented off from each other. In many cases, this resulted in both of us working at cross purposes to one another or even getting in each other's way.

As an example, we had gone out of the system to order a flotation chamber, to use as a decompression module following hours of remote viewing. It took approximately two years from when we ordered it till it was delivered. Since it was a somewhat peculiar purchase for the United States Army at the time, John's department was asked to handle it by the general. When John tried to deliver it, I told him he had the wrong address and he'd have to go deliver it to whomever had ordered it, which of course was not us. It ended up in a field storage depot at Meade for another year before we hired some furniture movers to retrieve it and bring to our building.

Sometimes the general or the chief of staff would forget who did and did not have authorization to enter our facility. In more than one case a person who arrived at the door under orders from the chief of staff or the general was made to sit in his or her car for an hour while we tracked down the appropriate clearance. In one case, a ranking officer decided he didn't have to do that and tried to force his way inside. To this day, he has no idea how near he came to a closeup view of the working end of the .45 automatic I was pulling from the back of my belt. Things were beginning to get a little bit out of hand.

Home life was deteriorating fast. I sort of broke the camel's back when I announced that I was going to be buying a piece of land in the valley adjacent to The Monroe Institute. It was a nice lot of about five acres, buried in the woods in the same valley in which the Institute was located. Bob Monroe had actually purchased about 800 acres, or nearly a complete valley surrounded by hills, and decided to share it with friends. He had broken it up into 79 lots of varying sizes, which he was now offering for sale. I decided to buy one. Peggy really didn't say much, but did ask me what I intended to do with it. I told her that I was going to build a small cabin on it, a place that I could go on weekends to relax. I closed the deal with Bob, and Peggy and I traveled down to the property a couple of weekends later to begin construction on the cabin.

The cabin was a small thing, comprising only about 400 square feet, and all one level. I put in 12x12 pressure-treated footers and began building a support deck. About the time the support deck was completed, we had our first fight over the property. It actually followed a meeting we attended that was called a "New Land Property Owners Meeting."

(A lot of people thought the term "New Land" had some special meaning to Bob, but the name happened merely because when Bob and his wife, Nancy, were looking for property to buy, and looking at a number of areas simultaneously, one day he was going out to visit the location on which the Institute now stands, and Nancy asked him where he was going. He simply replied, "I'm going over to the new land," and the name stuck.)

Attending the meeting, Peggy was able to meet quite a few of the other people who had bought land and were either building or living nearby. In those days, the meetings were more for social than business reasons. Among some of the participants were younger women, who were clearly unattached and obviously came across in some way challenging to Peggy. It could have been the way we were being greeted by the others, or it could have been their interest more in me than her, because I had attended one of the seminars. Certainly, one of my trainers, Melissa, was attractive, and she owned a house there and was acting as if we were old friends. In any event, for one reason or another, Peggy got angry. She didn't say anything while we were at the meeting, but she certainly did on the long three-and-a-half-hour drive back to Fort Meade. By the time we returned, she made it very clear that she did not want anything to do with the Institute, Bob Monroe, the cabin, or anything else that might create a connection there. I was deaf in one ear from the ride, so I went to bed in the guest room.

The next day, as I was leaving for work, Peggy informed me that I would have to find another job or else. My normal hour cool-down period that day extended to something like three hours. I was beginning to feel like a slave—chained to the job, the viewing, a pitiful small area surrounding my desk, and the space of my mind. That's when everyone always asks themselves what else can get worse, right? I got a call out of the clear blue from my son, Scott.

It had been nine years since I had seen him. When I got over the first few seconds of shock, I asked him how he was doing.

"Well, that's what I'm calling you about," was his response. He proceeded to tell me that he was being harassed at school by a lot of bullies and there were a lot of racial incidents. He said his grades sucked. He had thought about it and decided that he was going to leave Miami and come to live with me.

I went numb all over. How do you tell a very young child that he is trying to jump from the frying pan into the fire, when your heart is yelling, "Go get him"? There was nothing more that I could want than to be with my son again, but where he was, he at least had a home to come home to. Peggy and I were at each other's throats; I was the only one doing the remote viewing at work; and I was close to the breaking point emotionally. I had to make the right decision in a handful of seconds, and it had to be the right one for him and not me.

I told him that if he moved in with me, I would expect that his grades could never fall below a B—actually, I said, A's would be better. I would expect him to follow my rules, and they might be even stricter than his mother's. And, he'd lose contact with all his friends. I reminded him that I would also have to be at work all day, and the time we could spend together at that moment wouldn't be too great.

I listened to a huge sigh across the phone line. I could feel the last of the air leaking from his rescue boat. My very soul felt as though someone had poured it full of molten lead. God, it's hard even now, remembering how much my heart hurt right at that moment. I could taste his pain, when I hoarsely asked him to put his mother on the phone.

She told me which public school he was in and my heart sank. It was probably one of the toughest schools in Miami from a small kid's perspective—lots of gang violence and all the other possible problems that could exist in a single school. I asked her to move him to my old high school. I was sure that if she went down there and spoke with someone and they knew he was my son, they'd find a way of getting him in. I discussed his home situation and she assured me that while she was trying to hold the line with him, it was mostly a school issue.

I hung up hoping she would carry through, which she did. I wrote Scott a letter, hoping that it would explain how I was feeling, and I received it back in the mail unopened some weeks later.

I was extremely depressed for a long time. There wasn't anyone at work I could talk with about it. Had Ken still been there, I probably would have discussed it with him. But, he wasn't, so I bottled it all up. I would sometimes sit at night in my living room, watching the moon cross the horizon through the window. It seemed like seven lifetimes ago that I had wondered what a blood-colored moon looked like on the other side of the world. Now I knew. It looks exactly the same no matter where you're standing, and like the moon, no matter where you stand, all your folly and all your human strengths or weaknesses stand with you.

I went back to work, trying to do the best I could with the targets that were still pouring in through the project door, but I was mentally stretched about as thin as I could be. By the end of the following week, I received word that my father had finally lost his war with throat cancer, and Peggy and I headed back down south to bury him next to my mother.

When we arrived in Miami, we got a room at a local motel and went immediately to the morgue to sign the release forms for the transfer of his body to the funeral home. I asked them for his possessions and they told me there weren't any. That's when I lost it. All his life, my dad had worn a simple wedding band and it had never been off his finger. If he had wanted to remove it, he couldn't have done so without cutting his finger off or the band itself. It was welded into the calluses at the base of his finger and palm. I asked to see the body and the clothes he was brought in with. They could find his body but not the clothes. His ring finger had the deep white groove where the ring had been, but it wasn't there now. I demanded to see the head coroner and when he came into the room I pulled my identification out and pushed it into his face.

"See this! I'm an Army intelligence officer. You find my father's wedding band, or you'll wish you never met me."

Peggy was pulling on my arm and telling me to calm down. I guess I was a bit out of control. But in minutes they found his clothing, wallet (probably with more money in it than he came in with), and the gold band they had cut from his finger. I don't remember much after that, except noting that the death certificate stated "Death from Malnutrition." When they forced him into the hospital, he refused to eat. Whenever they attempted to put a tube in him, he'd find some way to rip it out. At least they were honest about his having starved himself to death.

If it sounds like I have a lot of rage here, I do. It is plain to me that there are separate medical facilities in this country for different people and the differences really aren't based on color or race, it just looks that way. It's based on how much money you have or what kind of a credit rating you can muster. Someone can be a good human being all their life, they can be honorable and just, even-handed, as well as caring about others. But, if he or she doesn't have the right kind of bank account, he or she will get the minimum. I'm not talking about just my father here, or my mother. I'm talking—from experience—about half the combat vets who live in this fine country. I challenge anyone who thinks they're taken care of in some automatic way, to go out on the street and check it out for themself. There's a lot of eyewash going on.

I returned from Miami with a heavy heart and somewhat past exhaustion.

My trip down to The Monroe Institute had made a noticeable difference in my remote viewing. Even if no one else noticed it, I felt certain that if I were to actually work personally with Bob Monroe over a longer period of time, I might even be able to learn to control my spontaneous out-of-body events. The Hemi-Sync tapes I was using were the only means I had of actually relaxing and putting my mind in a state where I could continue to do remote viewing. I told Fred what I thought and he agreed. So I generated a ten-page request and recommendation on how I could spend time with Bob Monroe and learn even more. I attached an estimate for what it would cost and gave it to my boss. This document floated its way up the chain of command and was eventually approved. I picked up a check from the disbursing officer and Fred and I traveled back down to TMI for another visit with Mr. Monroe.

We proposed to Bob that I spend elongated weekends with him, working in his lab Friday through Monday, over the course of fourteen weeks. The intention would be that together he and I would develop and cut a specific Hemi-Sync–style tape that would be tailored for my use in learning to control my out-of-body experiences, as well as toward further improving my remote viewing. He agreed that he could help.

Back at Fort Meade, Peggy took the news quietly and unemotionally. We were trying to calm things down between us, and things actually seemed to be getting better.

The problem was, now I would be leaving Thursday night for the Institute, and working through until I returned sometime on Monday. Tuesday through Thursday I would continue to do remote viewing. It was hoped that during my absence Tom could begin to carry some of the remote viewing load.

Just prior to my beginning with Monroe, Robert Cowart had begun having severe pains in his back, along one side of his spine. It actually in some ways resembled the beginnings of Hartleigh's problems. So, Robert started making trips to Walter Reed Medical Center to get it checked out. As it got worse, he stopped traveling to the West Coast for training with Ingo. This left only Tom. Tom once showed me two of his best remote viewings and they looked very impressive. When I pressed to find out if they had been blind or double blind, he said he couldn't go into the specific methods he was using because he was under orders not to discuss it with me. Again, I was being pushed away from the subject matter and the new guys. I backed off.

Aside from those two remote viewings, I never saw either Robert or Tom perform an operational remote viewing. My sense at the time was that the office was in deep trouble. It was apparent to me, if no one else, that I was the only one doing remote viewing in the project, and at the time I was seeing no evidence of anyone to follow. I started reminding them that my retirement date was less than a year away. I didn't actually have to retire, because I was only hitting my twenty-year mark, and could have stayed another ten years. But, I knew if I continued at the pace I was keeping, I would never make it to thirty years. I left the following Thursday evening for The Monroe Institute and my first long weekend with Bob.

The schedule was pure Bob. We'd start at a very reasonable 9:00 A.M., and work until Bob got tired, which was usually around 1:00 P.M. He'd retire for a nap—what he usually called "waiting for a long-distance call from overseas"—then we'd begin again around 3:00 P.M. and work a couple more hours. If he extended the hours, it was usually in the evening. Sometimes we'd work together until seven or eight.

The first six days we spent cutting a tape, which he said would only work with me. Since he wasn't absolutely sure how his mixture of set signals would affect me, he started with a baseline signal and we built from there. The signals were modified as we went, dependent on my subjective reporting. Sometimes he would tweak the frequency just a bit and I'd have a sudden urge to urinate. At other times he'd tweak the signal a little bit and I suddenly couldn't remember what the word "color" meant, and couldn't describe anything with color in it. It was all fascinating, but eventually we developed a very powerful tape that would actually make me feel as though my entire body was vibrating and hovering about six inches off the bed in the control room. From there, it was increment by increment, learning how to roll over without moving my body, all the while doing practice remote viewing from sealed envelopes and what he liked to call exploration sessions.

The exploration sessions were interesting. He was continually tweaking the dials while I was exploring, and watching my physiological response as reported though electrodes. I always felt as though I was completely detached from my body and stretched beyond time and space. I learned to completely disassociate myself from the reality around me and to immerse myself in another place in space/time. As we progressed, things became easier and easier for me, and the input became clearer. During actual remote viewings we noticed that the electrodes recording my leg and arm voltages would actually invert. You could watch them on the meter as one side dropped and the other rose until they completely inverted and began traveling in the opposite direction. Bob seemed to think that this was exciting and very meaningful. When we demonstrated it to Fred, he seemed to think so too. But, I wasn't so sure. Maybe my body had always done this no matter what I was doing, as long as I was relaxing. In fact, I learned much later that my body does exactly the same thing as I'm going to sleep. As things progressed and got better, Fred started showing up on some weekends to observe. One weekend he brought some tasking in a sealed envelope, which he handed to Bob. I asked him where it came from and he said he couldn't tell me.

Detailed descriptions of this tasking and the results are in my first published book, *Mind Trek*. The seven sets of coordinates turned out to be all located on the surface of Mars. Even I was stunned by the result.

The weekends came to an end sooner than I expected. Time flies when you are having fun, I guess. On my return to the unit, I wrote a report about the events that occurred and my experiences and recommended the exposure for any serious remote viewer. This report was passed upward through the command and eventually reached the headquarters and the general. He liked what he saw, and decided that there should be some kind of a program for his other officers—something that would help to open his staff's minds, and give them a leg up on thinking out of the box.

In addition to intelligence collection, I believe the general saw remote viewing as a method of actually thinking out of the box to the extent of being able to see or realize answers to problems that would not normally be considered. In this sense I believe he was very much ahead of his time.

In any event, because of our relationship with The Monroe Institute and Bob's senior staff, our office was contacted and I drove into Arlington, where I spent an entire afternoon in the general's office describing my experiences while at The Monroe Institute.

An uncomfortable feeling was beginning to grow in my gut. I was beginning to get a sense that something else was going on that I wasn't quite seeing. Within a week of my visit with the general, our office was tasked with developing a program at The Monroe Institute that would benefit the common officer in the headquarters. At the same time, the general was starting to hold parties where he would invite in only certain, hand-selected people to participate in trying to bend spoons with their minds.

When I had the discussion about the Institute with the general, I had stated that I didn't feel it was something the average officer in his command should participate in. Someone who wasn't accustomed to thinking in an open way about the paranormal or about unusual events in their life, or someone who was locked into a specifically restrictive religious belief that didn't allow for such activity, could find this severely damaging. One only had to look at my own life to see that at a minimum it was terribly corrosive to my close relationships. But I guess the message didn't get through or wasn't given much of a priority.

Part of the difficulty in setting up a program like a Gateway at the Institute for INSCOM officers was that it couldn't look like what it was. The program also couldn't mix INSCOM officer personnel with civilians. The command was worried, and rightly so, about what information might be shared with strangers in the open discussions after tape sessions. So, Bob Monroe and Nancy Honeycutt, his executive director, were asked if they could develop a program similar to the Gateway Seminar, only for handpicked INSCOM personnel. They agreed that it could be done, but only within certain restrictions.

Nancy Honeycutt had been involved with the creation of the Institute from the very beginning. She had started out as the only full-time employee, supporting all of the work and research involved. Her participation involved acting as personal secretary, one of the first trainers, full-time office manager, courier—and she had even soldered most of the connections in the wiring harnesses they used for programs in local motels before he was able to relocate to a permanent building. She was one of his first explorers to be experimented on with his Hemi-Sync system of frequencies in the development of the specific tapes now used in programs today. Having such a wide range of experience, she was able to completely redesign the normal Gateway Program and tone it down to a military group within a matter of a few weeks. They called it the RAPT program, for "Rapid Acquisition Personnel Training."

Still having considerable reservations about such overt military participation in such a program, I brought my concerns to the headquarters in a written memorandum, which I delivered on August 23, 1983. In part it said:

"The experience is intended to expand man's consciousness and broaden his perception of reality. This is accomplished through a patented technology, which synchronizes right/left brain interaction and produces peak amplitude within the optimum brain wave activity areas. This allows thought while in higher-order brain wave states conducive to original thinking and/or holistic idea formulation."

As to how the program actually operated, I responded that it was "six days of intensive tape exercises, with each tape followed by a discussion relevant to the experience. This could range from personal (emotional), to group (intellectual) by nature. Approximately one- to two-hour discussion periods with Robert Monroe were presented in the adjoining David Francis Hall. Topics covered there were generally philosophic in nature. Various films and tapes were presented following the above talks, which were designed to enhance the overall experience. Talks were also given by other TMI personnel, with direct reference to the professional/medical association, New Land concepts, and may include a tour of the newly constructed M.I.A.S. experimental laboratory." Back then, M.I.A.S. stood for "Monroe Institute for Applied Sciences," which was later changed to "The Monroe Institute."

Regarding what could be expected, I simply stated: "Intellectual horizons would be broadened and new concepts of perception would be unavoidable. Light and heavy emotion-packed responses will result from the intensive tape experience. The experience can be expected to alter the participant's personality with regard to interpersonal relationships."

I was emphatic in noting: "While out-of-body experiences

(OBEs) were known to spontaneously occur as a result of the technology used, this was not the purpose of the program. Personal value derived was completely dependent on the degree of participation or effort which anyone put into the experience."

I explained, "M.I.A.S. does not 'push' a specific philosophic, spiritual, or intellectual position on anyone. They do try to open the human concept of experience and consciousness."

I stressed, "The group identity will have a direct result on the effectiveness of the experience. In this case because of the all–"military minded" group, unless participants across the board are willing, and urged to divest themselves of peer pressure, rank consciousness, ego-based self protectiveness, etc., the experience of the whole would be seriously diluted."

I strongly recommended that participants "have no expectations other than to be "open minded" about the process, that they "give and participate 100 percent," and "enjoy the experience more as a fun or human thing to do, versus work oriented." I recommended they "dress in shorts and tee shirt, and carry along a bathing suit." I also reported, "Fasting during the seminar, or conscious control of the amount of food intake has been known to enhance the experience." I suggested they "prepare to spend free time in a physical exercise (e.g., jogging, swimming, hiking, etc.). This will assist in 'grounding' the participant, which in turn greatly enhances the experience."

Lastly, I warned the general, "Not all of the people residing on the property or those who frequent or visit the center as guests are friendly to the U.S. government or Army. Some can be particularly caustic with regard toward 'intelligence' type personnel involvement with M.I.A.S. During my most recent visit it was clearly established by personnel (other than M.I.A.S. employees) that they were very much aware that U.S. Army, specifically U.S. Army intelligence, personnel were coming to attend a seminar."

The command responded positively, sending a message to INSCOM commanders throughout the world notifying them of the initiation of the RAPT program and recommending that the local commanders personally interview applicants who wanted to participate, and use the interview to determine acceptability based on the following areas of concern: the person's "ability to approach new technology with an open mind, ability to objectify and evaluate complete new methods of thinking presented, ability to suggest applications based on new methods within an INSCOM operational framework, ability to apply newly learned skills in a personal/professional scenario, and ability to construct testing/evaluation procedures to determine the effects of the new technology." During interviews, commanders were requested "to stress that RAPT is strictly a voluntary training program, which may be declined without prejudice."

As a result of the message, headquarters was swamped with requests, and the word spread to the Office of the ACSI—where it was badly received. They had already gotten rumors and comments regarding General Stubblebine's spoon-bending parties, and this was like icing on the cake. People I knew who worked in the ACSI office called me. They were concerned about the direction in which the general was driving INSCOM and his vision, and they were even more concerned about the direct involvement of personnel from the Grill Flame unit within that context. (I went to a lot of trouble to meet with the general in private and passed on those concerns, advising that continuing to pursue his course of action could result in a personal penalty or some negative recourse from the ACSI himself.)

The first two RAPT programs were filled to capacity. Participants included the INSCOM commander; a couple of Army senior staff-level chaplains; senior commanders from Hawaii, Panama, Germany, Okinawa; the command psychologist; INSCOM chief of staff; field operations people; counterintelligence agents; Special Action's Branch members; and even a commander from outside INSCOM. Comments on the effectiveness of the program and people's feelings toward it ranged from "I don't get it" to "absolutely outstanding." No negative comments were filed.

The third RAPT program created a problem.

The Institute requires that anyone wishing to attend their programs fill out a questionnaire that details his or her history, with specific emphasis on the medical, emotional, and mental. The reasons for this are apparent. The program is intense and it's felt that someone with difficulty in any of these areas could be affected adversely. People are sometimes asked for approval from their doctor before they are accepted to a program. Until the third RAPT program, of thousands of participants only a few had had problems, which were not serious. In those cases, people had not filled out the questionnaire honestly—omitting salient facts.

From the outset, INSCOM was not willing to share the personal information contained within this questionnaire, which is understandable, given the nature of their employees. An agreement was made in writing that the INSCOM staff psychologist would interview the possible attendees and certify that they met the requirements and were not at risk. This he did.

But when the third RAPT group was organized, one of the attendees had to withdraw the day before departure as a result of illness in his family. That man was in turn replaced by a man who wasn't properly interviewed. He had also omitted certain facts about his background when he had entered the Army, which of course had never been entered into his record. This resulted in an incident during the program that required the man be removed and taken to Walter Reed Medical Center for treatment. The man was not institutionalized as has been rumored. He was simply shaken by some of his experiences in the seminar and unable to cope with the results. He later returned to duty with no long-lasting or ill effects. Even though it was later discovered that the man had been withholding information that was pertinent, it still resulted in the RAPT program being terminated by order of the ACSI himself. Back then, it was an unfair judgment call in the eyes of some, but probably a rational one given the political climate of the time.

The incident could have been worse. The professionalism of TMI employees prevented it from escalating—specifically Nancy Honeycutt, the Institute's director, who brought the situation under control, and Bill Schul, a professional clinical psychologist and one of the program trainers.

In spite of those facts, a lot of negative blowback came down on the Institute. The military initially refused to pay the Institute for the final RAPT program, a situation that I found both deplorable and unacceptable, and one I personally brought to the attention of the INSCOM chief of staff, who then approved payment.

Our project's unavoidable involvement resulted in negative consequences in the Grill Flame project that further separated us from our peers at INSCOM, and within the Army intelligence community—an unfair knee-jerk reaction based purely on fear of the unknown.

Chapter Eleven

End of the Line

At this time Peggy and I finally reached our personal Waterloo. I was totally exhausted, so I decided to submit my retirement papers at the twenty-year mark instead of going for thirty. When I first brought this up to her, she seemed to be inordinately pleased. What I didn't know was that she saw this as a way of getting me away from the project, away from my involvement with TMI (or at least their influence), and starting all over again. Only, in her mind this meant I would be quitting the Army and moving to St. Louis, Missouri, where all of her family lived—three sisters, her single mother, and single grandmother.

This was not something I was contemplating at all. I had already decided to build my retirement home on the piece of land I was paying for in the Blue Ridge Mountains.

Peggy and I were sitting at dinner about a week after this initial argument when she began telling me how excited she was that we'd be moving to St. Louis and that she could finally be close to her family.

"What about my family?" I asked.

What started as a calm and warm conversation quickly turned to an exchange of tar-covered, flaming spitballs. We set the dining area on fire, and half the house, as we raged at one another, moving from room to room. There was no way I was going to move to St. Louis, and there was no way she was going to move anywhere else.

I lay awake all that night, thinking about the arguments and the anger in our lives and realized that I had really been remiss in taking responsibility for my actions. In reality, I had been keeping silent for years when I probably shouldn't have, in an attempt to preserve a marriage that probably should not have occurred in the first place. It wasn't that I didn't love Peggy. I had always loved her. She surely didn't deserve the treatment I had been giving her. But I was doing everything I possibly could in an unconscious attempt to "not fail" at my second marriage. I now realized that I had been hurt so badly by the first failure, I was doing whatever it took to maintain the second just to prove I was not a failure. In fact, I was driving both her and me insane. To continue with such folly was stupid. I would have to take responsibility for all the bad times that I had put her through, and be honest with myself. It just wasn't working. I'd have to take the hits, whatever pain it would cause, and be up front with her.

The following day, I told her what I had been thinking, and said that it would only be to both our detriments to continue the relationship. I felt we should separate and file for divorce. At first she tried to argue with me about it, then she went into an even greater rage. But, in the end, I think she understood that it just wasn't working out for either one of us. I told her she could take anything she wanted, her pick of the cars, and whatever settlement she decided on would be fine. Within the week, we both went to the judge advocate general's office on base to fill out the paperwork. She got the Army lawyer; I got the Marine (hoorah); and we amicably parted company.

In hindsight, the first couple of years I was married to Peggy were absolutely bliss-filled. She was and still is a lovely lady. Her Irish temper and wonderful wit I suppose she inherited from her grandmother. All of her family were always very gracious to me and are good people. The last five years should never have happened. I put her through a miserable time and take full responsibility for it. I was too proud to let go of the idea that I must not fail at marriage again. We both suffered the consequences.

Remote viewing was beginning to take its toll. I had grown a beard and was becoming more and more of a recluse, staying to my little cubical except when I needed to cross the street for an RV mission.

I received a call from the chief warrant at Branch, CW3 Mooney, who stated officially that my competitive status for promotion was dead in the water. In his words, because selection was based solely on

The Stargate Chronicles

performance (that is for warrant officers—within their MOS), and that it was judged by the content of the filed officer evaluation review (OER) forms—forms which reflected that I had been out of MOS for an extended period of time, I was no longer competitive.

He also noted that use of a warrant officer out of primary MOS was in direct contravention with Army Regulation 611-112, paragraphs 17d and e, and based on that fact, I was to be immediately reassigned by the Department of the Army. Furthermore, a formal congressional complaint had been filed by one of my peers, CW2 Gary M. Bosch, naming me specifically as the reason he was being sent to Korea on hardship assignment, while I had been residing in some easy-duty stateside assignment for more than sixty months. He further advised that any request by me for a school would be rejected, any further officer evaluation form that showed me out of MOS would be rejected and returned, and my track record was not redeemable.

As a result, I was immediately moved by the commander INSCOM into the Military Intelligence Excepted Career Program (Nickname: GREAT SKILL). In essence, I vanished from the Department of the Army. My future officer evaluation forms were filled out by the colonel I worked for, endorsed by the assistant deputy chief of staff for operations—human intelligence, and from that point on only seen by a file clerk.

While I can't talk about the specific remote viewing that I was doing during this time, some of the statements within my OER forms reflect the level of mission I was participating in. All of my OER forms filed while assigned to the project were maximum OERs. In other words, I couldn't score any higher than I did. Some examples of statements taken from these OERs are:

"Chief Warrant Officer McMoneagle has provided direct support to six major intelligence collection projects controlled by Army and National intelligence agencies. The resulting intelligence, unavailable from any other intelligence source, was determined accurate and of highest value. In addition to these operational requirements, he installed the first fully automated information system replacing a time-consuming manual procedure. He designed and installed all of the operational software, initiated personnel training and performed all the duties as the "sole" system administrator. As a result of his efforts the administration burden of processing intelligence reports has been reduced by more than fifty percent.

"(He) directly participated in collection missions against 213 areas of interest to United States intelligence agencies. Collection of the above intelligence resulted in a substantial number of product reports, resulting in valuable information being provided to the highest levels of the government.

"(He) has been directly involved in the collection of information against 21 separate targets of high interest to U.S. intelligence agencies. The reports submitted due largely to CW2 McMoneagle's efforts have resulted in valuable information being provided to the highest levels of the government."

My senior rater comments are pertinent to the previous comments by the Branch warrant who, at the time, really wanted to see me thrown out of his Army.

"CW2 McMoneagle is a topnotch professional. He has performed in an outstanding manner in a very sensitive intelligence project. He is a prize for the Army. He has the administrative, management, and leadership ability to handle tough jobs at the highest levels of government. His potential far exceeds the narrow aspects of military intelligence operations. He can handle several actions simultaneously and would fit well into fast moving, demanding positions where the Army's best warrant officers are needed. Select for advanced schooling; promote to CW3 ahead of his contemporaries."

In another: "(He) continually demonstrates extraordinary ability to absorb and explain very complex problems and concepts. He is self-motivated, motivates others by example. Thrives under pressure. Always ready to assume additional responsibilities. His integrity and moral courage are above reproach. Not a yes man."

To this, I would add the following statement by the CIA Public Affairs Office, on remote viewing, which is dated September 6, 1995, 05:38 P.M.:

> As mandated by Congress, CIA is reviewing available information and past research programs concerning parapsychological phenomena, mainly "remote viewing," to determine whether they might have any utility for intelligence collection.
>
> - CIA sponsored research on this subject in the 1970s.
> - At that time, the program—always considered speculative and controversial—was determined to be unpromising.
> - CIA is also in the process of declassifying the program's history.

> We expect to complete the current review this autumn and to make a recommendation regarding any future work by the U.S. Intelligence Community in this area.

The report they reference that eventually came out was the American Institutes for Research (AIR) report, which I address later on in this book as a separate issue.

The whole point of the above is to convey the fact that while effective remote viewing was taking place, and was being reflected in my personal OER forms, it was disappearing into a black hole. Army intelligence, and nearly all other intelligence agencies in the American government, was having not only the cake, but the ice cream also, and no one was picking up the tab.

Captains Tom McNear and Robert Cowart, who had arrived in August of 1981, had been in training every other two weeks at SRI for nearly eighteen months. But they were still just shy of completing the first two stages of a six-stage training system. (To be exact, a portion of their training period, about four months, shouldn't be counted. We were forced to stand down for that period as a result of a congressionally directed hiatus. This was in part because of the knee-jerk reaction to the incident at The Monroe Institute.)

Tom's initial examples of RV at SRI showed high promise, but Robert was beginning to suffer from a bad back, not too unlike the discomfort Hartleigh had been dealing with before his death. In fact, I believe there was some overlay between Hartleigh's departure and subsequent death and Robert and Tom's arrival. I remember them as knowing one another.

Robert's pain eventually reached a point where he was hospitalized and they discovered that he had a cancerous tumor running along his spine. At almost the same time, our long-time secretary, Gemma Foreman, discovered that she also had cancer. Both began treatments about the same time.

The operation that removed the tumor from Robert's back resulted in some paralysis in his legs. He stuck it out with the project as long as he could, but was eventually medically discharged and left the area, permanently riding in a wheelchair. Gemma also died quite soon afterward.

As we neared the middle of 1983, things were not looking good in terms of replacement viewers. Tom seemed to be coming along well with Ingo's training, but it was taking too long and he wasn't yet operational. I had become a nonentity within the Army, although those using me didn't view me that way—at least, not judging by the levels of tasking that was being thrust on us. The numbers of agencies were increasing, as well as the numbers of problems.

One thing I did to alleviate some of the pressure was to bring automation into the project, as cited in one of my OERs, noted previously. Up until this time, we were doing everything by hand, with carbon paper or copiers. Because I had been one of the first to design and use automated systems to drive both intelligence collection systems and perform analysis, I wrote a feasibility paper suggesting that installing a fully automated support system would relieve much of the office burden and create an essential background database for remote viewing information, analysis, and for cross-tracking results, remote viewers, and intelligence content. I felt this would prove to be invaluable from a historical standpoint.

My paper was received positively and I was authorized by the head of Human Intelligence Collection to draw the funds to buy the equipment. I bought the latest and most versatile WANG system available at that time. It was terribly expensive. It had fully removable stacked hard disk drives, which could be secured in a safe, and once removed, left nothing resident within the system. The system could be programmed using COBOL, with subroutines in BASIC and math subroutines in FORTRAN IV, the languages I was familiar with at the time. Since I was the only one in the office who had ever seen a computer up close, I also had to deal with writing out the standards for operating it and entering and extracting data. (This helped me adjust to my world, which was growing smaller and smaller. I was now only allowed to converse with Fred during RV operations, and the new boss, Lieutenant Colonel Bee.)

I remember getting a call from the automatic data processing officer at the headquarters in Arlington Hall Station, asking me if I actually had a WANG system. When I said yes, he was amazed, because they wouldn't authorize him one. It was more advanced than his IBM equipment, which still used old-fashioned punch cards, while I only had to save my programming to a removable disc and could back it up that way, doing everything virtually via the screen. I understand that when I left the unit in September 1984, within a couple of weeks the equipment was moved to the headquarters, where they said they could get more use from it. Not really a bad move, because it opened the door for the unit to obtain some of the first desktop computer systems, which were more conducive to the type of work being done there. If others in the command had been encouraged to open their minds, I believe the leap to desktops would have occurred much earlier.

At the end of 1983, the boss called me in and informed me that they had found a solution to the manpower problem. General Stubblebine had passed him a list of people he had met on his world travels who showed high levels of psychic functioning and the general wanted us to go out, interview them, and if appropriate, recruit them. This entailed a ten-day whirlwind overseas tour of six bases, where we sat and talked with potential future remote viewers. Before setting out on this debacle, I wrote a memorandum (which is still classified) stating my objections to this form of recruitment, as it abandoned the original methodology used for selection, which worked very well and should work again. There was no way you could tell, simply by talking to them, if people were psychic or would make stable remote viewers. But the memo was disregarded and we made the trip in early 1984.

Fred spoke with me just prior to departure and explained that if anyone could tell that someone would be a good remote viewer, it would be me. In other words, let the force guide me.

At the same time, unknown to me, a decision had been made to send three more officers to Ingo for training, even though Tom had only finished the first two stages and none of the follow-on stages had even been outlined. Tom told me later that he had a sense that Ingo was putting it together as he went, using Tom as sort of a guide, basing it on his ability to conform. A decision was also made to transfer the training from SRI in California to an office located closer to Ingo's home in New York City. The three people chosen to be additional trainees were Capt. Paul Smith, another captain I can't name and a woman civilian analyst from the headquarters.

Lieutenant Colonel Bee told me that all these people were selected based on a single recommendation from Mr. Swann, actually a demand, that they "not be" natural psychics. He said that his requirement was for otherwise bright and intelligent officers.

I have to state that I honestly understand Ingo's desire here. After the whirlwind trip and interviews with the proposed list of psychics (all considered to be naturally talented), my recommendation was to hire Lyn Buchanan and if possible rehire Mel Riley. My reasons were simply that as much talent as any of these people might or might not possess—it was impossible to say without testing—regardless, they would have to be amenable to altering their methods to fit within the severely restrictive protocols required in remote viewing. Most were not. In fact, a couple of them stated up front they would not alter their methods for anyone, under any condition.

Having said this, even with the potential being shown by the early stages of Tom's work, I felt it was way too early to introduce "nontalented" people to the project using an iffy or unproven training system. Not only was my concern disregarded, they added a fourth person to the list—Capt. Ed Dames, who was already known to others within the Fort Meade area as being obsessed with UFOs and extraterrestrials. I thought this was really unnecessary and said so. The boss told me that he wasn't being trained by Ingo to be a remote viewer, but was being trained so that he could understand how to "run" remote viewers—someone to give a break to Fred, who was also exhausted, being the only person now capable of running the remote viewing sessions. I filed my report from the trip and capitulated by formally filing my request for retirement.

I left the project prior to Tom's being able to demonstrate the results of his training with Ingo. I've since talked with Tom a little about his experience with the training. He states: "I believe Ingo's training worked. I feel like I was able to produce the necessary information about the site using Ingo's method, but that was by focusing on the process and not the site, as Ingo always instructed. I don't know how to say this—by using Ingo's method, the information came through, but I rarely felt like I (me, Tom) got the site. I got the information, but it was more like the site got me."

Tom said that his first-ever site, which he did with Fred as monitor and me as an outbounder, using the old SRI method, was the first time he actually "knew" he got the site, that he was actually there. With Ingo's method, he rarely felt he was there or at the site. The key difference, as Tom explained it to me, was that one method felt noninstructed and natural, and he felt like he was at the site and experiencing it, while with Ingo's method he felt more like he stayed in the room and the information about the site came to him.

These are important differences, because they indicate to me a possibility that Tom had a considerable amount of natural ability, the key ingredient, which everyone keeps saying isn't necessary with Ingo's training technique. I believe Ingo's training system works to some degree, but only with people who have demonstrated a natural talent for remote viewing.

I do know that Ingo was forced into an impossible situation. The contract monitor at SRI and someone at the command level in INSCOM were forcing the issue. Whether Ingo was ready or not, whether he had completed his testing of his training methods, and whether naturally talented people rather than nonnaturally talented should have used it will never be known. The higher-ups wanted training, and they wanted it right then and there. So it was done. I think this did a disservice to Mr. Swann, the United State Army and some of its personnel, and eventually set the stage for tearing the unit apart. But then, who am I to be complaining? I had submitted my retirement papers and it was none of my business.

A request for retirement is just that—a request. The Army doesn't have to accept it. But, because the program was voluntary, there was little anyone could do to prevent it from being filed. I put the papers into the system and was told to expect an answer in approximately two weeks.

Five weeks went by, and it was as if my papers had vanished into a black hole. I called the man who was supposed to be driving the papers through the system and he was surprised by my call. He had shredded them a month earlier—at my request!

Enraged, I got into my car and drove over to his office. When I got there, I asked to see the signed request to have them withdrawn. He couldn't produce it. I asked him why he shredded them. His response was that when the commander of INSCOM saw them, he said he it was an obvious mistake, and that he was sending them back. When he got them, he shredded them, thinking I had agreed. After all, you never argue with the general. Well—almost never.

I called the general's private secretary and she said he wasn't in, so I asked to speak with the chief of staff. I told him what happened. He said the general had told him not to worry about it, "We can talk him into staying." He then asked me what would it take to induce me into staying on indefinitely.

My response was, "Nothing."

"Well, what if you retired from the Army and stayed on as a civilian employee of the Army?"

"No."

"How about GS-12?"

"No."

"How about GS-13?"

"No."

"Do you want a direct commission?"

"No."

"Do you want more money? To work as an independent contractor?"

"No."

"Well then, what in the hell is it that you want?"

I think my response was not what he expected. I said, "I just want to retire and go live in the country. I'm tired; there's no serious effort being made to replace me; and I'm not even allowed to talk to anyone in the same office with me."

He told me he would pass that along to the general. I sat down at the typewriter in the office I was standing in and retyped my request for retirement. I took a two-day leave and hand-carried it from office to office for signatures, the last office being General Stubblebine's.

When I carried it into his office and dropped it on his desk, I know he was certain that I was jumping ship. In my own mind, there was nothing else I could do. I was completely burned out. He signed the papers, but sadly, I think.

Part of my retirement request was that I got to use my accumulated sixty days of leave time as I wished. I tacked Thursdays and Fridays onto my weekends, giving me a three-day work week for the remainder of my service time, and planned a six-day Gateway Seminar at The Monroe Institute immediately. I continued to do remote viewings, but I think Fred sensed how tired I was. He began sliding more and more of the workload off onto Tom, who was doing fairly well, and Mel Riley was now back in the office, after returning from Europe, and he had always been an excellent viewer.

Just before departing for the Gateway Seminar, I was cleaning out some of my old files and noticed something that had been going on for some time. *For nearly two years,* they had been labeling my work with the numbers of viewers who had long since departed the unit, as an indication to anyone who paid any attention to statistics that they were fully operational with a handful of viewers of equal talent.

I confronted the boss with the information, and he told me that since they had been down to a single viewer for more than two years, they felt it would give me more protection. If anyone (presumably the enemy—whoever they might be), found out there was only one, they might get the idea that making me vanish would be a good idea. I didn't buy it then, and I still don't.

(I learned, many years later, that much of the original work by Hartleigh, Ken, and me was deliberately shredded. I could hypothesize that this was done to bury the fact that multiple viewer numbers were being used for single viewer[s]. But, I doubt that was the single greatest reason.)

I was leaving the office wondering where I would end up and what I would be doing. Once remote viewing gets under your skin, it's very difficult going cold turkey.

Chapter Twelve

Retirement

My second Gateway experience was better than my first, maybe because I arrived totally burned out, with no long shopping list of expectations in my pocket. My trainers were Bob Monroe's stepdaughter, Nancy Honeycutt, and her friend, a psychotherapist from Connecticut, Patricia Sable (now Baker, as in Kim Baker—race car driver/entrepreneur). It was a nice surprise seeing Nancy again. On the day she had met me previously on the back deck of the center building, she had no idea who I was. Now she knew that I was some kind of an intelligence agent with a greater-than-normal interest in the paranormal, in her father, and in what they were doing at The Monroe Institute. During my intake interview with Patricia, however, I simply said that I was a military warrant officer about to retire.

The entire week was significant because I was able to really chill out for the first time in years, and had a couple of interesting experiences. The first one requires some background if it is to be understood.

One day, way back at the beginning of my involvement with the special project, in late 1980, Fred and I were talking about the most embarrassing moments in our lives.

(For example, right after I had arrived at Arlington Hall Station, and having been pinned as a brand-new warrant officer, I was asked

The Stargate Chronicles

to sit in on a meeting in the War Room with General Rolya, two ranking diplomats from an allied country, and three additional Army generals representing other commands. Because I was representing my office, which was going to do a formal exchange with the specific country in question, I was dressed in my best uniform, with spit-shined shoes, and wearing all of my medals. After becoming as comfortable as one can be the first time at the twenty-four-person conference table, in the luxurious surroundings of what is essentially an executive meeting room behind vault doors, one of the people tasked with serving the function came around offering coffee. Of course, when everyone else took coffee, so did I. Unfortunately, I got a coffee cup with a cracked handle. When I picked it up, the handle came off and the cup, filled with very hot and freshly brewed coffee, dropped straight down the front of my dress uniform coat and into my lap. My slight grunting noise, a result of the highly heated fluid suddenly hitting me in the crotch, immediately snapped 23 pairs of eyes my way. So, there I sat with the coffee cup handle in my right hand, trying to act normal.

The general never broke stride. He stood up, carefully unbuttoned his dress uniform, and threw it across the room onto a chair remarking, "You're right, Mac. It's too hot for a coat in here." At which point, everyone else in the War Room removed their coats. The chief of staff had someone take my coat out to be cleaned while we were in the meeting, so that when we got up to leave, it looked as new and clean as when I came in. Embarrassing for me—quite. Would I follow that general anywhere on the planet, and cover his back? Hell yes!)

One of these "most embarrassing moments" happened back when I was a kid, maybe ten or eleven years of age. One of the best things about belonging to the Cub Scouts in Miami, Florida, which was being run by St. Mary's Cathedral, was getting out of the city—which meant getting out of the slums—for a few days. On one camping trip, we traveled out to an orange grove located in the extreme west of Miami, right on the edge of the Everglades. (Back then, the Everglades was a vast and mysterious swamp, where there are now million-dollar homes.)

We set up our tents and started playing a game called "Message to Garcia." This is where one kid has a message whispered into his ear and he gets twenty minutes to go hide, then he must make it in without being tagged and deliver the message by whispering it into the ear of the next kid. The real goal of the game you actually realize at the very end, when the last boy is asked to state the message to the group out loud, and it almost always turns out to have no resemblance whatsoever to the original message. Which is what the game is all about—clear communications and how important they can be.

We had been playing all afternoon, and around dusk it finally got to be my turn to go hide. I took off looking for the highest tree in the grove, which was about 150 acres. I had been watching the others and noticed that no one ever looked up. So, I had already made up my mind to find the largest orange tree I could and hide in it, which I did. I climbed up as high as I could go and wedged myself in the limbs and, because I was so tired, promptly fell asleep.

I told Fred, the next thing I know, I am awakened by the sound of my name being yelled by a lot of adults, who are spread out across the orange grove in a line, waving flashlights all about. It was about 4:00 A.M. when they found me. Embarrassing? Well—let's just say I missed the next three camping trips and pissed a lot of parents off. The worst part was that I ruined the game, because I couldn't remember the message.

Well, on the third day of Gateway, we were half way into the third tape of the day, when I suddenly felt as though someone had crawled into my CHEC unit (that's a Controlled Holistic Environmental Chamber)[10], and sat down on my knees. I opened my eyes, pulled off the headset to yell at them, and noticed that it was a woman I'd never met, and not a participant in the Seminar. She was from India, and appeared to be middle-aged. She had a small, painted dot between her eyes, gray streaks through her hair, and was on the pudgy side, wearing native Indian clothing. She wore no shoes, but was wearing decorative items around her ankles and arms. She looked strangely familiar, although I was sure that I had never met her. I pulled my legs back out of the way and asked her what she was doing. She said she was there to talk. I said I didn't know her, at which point she sort of winked and waved her hand—and I had a sudden and instant recall of having met her before. This wasn't a suggestion, or a totally new experience; it was just as if I suddenly

---

[10]Robert Monroe always liked acronyms and was a bit into the ash and flash. It was the showman in him.

recalled our previous meeting. It had happened when I fell asleep in the orange grove. As I had been falling asleep, she had suddenly appeared and took my hand and led me to a place that was rose colored and had a place for us to sit. There she had introduced herself and we had talked all about what I was going to do with my life.

She smiled at the look on my face, and of course I went into shock and could not respond at all. To suddenly have instant recall about having planned out your life—the good, the bad, and the ugly—was a bit overwhelming. I told her I couldn't remember her name, which she then laughingly told me.

"Karanja! My name is Karanja."

Her name appeared in my head as she said it. I saw it with funny markings over the *n* as well as between the *r* and the *a*. I wrote it down in my journal later so that I wouldn't forget it.

So, I said, "Okay, Karanja. Why are you here?"

To which she responded, laughingly, "Just to talk."

"And . . . this time, I get to remember what we talk about?" I tentatively asked.

She waved her hand and I awoke at the end of the tape.

I didn't know what to make of the experience. It totally overwhelmed me. I asked the guy sharing the room with me if he had heard us talking and he said no. He did say that he had experienced a very strange light in the room, though, which had passed the outside of the small black curtain that closed off his CHEC unit. He thought maybe I had walked across the room and sunlight had been reflected off something I was carrying.

I told Fred about it later when I returned to Meade and we've always referred to her as the Swamp Lady, because that was the first place I had been introduced to her.

What is she? Who is she?

Well, the best that I have been able to come up with so far is that she is some aspect of myself—some projection of self, which is maybe interested in whatever I may be protecting myself from. Some of those I've told about her say she is my guide. Maybe so, maybe not, but I really have no idea who she is. I just know that once in a very rare moment in space/time, I sometimes see her and we talk. What we talk about is beyond my reach until after it has happened.

I spent a great deal of time searching for the meaning of her name. I asked numerous people I knew or have met from India, as well as those who speak numerous dialects of Hindi. None were able to translate the name. Eventually, after I started working at Stanford Research Institute International (SRI) following my retirement, I spent a weekend attending a special exhibit of Hindu gods and deities at the museum in the main park in downtown San Francisco. In one of the rooms was a huge multilevel altar, with dozens of small statues displayed on it. On the very bottom shelf, toward the rear, was a tiny statue of a slightly pudgy woman in Indian garb. They listed her as a minor deity, with the name spelled Kiranja, which, translated from some archaic dialect, means "bringer or carrier or light."

Knowing what I do now, and thinking as I do now about how space/time might be imagined to work—I could have, at that precise point in time, created all of my experiences with her up until this very moment. You see, I believe we fool ourselves into thinking that things are linear simply because we normally experience them in that fashion. But in reality, anomalous events happen and we experience them outside of the linear-time framework. In a simple sense, it's like saying that since I will eventually know the answer to a question for which I currently have no answer—it will eventually be inside my head as knowledge. Therefore, if you change how you think about time, I can view the information as always being in my mind from the beginning. In other words, maybe information doesn't travel to us—it's just always there until it is necessary to complete the time/space framework.

One thing is for sure, she will always be one of the great mysteries in my life that will keep me interested in the paranormal and how reality might or might not work.

The second thing that happened at that specific Gateway was a simple and kind gesture that brought my third and final wife into my life. I was allowed to ride along to feed a couple of dogs.

One afternoon, during lunch, I was talking to Nancy Honeycutt, when she said that she had to go and feed Caesar. For some reason, the name conjured up an image of a huge cat, a Bengal tiger wearing heaving chains in a basement cage. Or perhaps a regal Doberman, guarding a small stone cottage in the woods. Whatever the image, it intrigued me, and I asked to go along. At first she was reluctant. I didn't know it, but the rules strictly forbid any of the trainers getting chummy with individual participants. These were rules she knew well, because these were rules she drafted for all the trainers. But, I pressed her and she finally relented.

We drove over to her home, an old farmhouse, sort of an ugly shade of faded yellow she quaintly called the "Col. Mustard House." She warned me that Caesar could at times be overly protective, but his son, Higgins, was only a puppy. So, I was nervously having images of major-large Doberman, and smaller, puppy Doberman who the larger Doberman would kill to protect. I tentatively moved to the backyard, while she entered her house calling out for them. She slid the rear deck door open, and out burst Caesar—all eight pounds of him. He looked like a blend of poodle, corgi, and terrier, with a sort of a schnauzer haircut. He came right over to me and stiffened, bristling at the neck and growled a low, guttural growl. Right behind him, with his ears hiked halfway up in the air, was two pounds of Higgins, his tail whipping back and forth.

She told me that Caesar was just checking me out. He'd calm down after a few minutes. He gave me a quick second look and then took off after Higgins. They had a great time in the yard.

Sitting under an old walnut tree, she told me about how little Caesar had looked at her a few years back when she had to go out to California to work. (For a couple of years she did sales work for a couple of major publishing houses selling textbooks to colleges on both the West and the East Coast, before coming back to work at the Institute as its director.) She said it broke her heart leaving him at home. It was evident that she loved her two little fur babies quite a bit. We just sat by the walnut tree and talked, and I felt something turning over inside me. It scared the hell out of me, though. There was no way that I would entertain any concept of a third marriage. I had already destroyed two; a third was out of the question. I tried very hard to stay away from her after that, but over time it became more and more difficult.

One of the things I had to do to prepare for retirement was take a complete physical at Walter Reed Medical Center. And, it was complete—properly crossing all the *t*'s and dotting all the *i*'s. They annotated the fact that I had severe disc disease and multiple hairline stress fractures throughout my spine, which qualified me for 30 percent disability. No surprise to me, because I had spent the past sixteen years living with pain. Surprisingly, I also got another 10 percent for arthritis in my left wrist, right hand, and spine, a result of other injuries I sustained during service.

Then I learned one of the interesting things about military service they don't tell you when you sign up and are doing your time. Even if your disability is severe enough that you can no longer work to support your family, it doesn't mean anything in terms of additional money.

Congress passed a law over a hundred years ago that prevents retired veterans from receiving both retirement pay and whatever percentage of disability they end up with as a result of wounds or injuries sustained in service to the country. In fact, once you are retired, you get to pay your own disability. For every dollar you receive in disability, you have a dollar deducted from your retirement salary. The only good part is that the percentage paid in disability is not taxed.

Now, if, as a retired military officer or enlisted man, you go to work for the government after you retire, then you retire from government service, the disability—whatever percentage it might be—can be a result of government service and not military service and you can draw your full retirement and disability. Or, if you are a congressman or senator and you are disabled while serving (even just one term), you can draw both retirement and full disability. Or of course if you are the president of the United States, who is also the commander in chief, you can draw both because you would draw it as the president and not as commander.

If I sound a bit peeved here, it's because I am. Any of my readers who believes that the military veterans who are retired and 100 percent disabled are well cared for should check it out. They aren't. Men who make it to retirement and end up crippled as a result of earlier wounds or injuries while in service, and who are now stuck in wheelchairs, get to pay their own disability. This is a tragedy, especially when they are in their early forties, and their kids are hitting college age, or the family needs medical insurance, or a home, or food. Try it as a retired sergeant first class with three kids, living with some bizarre disease they found in your blood as a result of kicking in the wrong bunker door over in Iraq back in 1991—a disease that won't let you roll out of bed.

It's an unconscionable crime that the bills of war are always paid when it comes to a new multibillion-dollar technology, but the cost in human terms—like the lives of Americans—always seems to get lost somewhere in the shuffle. Excepting of course everyone else who serves, but not in the military. I suppose the government contractors and other lobby groups are much stronger than the ones representing the military retiree, or maybe those in the retiree lobby serve two masters.

I won't apologize for the strength of my feelings on this issue. I've seen too many of my compatriots go down hard after significant sacrifices on behalf of their country. The people who are making the decisions to send soldiers to war also make the decisions not to care for them afterward.

While in Walter Reed, they also gave me a full-blown heart stress test on a treadmill connected to a computer. They put me through a grueling 45 minutes of jogging up and down hill, which got my heart rate up to about 225 beats per minute for about a ten-minute stretch of simulated hill climb. The computer declared me (aside from my entire spine, which the testing actually trashed again) as fit as someone age 39 should be. I limped out of Walter Reed satisfied that there wasn't anything too terribly wrong with me.

The following week, one of the strangest incidents in my career occurred. When I walked into the office on a Thursday morning, the boss asked me to give the chief of staff a call. He said it was urgent. I called him right away. When the chief of staff took the phone from his secretary, he immediately started chewing on me like a piranha. He said he was going to have the military police pick me up and bring me to Arlington Hall Station in irons. He was absolutely infuriated like I had never before heard him. When he finally stopped yelling into the phone, I asked him what in the hell it was that I was supposed to have done.

"You mean you don't know?" he responded, incredulous.

"No. I haven't got a clue, Colonel," I yelled back.

He took a deep breath. "We have a formal signed complaint from a lieutenant colonel doctor at Walter Reed who says he was physically assaulted by you last week."

I had been there the Monday before for the retirement physical and had not even seen a lieutenant colonel, never mind assaulted one. I tentatively asked, "When was this supposed to have occurred?" I could hear him shuffling papers.

"Wednesday afternoon."

I let my breath out in relief. I didn't even know that I had been holding it. "Well, it wasn't me. I was standing in the Capitol building with the assistant deputy chief of staff for HUMINT, and my boss," I replied.

More paper shuffling.

"Something's wrong here then," he replied. "He says in his statement that he identified you by the identification badge on your dress greens. He describes you almost perfectly head to toes. And, he claims you jumped him in a deserted corridor for no reason."

"It wasn't me," I exclaimed again, repeating what I had said before.

He didn't believe me.

"I want you in my office in an hour!" he said, then hung up.

I went to my boss and told him what had happened and he went with me to the chief of staff's office at Arlington. When we got there, there was a lieutenant colonel in the outer office, who nervously watched us as we entered. The chief of staff's secretary announced our arrival and he came out to meet us.

Looking at the lieutenant colonel with the medical insignia on his collar, he asked, "Is this the guy?" pointing to me.

The lieutenant colonel nodded in the affirmative, but watched me really carefully, nervously. I guess he was afraid that I'd be jumping him again.

"Well, I wasn't at Walter Reed on Wednesday. I was there on Monday getting my retirement physical, and this man," I pointed to the lieutenant colonel, "is a liar."

All hell broke loose when I called him a liar. The commotion was loud enough to bring the general in from across the hall, asking what was going on. The chief of staff explained the entire situation.

The general picked up the phone and called the assistant deputy chief of staff for HUMINT, and asked him where he was on Wednesday. After a few minutes he asked him who was with him. Nodding his head, he hung up the phone and looked toward the lieutenant colonel.

"Well, sir. You are wrong. This man," he said, pointing to me, "was in a room of the Rayburn Building at the Capitol with the assistant deputy chief of staff for HUMINT, his boss here, and two congressmen and a senator when you were assaulted."

The room became very quiet. The lieutenant colonel medical officer had the most perplexed look on his face. He just picked up his briefcase and turned and walked out of the office. The chief of staff dropped the paperwork in his secretary's wastebasket on the way back to his office. Everyone just sort of walked away from me.

"Well?" My boss inquired. "You coming?"

I followed him out to the car and we drove back to Fort Meade. To this day, I haven't got a clue to what has to be the strangest incident in my twenty years in the Army. On the way back to Meade, my boss kept ribbing me about beating up on people while out of body. At that point in my service there were only two other McMoneagles serving in any service of the DoD that I was aware of, neither of them locally and neither of them relatives.

I was spending more and more time down in the Charlottesville area, and less time at Fort Meade. When I was in my quarters on base it was uncomfortable. I was alone with my dog, Barney, and we were missing things like the stereo and some of the other things that make a home more livable. We'd spend a lot of time together taking longer and longer walks on base. It was also uncomfortable being there alone in the middle of the week, especially during the day. Some of the other wives in the quadrangle of town homes knew that I was permanently separated from Peggy and would show up at my door, sometimes looking for an extra light bulb, but mostly looking for other things. I stayed away as much as possible.

When I drove south, I took Barney along with me on a few of the runs. He really liked riding in the car. He'd sit up front like a regular passenger and watch stuff go by. He really loved looking at cows. I think he thought they were just larger dogs.

On one of my trips down to the Institute I brought him by Nancy's house to meet Caesar. It was a really big mistake. Barney and I had had a fight with a pack of dogs on Fort Meade. We were jumped by a pack of four dogs, all family pets that people had let out to roam the neighborhood after dark—a malamute, an Irish setter, a German shepherd, and a springer spaniel. I put the malamute in a parked car, the springer spaniel in a dumpster, and killed the German shepherd. Barney killed the leader, the Irish setter, and kept the German shepherd at bay until I had a chance to defend myself. I spent three days in the contagious infection ward at Fort Meade's hospital, getting my wounds scrubbed out every two to four hours. After that, Barney would never let another dog get close to me—even smaller ones like Caesar and Higgins. Caesar, protecting his territory, of course charged right up growling. Barney snatched him up like a roll of paper towels and took off across the yard with him, shaking him like a rag doll. Higgins took off for cover. I took off after Barney with an umbrella. Barney wasn't afraid of much, but snapping any umbrella open in front of him really generated a great startle response. Barney startled—Caesar hit the ground running, no worse for wear, and I reconnected Barney's leash.

In the beginning, whenever I visited Nancy, we would put Barney on the second floor and keep the other two dogs downstairs. Otherwise, Barney was always kept on a leash, especially when I walked him. I could tell it was putting a strain on her, and on all the other four-legged ones. I knew in my heart that it was only a matter of time until Barney would get another shot at Caesar or Higgins—and the next time we might not be so lucky.

I knew if there was ever going to be a permanent relationship between Nancy and me, I was going to have to give Barney up. I thought about it a lot and we discussed it a number of times. We even considered turning the oversized garage into a kennel, and connecting it to a full-sized, covered run outside. A grand idea, but I just couldn't envision being able to watch him like a hawk all the time. In my own mind, it would have been too much to ask her to give up both of her dogs for my sake. It was just one more of those incredibly painful events in one's life that one has to deal with. It was certainly one of the most painful in my life up until that point. Barney was my friend and confidant, something you don't have a lot of in the intelligence business. I could share time with him and he made no demands, other than to be there with me, sharing in whatever I was doing. He even carried his own food and water in a set of saddlebags I had made for him. It wasn't the same as a relationship with another person. That's always a two-way street. With Barney it always felt like it was one way—him to me. It didn't take much to have him crawl up next to me on a couch and lay his head in my lap, or give me a gentle woof when my alarm had run down. His demands were quite simple—"Just take care of me."

That's the part that made it so painful. He wasn't asking much, but it was more than I could manage.

It was equally hard on Nancy. Actually, I should begin to refer to her by her nickname, Scooter. (When she was a tiny baby, the woman who helped take care of her started calling her Scooter, after small little cakes they used to sell with the same name.) She had really strong feelings about the issue as well. She would have done anything I asked, modified any part of the house, or done almost anything to ensure keeping Barney and me together. That was one of the things I fell in love with Scooter for—she always put herself in someone else's shoes before she made judgments about them or made comments about the situations they were in. In this case, I knew she was imagining how it would feel for her to give up her own two dogs and it generated an almost unbearable amount of imagined grief for her. But, it was one of those things in life that has to be done, and it was really my decision all along. I told her that I was going to find a solution and that it probably meant giving Barney up to another good home. I can't think of too many other times that I've seen her cry so hard or feel so bad about something she couldn't do anything about.

When I got back to Fort Meade, I sat down at the kitchen table and wrote a letter from Barney to whomever the new owner might end up being. In it, I explained that I (speaking for Barney) was overly protective of my family members, that I really liked hot dogs a lot. I listed my favorite words, especially the ones I knew really well, like sit, stay, lay, that sort of thing, then explained that more than anything, I loved being with family and riding in the car. I took Barney to his vet—who absolutely loved him anyway—and she started looking for a new home for him. Within a few weeks, a saleswoman saw the letter that I had written for him. She worked the Southwest territories and wanted a traveling companion to protect her and her things. When she sat down in the vet's office and they let Barney in, he went over to the couch, climbed up, and laid his head in her lap—about as sure a sign as any could be. I received a single letter from the woman after the first sales trip that Barney accompanied her on. It was quite simple and straightforward—the message, abbreviated, was "I love Barney, he loves me, and you can't have him back." So, in my heart, I am eternally grateful to the woman who gave Barney his new home and role in life. He was almost trained for it. But even now, I keep a folder with pictures of Barney on my desk. He will always have—as all my fur children do—a very special place in my heart.

When I got within about six weeks of retirement, I began moving my stuff down to the Col. Mustard House, near Nellysford, Virginia. By the time I reached retirement, I was living in Nelson County, Virginia, deep within the Blue Ridge Mountains and commuting to Fort George G. Meade, Maryland, deep within city concrete and impossible traffic. On a good day it was a drive of about three hours and 45 minutes. So, leaving for work my final weeks at Meade meant hitting the road around 4:10 A.M., something I was perfectly comfortable with. It gave me a lot of time to think about what I was planning and doing. The most difficult decision I was going to have to make was whether or not I could commit to another serious relationship. I had done so much damage to myself and others in my first two attempts that I didn't want to spoil a good thing by reliving history.

I thought long and hard about making the decision, spending weeks agonizing over it before finally making up my mind. Eventually, logic and good sense won out.

Having been a soldier for twenty years, I knew that death could come out of nowhere at any time. Having had the near-death experience in Austria in 1970, I was also aware that nothing really matters in life other than that you are living it true to yourself. For quite a few years I had forgotten that. Scooter was now gently reminding me, in her own way.

I decided the only way I could ever muck up a third marriage was to be in one, and the only way *not* to muck it up was to try to do the best I could without constantly living in fear of the consequences. I came to the conclusion that a decision about marriage has to be made without fear. I decided the only fear I had at that time was not being with her. I loved her too much and just couldn't walk away from her.

Because I was in a black project, and very few people knew me, my retirement ceremony was held *in camera,* secretly and quietly within the project building. Scooter was invited to attend and the building was sanitized for her benefit. I was very surprised when the assistant deputy chief of staff for HUMINT called everyone to attention and presented me with an award, the Legion of Merit. In my experience, few people receive them—usually those who have made major contributions at a much higher level in the bureaucracy. I was even more surprised to see that part of the certificate referred directly to the work I had done within the project.

When my boss handed me my final orders, he asked if there was anything I felt I had to say as a parting comment. The words I wanted to say were "I'm proud to say that I've done twenty years in the service of my country and am walking out the door with my integrity still intact." That would have been meaningful. But, instead I simply said, "I am proud to have served with so many good people and I have surprisingly managed to survive a career of twenty years without anyone ever having to give me a direct order." This was kind of a small dig about how difficult it was to get me to do anything in any other way than my own. I shook everyone's hand and we left. Because I'm psychic, I knew what they didn't—it wouldn't be the last time that I'd be seeing them—and it wasn't.

Scooter drove me and my gradually growing folder of papers around the base for a couple of hours while I was formally checked out of everything. She held my hand while I exchanged my active-duty ID card for one showing that I was retired; she helped me scrape the bumper stickers off my car; and she looked the other way while I deregistered my firearms and threw them into the trunk. These don't sound like very important things today, but back then, when I was doing it for the final time, I was choking all the while on a very large lump in my throat.

On that final day, I was not only leaving the special project where I had spent 71 months doing remote viewing, but I was also walking away from twenty years of service to my country in what could only be described as having been a major love/hate relationship, especially the 151 months—that's twelve years and seven months—that I had served continuously overseas. My multiple tours of duty in Europe, the Far East, and various islands had all been active (real mission) tours during the Cold War and there was almost as much satisfaction about what I had been able to accomplish, as there was a trail of destruction in my relationships with people—and not just ex-wives.

Serving in the kinds of intelligence positions I had been in, I hadn't made more than a handful of friends in my entire twenty years of service—not lasting ones anyway. There wasn't much to show for a large chunk of my history. Most of what I had accomplished over those years was and still is classified. So, in any of my new endeavors there would be little that I could share with anyone I might meet or make friends with. I could envision the following repetitive scenario:

> POSSIBLE NEW FRIEND (PNF): "You did what for twenty years?"
> ME: "I was an intelligence officer in the Army."
> PNF: "Doing what exactly?"
> ME: "A little of this, a little of that."
> PNF: "Oh. Er . . . I see."
> ME: "What do you do?"

PNF: *"I'm a commodities broker for a major bank in New York. We generate capital . . . etc., etc."*

As you can see, with a history like mine, you can really generate a great deal of interest in yourself as a human being. It's almost guaranteed to convince someone to invite you over for dinner to chew the fat.

Right after my retirement, I took six months off and wrote a book. It is a still-unpublished novel originally titled *Gods That People Play*. It's filled with all the stuff I couldn't put anywhere else because it was too gruesome. It's a horror story. I don't think Scooter particularly enjoyed reading the manuscript. The part about the elevator door opening and the severed head rolling out into the hallway really got to her. I know my new friend and agent in New York, Ms. Eleanor Friede, called me at 2:00 one morning and her exact words were "Thanks a lot you son of a bitch, now I can't sleep." (Everyone who knows her knows that Eleanor was never a person to mince words or feelings. I love her dearly for it. She's retired now, and her partner has to deal with me, which is no easy task.)

Anyway, the book was about an underground lab somewhere in the desert where they were injecting a very special mix of DNA into animals to increase their intelligence. Step two was the small step up to humankind, or designer beings who could be used as weapons. Step three . . . well . . . maybe one day I'll get it published.

The other reason I wrote the book was because things suddenly were not faring very well in the remote viewing world. Right after I retired, General Stubblebine retired as well. He got into it one too many times with his own boss and a decision was finally made by the ACSI to replace him with someone who wasn't quite so progressive. So, the new INSCOM commander became a Maj. Gen. Harry Soyster, who had a reputation for being anti-anything-paranormal, the immediate effect being a termination of funds and spaces required to run the project. This affected both the special project at Fort Meade and the lab at SRI-International in California.

This was not a decision based on common sense or anything else material to the endeavor. It was one I believe was made purely at the request of those who didn't want to be caught dead standing next to a psychic. While we had been making a lot of friends in the clandestine world of intelligence gathering by providing valuable support, we were also scaring the shit out of a lot of people who owed their positions, promotions, and livelihood to politics, and were talking a good talk, but never walking the walk. It wasn't fear that we'd know their deepest and darkest secrets, it was plain old-fashioned fear—that if someone caught them supporting something they themselves would naturally ridicule, then by association they too would be ridiculed as well. Simply put, they didn't have the stomach or the courage for it.

All the funding had been approved on a year-to-year basis, and only then based on how effective the unit was in supporting the tasking agencies. These reviews were made semiannually at the Senate and House select subcommittee level, where the work results were reviewed within the context in which it was happening. So, decisions for renewal, funding, and a continued use of our particular approach to intelligence collection wasn't being made lightly, nor were these decisions being made by some crazed monkey hiding out in a bell tower.

In fact, a number of times I traveled to one of the buildings on Capitol Hill and sat in front of one of those committees and was asked to demonstrate my remote viewing ability. In many of those cases they would not let us bring a folder full of possible targets to pick from, which would have been a better protocol, but we had to respond to targets a senator or congressman, or one of their aides, had preselected and brought into the room. It is a terrible shame that some of these events were not photographed or recorded—or maybe they were, but not to my knowledge.

Sometimes the targeted envelopes were presented wrapped in a thin sheet of lead. A precaution to prevent me from using my x-ray vision, I'm sure.

In one case, I knew I would have to do a remote viewing for the head of an agency. The specific agency unfortunately cannot be named here, but it has its very own acronym and is in the top six. I was nervous about the possible outcome because my boss at the time informed me the day before that based on its outcome we might or might not be in business the following month. So I decided to do the remote viewing ahead of time, before we ever left the office.

A few days later, when we were comfortably seated in front of the "senior executive" for that agency, he made a big deal over carefully pulling the target envelope out of a briefcase with a combination dial lock. I then made an equally big deal out of pulling a folder out of my own briefcase, which contained his result. At the time, it was impossible to tell from the expression on his face if he was impressed or not, and he never said a word. He just carefully locked both the envelope and folder away after reading the information. I never got to see what was in the envelope, so I never got any direct feedback, but we soon started getting a lot of tasking out of his office. I guess in hindsight I actually did know what was in the envelope, or I would have gotten feedback—only it would have been negative. Sometimes feedback can be detrimental to your work—something seldom mentioned by many claiming remote viewing expertise.

Immediately after retiring from the Army, I submitted a request for employment to the laboratory at SRI. I thought this would be a place I could continue to pursue remote viewing, but under somewhat less stress. I also felt that I could contribute to the continuing research by volunteering my expertise. But I received no response at all to the first two letters I sent to SRI. During this same time, I submitted a formal proposal for a training program to my old office, with a suggestion that if they needed assistance I could be hired as an independent contractor.[11] I also proposed a completely new type of system for manipulating the database materials and tracking remote viewers and their idiosyncrasies. It was already clear to me from the conditions of the office when I left that they were going to have increasing difficulty and I felt I could at a minimum search out and identify specific talent areas using some new ideas that I had been cooking for some time.

I never got any of the proposals back from my old office. In fact, I never got any of my submitted materials back from my old office. What I did get was a telephone call from Lieutenant Colonel Bee. He said, in very clear words, they weren't interested. It was also clear from my short discussion with him, that they were totally pissed off for my having retired and wanted nothing further to do with me. This was made emphatically clear with the suggestion that I not call there any more. In a sense I could understand their feeling, but in another sense, I had the right to the same respect that any other person would have submitting a proposal. It left me feeling like an abandoned stepchild.

---

[11]Excerpts and portions of this original proposal showed up in what is called the CRV Training Manual that can now be found displayed on the Internet. Of course it is used out of context and leaves out the entire suggestion for using a selection and testing criteria for identifying remote viewers before they are exposed to any form of training.

Since I had moved in with Scooter, I was also beginning to feel guilty watching her drive off to the Institute office every morning while I sat around the house. I functioned well as a "built-in heating module" for Caesar and Higgins, but I was getting anxious about doing something else more helpful. So, one evening Scooter and I discussed the possibility of starting a company and selling consulting services using remote viewing as an application for business. I wasn't sure I could produce enough work to justify it, but we decided to go ahead and create the company anyway. We agreed that we would give it two years to see if it would succeed. As a result, within sixty days of my retirement, Intuitive Intelligence Applications, Inc., was born as a Virginia corporation. Now, all I needed to do was find some work.

This time, rather than write, I called the lab at SRI and asked them to please ask Hal to give me a call. A few days later, Hal finally called me back. In response to my query about my letters, he asked me if I would fly out and talk with him. He offered to pick up the tab, so I accepted. Hal was very clear in making me understand that it wasn't a job offer, but he was willing to talk about it, so I went.

I met with Hal at a pancake house within walking distance of the lab. We couldn't meet at the lab because my clearances had been retired along with me a few months before. In our discussion over breakfast, I learned that he had been reluctant to respond to my letters for a number of reasons.

First, he said they only had funding for about another year and a half. That meant he was already looking for new funding, and they'd need as much of the remaining funding as possible to continue operations until they found the new source.

Then, after hesitating for a number of minutes and playing with his pancakes, he finally said that he had been informed by people from my old office that I was unable to do remote viewing without a very specific kind of monitoring and that he'd been told that it was specific enough that it would make me very difficult to work with under laboratory conditions. This was totally unexpected, and shocked me.

I asked who had told him this and he responded that he had gotten it from the boss, and the boss had based it on information provided by the operations side of the house.

I couldn't believe my ears. I just kind of sat there. It hurt and angered me at the same time. I poured some more coffee while I fought the urge to start cursing and throwing things. After a few minutes of silence I said that this information was totally wrong—he had been grossly misinformed. I told him that I didn't even need a monitor to do my remote viewing. In fact, I explained, I had spent the better part of my career as a remote viewer teaching myself to do remote viewing under any circumstances. I just couldn't understand why someone in my old office would have said those things. In fact, at the time, I wasn't sure he wasn't shining me on.

We sat there for a bit not talking. Finally I offered him a suggestion. He could hire me as a remote viewer on a test basis, week by week. If after a trial period he found that he wasn't satisfied with my viewing, or that I couldn't carry my own weight at the lab, we could call it quits and part as friends. He agreed and I got a temporary contract for three month's work at the SRI lab. My clearances were reactivated, transferred, and reinstated. I processed into the lab and started work the following month.

Since that conversation with Hal back in early 1985, two other people working at SRI have confirmed that some of the people in my old office had done their best to sabotage any possibility of my employment at SRI. But depending on who was telling the story, the names seemed to change. I have never had any way of knowing who specifically pushed the issue from my old office. I have always preferred to believe that it wasn't the people whom I considered friends. It just wasn't within the character of friends to do that to one another—for any reason—even if they had been ordered to. But, it was clear from what I was being told that someone at Fort Meade, probably somewhere in the management, was trying to prevent my working for SRI. Whoever it was may have been using a number of others, or at least their names, as a cover. Whoever it was failed miserably, because I was now an employee of the SRI lab.

Within a few weeks of my beginning work there, my contract was renewed for a year, then again, repetitively, for every year the project operated out of SRI.

It really felt good working at the lab, because the environment wasn't as charged as at Fort Meade. I was also making considerably more money than as a remote viewing warrant officer. It wasn't Mercedes Benz time, but I wasn't worried about paying bills either. Mostly, it felt good to be contributing again.

At first I was disappointed in not getting to see Ingo very much or spend time with him because he was always in New York when I was in California, or in California when I was in Virginia. But, it didn't take a professor of logic to understand that keeping us apart was probably deliberate. At the time I didn't understand why and I still don't, although I now have some theories.

As was done at Fort Meade, I was assigned a number identifier in the lab at SRI, which was #372. This meant that now my remote viewing work was showing up as 001, 518, 508, 776, 345, and 372 and also under some of the numbers that had been used for Hartleigh, Ken, and others. At least as long as I was with the lab my number remained, and still remains, the same.

It didn't take long for some of the agencies that I had been supporting at Fort Meade to notice that I had moved, as there was an increase in requests for operational support from the lab—which I was sure didn't go over in a really big way with my old office.

Chapter Thirteen

Exploring New Territories

With a good income and finally settled into Col. Mustard House, Scooter and I finally set our wedding date for Thanksgiving Day, November 22, 1984. I had just received my final divorce papers from Peggy and was getting used to being no longer tuned to God, country, and flag. It was strange, but not uncomfortable, because it finally gave me a chance to relax a bit. Let someone else worry about all that world security stuff for the time being.

We planned our wedding to be held at home. We asked Scooter's uncle, Judge Carleton Penn, her mother's brother, to officiate over our vows, which he agreed to do. As if that weren't great enough, he also offered to make some of his world-famous Southern-recipe oyster stuffing for the turkey. He sat on the bench up in Loudon County, Virginia, for many years. (Now retired, he still sits on the bench in other counties throughout Virginia; in fact, I think he works even harder since his retirement.)

Judge Penn is one of the fairest minded individuals I have ever met. He is very clear about his own opinions and ideas about things, but he also doesn't let his own feelings enter into his judgments regarding the law. I believe that this great force of character was at least partially formed while he served as a lieutenant in the Marine Corps fighting in the caldron of war on Peleliu Island in the Pacific. (Putting it into perspective, the 1st Marine Division suffered casualties including 1,121 killed, 5,142 wounded, and 73 missing. That's a 36 percent casualty rate, of which he was one. Those losses resulted in tens of thousands of Japanese dead—an enormous battle in which the Marines were greatly outnumbered.)

Scooter's father, A.J. "Bud" Honeycutt, was also a Marine lieutenant fighting on the same island. They were friends at the time as well as comrades in arms. Scooter's father had the privilege of hauling a field artillery piece up the side of a mountain while fighting for every foot of ground they dragged it across. I have to add that her father is a retired Marine lieutenant colonel who fought in three wars—WWII, Korea, and Vietnam. He is a complex man, an honorable man, and a man loved by a lot of people in the mountains of North Carolina where he now teaches Sunday school at the local Methodist church and helps run a hospice for the dying.

The wedding was very close, personal, and attended only by family—which, for me, made it a memorable and emotional event. One problem gilded the event with a bit of mirth. Early in the morning of our wedding day, Scooter cut the wrapping off the turkey and discovered that it had spoiled. So, there we were, about 7:30 A.M. with the smelliest bird in the county and our wedding a few hours out.

When you live out in the country, 25 miles from any major city, it can be a problem replacing a turkey on Thanksgiving morning. I was scrambling. I hit three gas/quick shops before discovering a single frozen, rock-hard, twenty-six-pounder sitting in the back of a canned juice and ice freezer. I was afraid to check the "sell by date," and instead rushed it home to defrost. The only place large enough to fill with cold water to thaw it was the bathtub—which wouldn't hold water. So, between getting the rest of the house ready, I kept going in every ten or fifteen minutes to refill the bathtub. Luckily we had another shower, or we would have taken our showers straddling the turkey as well. By the time we were dressed and family began arriving, I was sitting with my suit pants rolled up, shoes and socks off, holding my right heel in the drain to keep the tub from leaking, while holding the bobbing turkey under water with my left foot. It took longer than I can recall to thaw the bird, so the actual wedding ceremony was repeatedly set back a number of hours. But it turned out to be a very fine turkey. It was also the first time that I had an opportunity to see most of the family in one room together, which pleased me and I know brought a lot of joy to my new wife, Scooter.

They say if you ever want to see what your wife will eventually be like, look at her mother. On our wedding day, Scooter's mom, also a Nancy, was as always the perfect Southern lady. I knew in my heart that I was one lucky man.

Early in 1985 we got into some very interesting targets at the lab, experimenting with words and language. The man who became my monitor for much of the time I was doing remote viewing was Dr. Nevin Lantz, a clinical psychologist. I also got to work again with Dr. Edwin May, who had been at the lab almost since its beginnings. Ed, Nevin, and I hit it off right from the start. Martha Thompson, the secretary, had a wonderfully dry sense of humor that I really liked; we became close friends as well. Beverly Humphries, the staff intelligence person, had dual undergraduate degrees from Stanford in the classics and anthropology and was a lot of fun to hang out with, even away from the office. With a great sense of humor, she was always up for a trip to the local miniature golf or Ming's for a Chinese lunch special. Russell Targ had already departed, I believe sometime in 1983, but Ingo Swann was still there, as well as other viewers—Hella Hammid, a professional photographer and lovely lady from Los Angeles; and two others I will call Keith and Gary.

There was also a man by the name of Jim Salyer who was the government's contract monitor and a hard man to get along with, although he and I never had any problems. All in all, it was quite a team, and team it was for the most part. We liked working with one another and everyone tried to make whatever we were doing fun.

As an example, in one series of experiments, which included a number of outbounder targets and trips to visit them, Ed had to hang out in a graveyard that had been randomly chosen as a target. While there, he picked a flower from an urn and laid himself out on the top of a grave slab, holding the flower over his heart, which of course was viewed as somewhat mysterious by those walking by. But it made a great target.

If the target turned out to be a restaurant, we'd sometimes eat there on our return for feedback. The differences in results, in my opinion, were phenomenal when it was fun to do, instead of being viewed as "a must do" chore.

In the first part of 1985 we did a series of targets that were "words." It was a complicated experiment, one that hadn't been tried before. It involved one team of people being located in the remote viewing room of the radio physics lab, while a second team was located all the way across the SRI compound in a trailer. The second team, the targeted team, consisted of Beverly, Nevin, or a third person. Their job was to generate a six-digit number using a pseudo random number generator. The first four digits were used as the designated page numbers in an Oxford dictionary, one of those gigantic seventy-pound books you couldn't steal from a library.

Once they turned to the appropriately designated page, they would count down from the upper left column as many lines as the number of the last two digits of the set. From that point they would use the next five-letter word as the target word. This would be spelled out along the edge of a blackboard by using gigantic letters printed in black on a white 12x12-inch card.

Once they had the target up, they would call the remote viewing room, say "ready," and hang up. As a remote viewer I would then be asked to concentrate on the blackboard (which I had never seen) and tell them what the word was, letter by letter.

We wanted to know whether or not one specific letter would come in better than another, if the remote viewer could see the actual word, or—and this was the "hidden from the viewer" part of the experiment—whether the viewer would get the word even when the letters were scrambled or turned upside down.

It was a difficult experiment for a viewer. From the outset you are front-loaded with believing that the word is going to contain at least one vowel—an *a, e, i, o, u,* or *y*. You are front-loaded with the knowledge of an entire alphabet, which immediately suggests an unlimited number of possible combinations. You are also front-loaded knowing there will be five letters. In short, a piece of cake.

I did nine word sets and got the following results: of nine words, I got the entire word correct twice, the words "flies" and "input." Of the remaining seven I got three letters correct on two, and two letters correct on two, and the remaining three one letter correct.

One criticism of the experiment was that it should have been pretty easy nailing at least one letter simply by guessing *a, e,* or *i,* the most commonly used vowels. But in the seven words I missed, I got no vowels correct and in fact, didn't give a single vowel as a response, avoiding them like the plague.

Of the two words I nailed, "flies" was set up on the blackboard rail in order, but the word "input" was scrambled. I can't remember the order of scrambling, just that the cards were both out of order and sometimes upside down or backward (letters facing the wrong way, or the card actually blank side out.)

What I noticed most about the experiment was the fact that the "idea" conveyed by the word was transferred as information, not the individual letters. In other words, I wasn't seeing individual letters; I was seeing images in my mind of birds flying against a background of sky, planes taking off, or small buzzing insects hovering over rotting food.

At least two other remote viewers did equally well, which began to give me a clear impression of the remote viewing quality at the lab. I was beginning to understand that the lab at SRI worked in a totally different way than any other paranormal lab. They spent a great deal of time hunting for and locating high levels of talent in specific individuals. Then they tested the individuals they located. If the individuals they found could consistently produce good to excellent results, they would bring them in and use them for their experiments. This was producing a far better result than using volunteers from college classrooms, or other segments of SRI, or the local high schools.

It took a lot of time, effort, and expense to go out and do a presentation on remote viewing, test these larger groups of people, and finally winnow out the best through judging the individual results and retesting, but it made perfect sense. If you are going to study the paranormal, you go out and find people who can actually do what you want to study; you don't study a general population randomly in hopes of hitting someone who can do something that's considered extremely rare in the first place. I was beginning to understand why we got the results we did while other labs had such a hard time capturing PSI under the microscope of science.

But the remote viewers had to stay current and stay sharp. If you lost your edge for a lengthy period of time or burned out, you probably weren't going to be working as a remote viewer during the following contract period. This speaks volumes for Ingo, Hella, and the other remote viewer's abilities. They did years of uninterrupted work at SRI, some curtailed prematurely by death, as in the case of Hella, some retiring to pursue other more important issues in their lives, such as Ingo, and some still working for the same lab, although it is no longer located at SRI.

The other thing that took getting used to was the way things were set up inside the lab. Checks and counterchecks were set up, to ensure that the targets were always blind targets and the judging was also always done blind and without prejudice. The major assumption that was always underscored within the lab was an assumption that anyone in the lab could be cheating—viewers, researchers, or staff.

Rather than personalize it, we all accepted this as part of the cost of proving that whatever we accomplished was not in any way tainted with doubt. We had to do what we were doing without the slightest hint of irregularity, something I've never seen in any other laboratory, PSI lab or not.

Right when everything was going about as well as I could hope it would, my life was once again turned upside down.

Scooter and I were taking a June day off in 1985, spending it in the middle of Lake Miranon, a fourteen-acre lake in the middle of Robert Monroe's New Land subdivision. We were lying on a floating dock, anchored in the middle of the lake across from the dam—lounging in the early-afternoon sun, drinking iced tea, and just holding each other's hand—when it felt as though someone drove an iron spike through my upper left arm and shoulder. The pain quickly began to spread across my chest and down my arm. I knew immediately it was a heart attack—but I couldn't believe it. I shifted my weight and took a few deep breaths hoping it would go away. It only got worse. I must have made a grunting sound, or it was the look on my face that caused Scooter to ask me what was wrong.

"I slipped that disc out of place in my back," I replied calmly. "It really hurts this time."

"What do you want to do?" she asked.

"Maybe we'd better take a run in to the emergency room and have them x-ray it," I suggested, smiling. I didn't want to tell her that death was knocking at the door.

We loaded everything into the boat and calmly rowed back to shore. By the time we pulled the boat up onto the dam and carried everything down to the car, I felt as though a semitrailer was parked on my chest. I could feel my heart rate rising and the blood pulsing in my ears.

The most overwhelming emotion at the time was—sorrow at how much time I was going to miss being with Scooter. Nothing else seemed to matter. It just didn't seem fair that we spent a third of a lifetime hunting for and finally finding each other, only to have it so abbreviated. I didn't want to panic her, so I suggested that she take a shower and change out of her bathing suit before we drove to the hospital, which she did. I just changed and collapsed on the bed and waited for her. The pain was increasing, but I wasn't frightened, just very sad about it. I absolutely knew that I was going to die and there were only two things in my mind that concerned me. One was, when should I tell her what was really going on? I needed enough time to let her know that I loved her more than life itself and I wanted to tell her I was sorry for leaving her so soon. But, I also knew if I told her this, she might be injured trying to get me to a hospital.

I also wanted to be as awake and aware as possible during the dying process. I'd been through this once before but was confused then and didn't know what to do or what to expect. This time, I was going to be totally aware of what was going on during the entire process. This focus allowed me to put the pain aside, where I could sense it, but it no longer interfered with my thinking. By this time, my entire chest was on fire. When I put the pain aside and began to focus on what was actually happening around me, things began to slow down, almost as if a clock motor was beginning to rotate at a slower speed. We got into the car and began our long drive to the emergency room.

Many have asked me why we didn't just call 911, or the local fire department. Well, back then there was no 911 in Nelson County. The local fire department was a volunteer force, which was equipped to deal with some medical problems, but did not have a cardiovascular emergency trained technician on call. Since addresses were scattered throughout the county area, calling an ambulance would have meant that it could have driven around for the better part of an hour looking for the house. The best plan was a safe drive into the emergency room.

When we got to the halfway point, a decision had to be made between making a right turn and going to the University Hospital in Charlottesville, or making a left turn and going to the smaller country hospital in the smaller country town of Waynesboro. She asked me where I wanted to go and I said Waynesboro. I knew they could react to the problem a lot better probably in Charlottesville, but I didn't want to be drugged out of my awareness. So, she made the left and we raced over Afton Mountain and into Waynesboro proper.

I know we had to have hit every red light there was between entering the town and the emergency room. At each stop, I argued with myself over just telling her to pull over so that I could say good-bye to her before it was too late. And each time, a small voice inside me said, "Relax, you can make it another two minutes . . . it's only another two minutes." The more relaxed I became, the slower my heart would beat. The pain was there. I could reach out and touch it like a fire. I know if I had let it in at that point I would have passed out.

Eventually we pulled into the emergency entrance and she started to pull through to the parking lot. I stopped her. I couldn't sense my heart beating any longer. I was beginning to lose the feeling in my legs and arms, and my ears were beginning to give off a faint musical tone. My vision was becoming faded around the edges and I was going into tunnel vision. I instinctively knew that my heart had stopped. I reached over and took her hand and told her that I had lied and I was having a heart attack and that she should go inside and tell them my heart had just stopped. The last thing I remembered was the look of grief on her face as blackness closed in. I was overwhelmed with the sudden realization that I had not told her how much I loved her and how much she had meant to me. My last feeling was being very sad.

I wish I could say I saw God, or that I experienced a transition to a wonderful golden realm, but I didn't. It was as if in the blink of an eye, I was suddenly jolted awake and found myself lying flat on my back and looking up into the gentle eyes of a lovely older man who was looking into my eyes with a tiny flashlight.

"Welcome back," he said.

Indeed, my heart had gone into defibrillation and they wheeled me into the emergency room. While they brought in the crash cart, my heart stopped. Scooter called the only person she knew who was a heart doctor, and that was her mother's doctor—Dr. Gorsuch. His office was just down the street and he came over immediately. So, it was his kind face I saw when I first regained consciousness.

I spent the next six days fading in and out of physical reality. The heart attack had disturbed the electronics of my heart muscle and they couldn't seem to stabilize me. Every now and then it would either go back into defibrillation, or just go completely erratic and stop beating. Each time, I'd know it was happening, because of the funny feelings I'd get first in the tips of my fingers and toes. Wonderfully mystical and eerie sort of musical sound would come to my ears, too. It was almost unearthly. Whenever it happened, I'd press the emergency button and tell the nurse over the intercom that my heart was stopping and she'd hit the "code blue" button calling for the crash cart. It was very unnerving to the nurses working in the intensive care unit. I'm not sure they were used to someone telling them he was going to step out of the physical before actually doing so. Eventually, they stabilized me enough to take a chance on moving me to the University Hospital in Charlottesville, where I had open-heart surgery.[12]

I've continued to explore through reevaluation what I learned from my experiences as a result of my heart problems. Later heart attacks resulted in sometimes days spent in intensive care units. Each time, my heart was weakened, and each time I fought my way back to a healthier condition. I had a severe attack in 1988, another in 1990, then 1991, and again in 1993. It seemed that each one was a little less critical. As I went through extensive testing following each episode we discovered that I was slowly but surely collateralizing the rest of my heart muscle—enlarging the smaller vessels to help feed oxygenated blood to the areas where it was most needed. The way I did this was by coming to an understanding about the very clear differences between living and dying.

One thing they tell you when you've had a major heart attack is that your life activities will have to be significantly reduced. They emphasize it even more when you've had open-heart surgery. "You'll have to cut back on your activities and take it easy. Alter the way you live your life. You can't be as active as you once were," is the usual way it's presented to a patient. That may be true initially, but what they actually do when they say that to someone is they scare the hell out of them. The unsaid part that's being stressed is always "If you don't, you are going to die."

Well guess what? We are all going to die. From the very moment of our birth, we are going to die, and that is an unalterable fact. But no one really knows when. And no one knows what will keep us alive for longer or shorter periods of time.

Yes, people can say if you stop smoking, you will reduce your risk of lung cancer—and they are absolutely right. But what has that got to do with sudden death? Nothing. It's statistics playing around with your fear factor. It's hindsight judgment of the worse kind. What they should be saying is "We all have a finite time of existence in this reality within this thing we call life. We don't have a clue how long anyone is going to live. But, while you are here, live it, and live it well."

When I came home from the hospital, I felt like a Mack truck had run over me, caught me by the collar, and had dragged me down the highway a couple hundred meters. Back in 1985, they hadn't

---

[12]There are a great deal of details about this experience in my first book *Mind Trek* if you are inclined to pursue it.

quite gotten the science of cracking someone's chest down to what it is today. I figured very quickly that since I was still here, I was going to do something productive. There wasn't much I could do immediately after leaving the hospital. I was so weak I needed help sometimes getting up out of a chair. But I could still think. So, I decided to write another book. I called it *Pulling the Plug*.

What moved me to write it was an experience I had my first week after retirement. I was sitting in a hamburger place in Nellysford, Virginia, and overheard a couple of men talking at a table sitting behind me. One of them said something negative about Vietnam and the other commented that there were a lot of bad things people had done there, bringing up Mai Lai as an example. Neither of them had served in Southeast Asia, of course.

I introduced myself as a retired Army officer and suggested that more times than not it would be impossible to go back and properly judge something that might have happened within the circumstances of war. Using hindsight was especially the wrong way to go about it. To really understand it, you needed to talk with someone who was actually there and participated, and even then, you only got one perspective of a very complex issue. They both said they thought that was a crock. They both knew exactly what they would and would not do given certain circumstances.

I didn't argue with them, just smiled and went back to my sandwich. But it made me think. Most people don't really understand how everyone becomes a victim of circumstance in a war zone, and how we can be driven to do some things we might later regret. Now I was remembering that incident and decided to do something about it. I couldn't travel for some time to SRI. So I decided to write the book.

It's a good book, in that the reader really can identify with the primary character, who's idealistic and very righteous in his personal morality and integrity. As the book progresses, the reader experiences what the character experiences and doesn't notice how the reader's views are beginning to change. By the middle of the book, the reader is totally identified with the character and rooting him on. In the last third, the character finds himself in circumstances that are no longer black and white, but are becoming more and more gray. Some of his actions become more instinctive, very much reactions based in surviving the experience. All of a sudden, the reader realizes the righteous character they've been identifying with all along is doing things that are morally questionable, and not only does the reader feel these things are the right things to do, but the reader is hoping for even more. Suddenly, the reader comes face to face with what every young man or woman who's ever been to war comes to grips with—the fact that to survive, a human being will do almost anything. There's no real right or wrong to the actions one takes in survival, and judging a person's actions cannot be done in hindsight. To judge someone under such conditions requires you to be standing there and experiencing what that person is experiencing—the fear, the terror, the hopelessness of the situation.

Since 1985, it has been rejected more than 25 times. Everyone who has ever read it has loved it and I've never gotten a negative comment from an editor anywhere who has read it. I've even gotten a two-page hand-written note from an editor who apologized for never having served in Southeast Asia. But as much as everyone liked it, no one would publish it.

They said there was no market for Vietnam books—it's the war we lost. Or, no one would like it because it forces readers to face an ugly truth about themselves. It may also have been a bit too long. It was originally 790 pages (double-spaced). I've since gone back over it two or three times and have cut it back to about 565 pages in manuscript form. I also changed the name to *A Necessary Evil,* because no one understood what I meant by the original title. "Pulling the plug" is an expression I used to use when someone would cross the line of reason. If you push someone far enough and hard enough, he or she will eventually pull the plug and go for broke. I think anyone who's ever experienced combat will understand the term. Maybe there is a lesson somewhere here for the Israelis and Palestinians—put the plug back in.

It took only until the end of 1985 to finish it, an unbelievable accomplishment because the powerful heart medications I was taking wouldn't let me stay awake for more than a few hours at a time.

At SRI, some interesting things were happening. One day, Hal Puthoff was there and the next day he was gone. When I spoke with Ed, on one morning he said they were trying to find additional funding to keep the lab open, and the next day, he told me that Hal had moved on, leaving him in charge. I wished that there was something I could do to help the situation, but what they needed was breathing room and a new budget.

My old office had been grinding down to nearly a complete stop.

They now had Tom and Mel as viewers, but they were very busy looking for a new home. The new INSCOM commander was shutting them down. Regardless of the tasking sitting in the in box, he wanted no part of Stubblebine's legacy.

So, moving into 1986, I was trying to do more healing than viewing, when Ed contacted me and said he had obtained new funding. Would I continue to work with them? Of course, I agreed. Ed knew I was recovering, but began tasking me from time to time on a target-by-target basis—which was about all I could have handled anyway. A lot of the targeting came from agencies that had been tasking the unit in Meade. Most of them were priority targets; tasking the agencies couldn't live without.

We changed the operation a little bit, so that I could do the remote viewings from Virginia. Ed or Nevin would call me and tell me when I had a target in an envelope sitting on top of a specific table in the lab. I would work the target and forward the results back to them by fax or first class mail.

Most of the others who worked at the lab originally were still there, with the exception of Ingo, who had moved his training operations to an SRI office in New York City. He worked there until he was informed by the Army that his training was being terminated. When it happened, it was a great surprise to me and I remember thinking now no one would ever really know just how good it could have been, other than perhaps through Tom's remote viewing, which would be a reflection of his teaching. It was certainly unfair to Ingo, who had worked so hard to develop what the Army had asked him for.

In mid-1986, with the new contract at SRI and Scooter working full time as the director of The Monroe Institute, we decided we'd better start thinking about our own home. I wasn't sure just how long I was going to last (physically), and I had always dreamed of my own home, as had Scooter, so we started buying books and cutting our favorite rooms out of them—a bedroom here, a fireplace there, and laying them out on graph paper to adjust what we liked or didn't like. Eventually, we agreed on how our house should look on the inside and outside.

I spent three months drawing the engineering plans and writing out the specifications, then went into Richmond and applied for a contractor's license for the Commonwealth of Virginia. I was tested and passed. I took the plans, specifications, building permit, and license to our local banker and asked him for a construction loan, which was transferred to our account within a few hours. I didn't know it at the time, but from the contractor's license, he took for granted that I was by trade a general contractor, when the largest thing I had ever built until that point was a coffee table.

The house now looks simple, but was in fact very complicated. It is a three-way split-level with a full basement on one end. The center supporting foundation is quite an intricate work of art. There are no cross ties in the vaulted ceilings, because the design itself supports the outer ceiling-bearing walls. The house is 5,030 square feet, of which 3,630 are finished space—and we built the entire house together. I was in charge of actual construction and Scooter was in charge of selecting the appropriate paints, colors, stains, woods, carpets, floors, etc. By construction, I mean I actually did all of the construction with another man, Adrian Stilson, a friend who is probably one of the finest brick masons in Virginia. I hired a helper, who lives close by—Daniel Crawford—who never balked at anything I asked him to do. Both are truly good men. The three of us drove every nail and laid every block, and I did all the wiring, electrical, plumbing, and detail work myself. I believe my finest accomplishment is the hand-cut Vermont black-slate floor in the foyer, which is actually a suspended ceiling in the basement and weighs in at around four tons.

When Scooter and I started building, the best that I could do was drag a cinderblock around on the ground using both hands. I was unable to lift a two-by-four by myself because I was still healing from my heart surgery and previous heart attack. When we finished a week shy of one year later, I was throwing ¾-inch sheets of pressure-treated tongue-and-groove plywood from the first floor up onto the second floor.

I'd take a couple weeks every now and then and fly out to the West Coast to work in the lab, participating in experiments and doing whatever other tasking I couldn't do from home. It was hard being away from the construction site while I was doing the work at the lab, but it was also a good break for my body. I found that if you really want to do a better job at something paranormal, you have to find a way of balancing it out with something physical. It creates what I like to call a "rubber band effect."

One of the ideas we decided to pursue was doing a remote viewing while in the lucid dream state. Dr. Stephen LaBerge was running the sleep lab at Stanford University and we were able to talk him into participating with us in an experiment to see whether or not remote viewing could be accomplished while in the lucid dream state. Stephen is a fun sort of fellow with an intense interest in what goes on when we are in a state commonly referred to as sleep.

I flew out to the West Coast and reported to the sleep lab at Stanford. I had been playing with lucid dream states (LDS) for some time, as a result of having worked with Robert Monroe at his lab in 1983 and '84. I have always viewed LDS as a prelude to the OBE state of consciousness, or at least one of the last and easiest steps toward accomplishing a controlled OBE.

When I first arrived, Stephen asked if I had ever had an LDS experience, which I responded to in the affirmative. When I told him that I could control them and produce them pretty much at will, I think he humored me by pretending to accept my answer as the truth, but didn't really believe that I could.

Stephen's research is done as follows: The subject is what I call hard-wired to a 28-channel bilateral EEG, by having the leads superglued to the skin of their scalp. This takes some time, but does a good job of making contact and preventing the wires from coming loose while in the middle of tossing and turning on a bed.

The subject is shut inside a very well shielded and soundproofed cubical a little larger than the standard-size single bed. The walls of the cubical are about half a foot thick and very well insulated to eliminate sound—going in or coming out. Temperature, humidity, and light are well controlled within this chamber, and of course it guarantees that the subject can't get up and walk around during the experiment. There is a place where the subject can essentially plug their wire-head-umbilical into the wall.

In an adjacent room, well removed in terms of distance from the subject's sleeping chamber, scientists can sit and monitor the subject in the darkened room with an infrared camera, and can also see the bilateral output from the EEG on a computer screen. All of this data is time-hacked[13] and stored in a very large file for downloading later onto a more permanent disk for any future analysis.

Monitoring the subject, the scientists can see when the subject

---

[13]This means the data has markings on it that agree with time markings on cameras, clocks, and other recording devices, so all the data can be compared if necessary later to a specific time.

enters into each stage of sleep, the production of sleep spindles and eventually the REM nodes common to deep-sleep dreaming. So, it is impossible to fake the fact that you are sleeping and in a real dream state.

The LDS is when the subject is in a deep sleep dream state and recognizes the fact—that is, becomes consciously aware that he or she is dreaming and can then assume complete control of the state for whatever purpose the subject wants.

I didn't know that the subject can take it one iteration further and actually notify the observing scientists who are monitoring the EEG outputs on the computer screen, thereby letting them know that the subject is awake and aware inside his or her dream. The way this is done is quite simple.

For example, if I am in a dream and riding a bicycle down a dirt road in the country, and suddenly realize that I am actually dreaming, all I have to do is stop the bike, put down the kickstand, then, standing next to it in the dream state, look over both shoulders four times in rapid succession—left, right, left, right, etc.

In the EEG monitoring room, some very small spikes appear overlaid over the REM node, or within the REM activity being displayed. This is because, while in deep sleep dreaming, one of the few muscle sets that is not frozen by self-induced paralysis are the same muscles that cause the REM nodes in the first place—those operating the eyes.

The protocol we designed was that when they saw that I was actually in deep sleep dreaming and I was able to signal that I was awake and aware, I would describe a picture they had randomly selected and pinned to the wall of the lab in a sealed envelope.

If our experiment worked, we planned a further experiment where they would push a key on the keyboard for a computer that would activate a pseudorandom number generator running in the background, which would select a picture from a large group of pictures in a file and send it to a computer screen located in another room that no one had access to. (This room would be totally sealed, including duct tape along the edges of the doorframe.) Only the number of the picture was stored for later use in setting up an independent judging schema. But, we decided not to add this complication until it could be determined that we could produce sufficient LDS and subjects to study.

My job was to move out of body in my LDS state, enter the room by passing through the door, and view the picture on the computer screen.

Once I had thoroughly familiarized myself with the picture on the screen, I was to stand perfectly upright in front of the screen and once again send them a signal that I had collected the information, at which time they would then come into the sleeping room where the chamber was contained and wake me up to report.

When we started, I'm not sure anyone believed for a second that it would work. First I would have to fall asleep. Then I would have to dream. Once dreaming, I would have to remember that I had another job to do and become awake and aware. Then I would have to signal them. A target would have to be randomly chosen and projected in a sealed room. I would then have to access the target, study it, remember what it looked like, and signal them to awaken me. I would then report a description of the target onto a tape and draw it to the best of my recollection. No problem.

In the first experiment, I discovered a major problem with the protocol. I *actually was* riding a bike on a dirt road somewhere in the countryside when I realized I needed to be awake and aware and had another job to do. I signaled them, then realized I had no idea whatsoever where the lab was, never mind what door I was supposed to be entering. I just stood there in my dream wondering what to do next. After thinking about it for a while, I realized that since I controlled everything that was happening anyway, I'd simply close my "dream state eyes," click my heels together like Dorothy in the *Wizard of Oz*, and when I opened my eyes, I'd be standing in whatever the target actually was. If it was a picture of Roman ruins in the Syrian Desert, then that's where I would find myself standing. Hopefully, the target picture wouldn't be the core of an active volcano, or the inside of a working iron furnace. I wasn't sure what would happen under those circumstances.

I closed my eyes and clicked my heels and when I opened them, I found myself standing in a lovely Bavarian valley filled with wildflowers and surrounded with beautiful mountains. The incredible reality of the target took my breath away. I've decided that this target needs to be displayed in the book because it is nearly impossible otherwise to explain just how incredibly accurate the dream was in comparison to the actual targeted image on the computer screen.

I spent what seemed in dreamtime to be about an hour walking around inside the dream location, after which I stood by the small barn and signaled them that I was ready to come out of it.

When Stephen woke me up, it was almost a surrealistic feeling, coming into reality, which felt just like the state I just left. I spent a few minutes regrounding myself, then described my adventure on a tape and drew a sketch of the target picture, exactly as I perceived it from the viewpoint of my arrival. It was a nearly perfect match.

We did a number of these and I found the greater the depth of the feeling of reality I had in my LDS, the better I did on the target. But, there was an interesting sidebar, which was beginning to spook

The Stargate Chronicles

me after a few days in the sleep lab. I was beginning to have numerous back-to-back "false awakenings," thinking I had awakened when I hadn't. It's stepping from one LDS into another LDS, believing that you have actually come out of your sleep.

After signaling them that I was ready to be awakened at the end of an LDS adventure, Stephen came into the booth and shook my shoulder, waking me up. I spent a few moments becoming grounded in being awake, then turned on the tape recorder, recording my impressions of the target. I spent a bit of time drawing my impressions on the pad of paper, after which I announced that I needed to go to the bathroom.

Unplugging my wire umbilical from the booth wall, I walked out into the empty corridor and padded down to the men's room in my bare feet. Since we were running the experiments at night, there were no students in the basement lab area, so the light had been turned off in the men's room. I hit the switch and nothing happened.

Backing out of the men's room, I looked around for another switch on the exterior and, not finding one, just stood there for a moment. A janitor came around the corner and I stopped him.

"The lights don't work in the bathroom," I said.

He grunted and opened the door and hit the switch and the lights came on. I thanked him, and he grunted again, then continued on his way.

After finishing in the bathroom, on the way out I hit the switch to turn off the lights. They didn't go out. I hit the switch again and still they didn't go out. So, I carefully inspected the switch as I attempted to throw it a third time.

My finger was passing through it, as though it weren't there!

I just stood there for a few minutes confused. It was unbelievable. My finger was actually passing through the wall switch itself. I kept thinking, "Man! Wait till Stephen and Ed get a load of this."

Then I realized I must still be asleep. It shook me to the core. I was living a near perfect reality in every sense of the word that I had expected to live. If it was true, then there was one sure way of testing it. I stood totally still in the doorway to the bathroom and quickly looked over my left and right shoulders four times.

Stephen shook me awake in the sleeping chamber. It was true. I had done my entire debriefing in an LDS. I repeated the process, and detached my umbilical and padded down to the room where they were doing the monitoring. I wanted to tell them about my experience. When I entered the room, Stephen was working at the computer alone.

"Where's Ed?" I asked.

Stephen looked at me with puzzlement. "Ed who?"

I felt the blood run to my knees. Could I still be in an LDS?

Quickly, I looked rapidly over my left and right shoulders again, and almost immediately Stephen shook me awake again.

I didn't move. For the longest time I just lay on the bed, staring back at Stephen. Finally I said, "Am I awake?"

"I don't know. Are you?" he humorously asked back.

"How do I know when I'm awake?" I asked back without humor.

"I don't think it's possible to ever know when you are really awake," Stephen quickly returned. "Maybe life itself is one long lucid dream state."

I continued to lay there not moving. After what seemed like an eternity I sat up and looked around, feeling the walls of the booth and touching the cold floor with my bare feet. It felt real enough.

Looking up, I saw Stephen pulling up a chair at the small desk in the sleep room. He was preparing a set of connector cables, while he hummed a happy tune to himself. I watched fascinated as he leaned over and began gluing them to the head of a bear sitting in the chair next to the desk. "There, there, little fellow. This won't hurt at all."

I lay back down on the bed and closed my eyes. Was this ever going to end? I lay there a long time trying to think of a way out of the experience, but kept coming back to not being able to tell when I was really awake. Eventually, on the fifth try, I was able to describe the target, draw it, disconnect from the booth wall and walk outside, where a couple of early-morning students looked at me strangely. Nothing changed from that point on, so I've either lived a very long LDS, or I reverted back to reality, if there is one, after the seven-hour nap I took that day.

To be perfectly honest, the experience scared the hell out of me. I now know what it must be like to be detached completely from reality and not know what is real or not real. It must be something similar to what a schizophrenic episode must be like. I can only imagine what such an episode must be like when it involves paranoia or something even more sinister as an accompaniment.

We finished the experiment and got some really fine results, but it was not something I'd recommend trying to develop for remote viewing capability. The other side effect is that you never really get any rest while this is going on. You are continually being awakened in the middle of your deepest sleep cycle, which begins to wear you down about the end of the second day. You think you're getting sleep and rest, but you really aren't. I believe this only adds to the false awakening effect, as well as follow-on paranoia. If someone weren't stable when experiencing these things, I can only imagine what kind of changes it would make to his or her psyche.

It also gave some hints as to the verifiability of some of the things people talk about experiencing while in a paranormal or LD state of consciousness. It is very real to them, but it is not very real to all the rest of us sharing another LDS called life. I saw this experience as one more very good reason to ensure the stability and sanity of someone who was going to be exposed to any mind type of experimentation or exploration.

Chapter Fourteen

Research

Between then and the end of 1994, I participated in an additional few dozen experiment series, some requiring as many as 75 remote viewings, as well as another few dozen operational types of targets.

One operational target involved U.S. Marine Lt. Col. William Higgins, who was kidnapped in Lebanon on February 17, 1988. It was one of the most debilitating operations I worked on, because I, and a number of other remote viewers, were about as reasonably certain about our information regarding his location(s) and how he was being treated as we had ever been about anything. Ken Bell and I went so far as to volunteer to lead someone to his location in a rescue attempt. But, because we were one of the few sources of information, it was considered way beyond the realm of possibility to plan or execute a raid based on PSI sources. Many months later, when one of the suspects in the colonel's kidnapping and murder was apprehended, he confirmed that our locations had been correct in the last two cases of his movement, and we had also been correct regarding his treatment as well as the methods used that resulted in his subsequent death.

I was reminded of a similar case, which happened just after I retired. Between the time I retired from the Fort Meade unit and my hiring by SRI, I was contacted directly by an old friend who asked me to see if I could provide him with any information relative to a U.S.

intelligence agent named William Buckley. I provided him with a detailed description of almost ten days of torture and described his eventual murder in Beirut. This was also subsequently verified in newspaper articles, which were passed to me many months later. While my description of his initial holding area was incorrect, the description and location I had provided for where he died was almost exact. I could only think of General Dozier and how lucky he had been. Had it not been for the professionalism of the Italian police and counterterrorist agents on the ground in Italy, he might have shared a similar fate.

Between 1988 and the middle of 1994, I worked an additional five major terrorist incidents, involving the loss of many Americans, as well as the attempt on the World Trade Center buildings that occurred in February 1993. The results of these remote viewings continue to be classified and/or protected information.

A lot of changes took place between 1986 and 1995 within the project, the greatest being that it was transferred to the Defense Intelligence Agency. Toward the end of 1986, Tom McNear had decided to call it quits. I asked him why he left the project and he told me he had been there for three years and eight months and was getting bored with what was going on. He said he was receiving mediocre OERs and there was very little he could do about it. He felt the low quality of the OERs and the job descriptions they contained were not going to get him promoted. This was a surprise to me, because my OERs had been outstanding. It was apparent from his comments that some major changes had taken place within the unit. Something was wrong.

He said that he and the boss were not the best of friends, and since Rob had developed cancer and left the unit and Gemma had died from cancer it wasn't the same. He said he had spent so much time away from home during the long and exhausting training with Ingo in California and up in New York, that it was beginning to affect his marriage. This was not a surprise to me.

He said his wife felt he was also becoming more and more withdrawn and introverted, as a result of his duties with the project.

When he asked to be released from the project, at first they were reluctant to let him go. But he persisted and eventually they agreed. He said he left the unit with no respectable job descriptions; no significant contributions to his OERs, which had mediocre ratings; and he got no end-of-tour award of any sort.

When I asked him if he had finished his training, he said I would have to ask Ingo that. His memory was that the last three to four stages had not yet been completed.

Since Ingo's training program was ended prior to its completion, the remaining extension to his system had to have been created, developed, and finished within the unit. Knowing how close to the vest Ingo always held his information and methods, especially his training methods, I wasn't convinced at the time that anyone could have done that. As time passed, I became even less convinced. At the least, they would have been unable to read Ingo's mind with regard to *why* he might have done things a specific way.

During this same period, a number of new people had been added to Ingo's training schedule, none of whom could possibly have completed it in its entirety, given the time it had taken Tom up until that point. They might have finished the project's version of Ingo's training, but certainly not Ingo's.

After the project transferred to DIA, we attempted on two occasions to include the remote viewers at Fort Meade in experiments that we were running at the lab. We thought it would be of value to include them, in that it would provide them an opportunity to practice on targets with ground-truth feedback, and would give us additional remote viewer input to the experiments, which were designed to try and identify an area within the brain in which the remote viewing was taking place. These were preliminary experiments to those that we would later run at great expense in the National Laboratory at Los Alamos. As we had always attempted to do in the past, we liked to try and identify consistent viewing talent prior to using it in our more expensive and complicated lab trials.

Unfortunately, neither the management nor the remote viewers back at my old project were willing to participate. Both of these test phases were around early 1987.

During these experiments, we used a slightly modified protocol, which involved the use of black-and-white (versus color) photographs for targets, and in another version, we used moving films or videos as feedback for targets, versus a static photograph.

Ken Bell, Gary, and I, plus three other viewers at SRI, participated in these two experimental efforts long distance. The target photographs (or, in the case of the second trial, sometimes videos) were selected and displayed on a "target table" in Pennsylvania. Ken did his remote viewing from his home in Florida, I did mine from my home in Virginia, Gary did his from California, and the other viewers did theirs from Maryland, New York, and one other state I can no longer recall. All the results were forwarded to California, where they were mixed with other targets, then independently judged.

We had some very interesting results that helped guide us in our designs for the nonremote viewing protocols we would be using at the national lab in Los Alamos.

The viewers at Fort Meade participated half-heartedly in the first few targets, then ceased to cooperate. I was never sure if it was the viewers who were the problem or the management, but it reduced the numbers of people we felt we might have available for future studies.

At the same time, whenever we felt we could add something of importance to the method of targeting, method of collection, or method of analysis, we generated a formal report and outline of those findings and forwarded them with recommendations to the project at Fort Meade. Many years later we were distressed to find most of those packages stored in a security safe, having never been opened.

So, whatever was going on at Fort Meade was either very destructive to the viewers, or management, or both. We continued to pass along our concerns to those in charge at the DIA administrative level.

Subsequent to that period, we did interact with one of the viewers at Fort Meade who voluntarily subjected herself to the rigors of remote viewing under scientific controls at our lab. She more than proved her remote viewing capabilities in a number of experimental series and is currently still working with the lab today. Her name is Angela Ford and she has proven herself an exceptionally competent remote viewer in both research and applications areas. She dares to follow her convictions.

Following the cancellation of his training program, Ingo announced that he would be retiring from further work in the lab at SRI. (In spite of this, he also participated in data collection at Los Alamos.) He no longer visited the lab in California. I missed seeing him. He had spent a little more than a year doing an experiment that dealt with binary questions—those that can be answered with two possible responses—yes/no, up/down, zero/one, etc. In a run of double-blind challenges that ran into three digits, he maintained an accuracy that exceeded 90 percent, something I've never seen repeated. These kinds of targets are forced choice and some of the most difficult to answer accurately for any long period of time. His method in attacking the problem appeared to be extreme, at least to someone observing it from the outside, but his consistency in accuracy was astounding. I was very sorry to see him leave, because his originality and intelligence would be missed.

In the latter portion of 1987, we started our study at Los Alamos Laboratories. We used the facilities there because they had a specially shielded room that was able to cut out a specific frequency range of interference and equipment that operated inside the room that used what was state of the art back then—an MEG (magnetoencephalograph)[14] which was brand new technology back then. The equipment we used in Los Alamos had a seven-channel *SQUID* (Superconducting Quantum Interference Device) for monitoring the inner workings of the brain.[15]

One of the conditions for using the equipment was that there could be no metal in the room, or as little as possible. The equipment is so sensitive to electromagnetic fields that it would pick up the very tiny wishbone in the center of a woman's bra and ruin an experiment.

Since everyone is born with a different size and shape skull, but approximately the same size brain, the brain is enfolded just slightly differently inside each head. So, you couldn't just point the SQUIDs in the same direction to read the specific areas of interest on different individuals. This required multiple attempts to first locate the area to be monitored. Once it was tuned to an individual, we would run specific feedback studies with the idea of finding out what we could about what was going on inside the person's working mind.

In our initial attempts, we captured many hours of data, which then had to be processed. There was so much data, processing it took months using what was back then some very sophisticated computer systems. The end result was finding out that the length of the session (data collection duration) was too short to give us what we were looking for, so we had to do it all over again. This is one of the interesting things about doing something completely new in science—you don't have a yardstick to measure what you are doing the first time—so it sometimes takes multiple efforts to find the baseball field before you can get into the game.

---

[14] You can go to http://boojum.hut.fi/triennial/squid.html and see an example of what one is capable of measuring.

[15] You can go to http://www.remyc.com/squid.html and see what these do. There is now one located in San Diego that has 148 channels.

The way this testing was affecting me was quite different. I was having continuing heart problems at the time, because of the higher altitude at Los Alamos, which is up on a high plateau. So, when I was there and in the "box" (special room), I was dealing with continual breathing and pain difficulties. Being pinned face down, with my face pushed into a special holder that deforms to fit my contours, then having a huge machine pushed up against the back of my head, while having chest pain and breathing difficulties, then doing whatever I needed to do RV-wise for a few hours at a stretch was extremely difficult for me. After completing a full morning of these measurements, I would jump into my rental car and drive down to my hotel in Santa Fe, where I was at an altitude that was bearable. It would usually take four or five hours for me to begin to feel comfortable again. Everyone else was staying up at Los Alamos, so it was an extra hour drive for me in the mornings and evenings.

We were able to run a number of people through the system and it gave us a lot of data—or at least enough to formulate where we would go next. The following year, we returned to Los Alamos and collected data in a different experimental set that allowed us to begin to see the probable area within the brain where PSI might or might not be taking place. Unfortunately, the cost involved was extremely high. Even at a national laboratory, time scheduling was difficult and rental time for the equipment, support personnel, and post-hoc analysis equipment was very expensive—thousands of dollars per hour in some cases. The amount of data we collected required hundreds of hours in collecting, assimilating, and analyzing what we were looking for. These studies carried us up through the end of 1989, then were curtailed for lack of funding and the ability to find equipment that could carry us to the next step. There are now machines that go as high as 148 SQUIDs, and use computer support systems that are ten orders of magnitude higher than the equipment we were attempting to use in the late '80s. Hopefully, one day we will find enough funding to continue our search in this direction.

If we can identify the very small and specific area that always activates when actual PSI is happening, we will have developed a way of knowing when someone is being "psychic" and when he or she is not. This would be something that could prove to be extremely beneficial in our quest for understanding the phenomena, or using it to its highest capability.

Another condition that changed in the mid to late '80s was the way our work was being monitored. As head of the lab, Ed instituted a number of oversight committees to guarantee that we stayed within reasonable bounds. One difficulty in the study of PSI is that it is not only *possible* to delude oneself into thinking something that isn't true, in some cases, it is highly likely. It can happen to anyone. In an attempt to reduce this possibility, he created the committees.

There were three committees, but the most important of these was the Scientific Oversight Committee, which comprised nearly a dozen of the best minds in numerous fields of study. There were in fact two Nobel laureates on the committee. Ed ensured that none of the members of these committees had any positive or negative biases toward PSI. The members of the committees had walk-in privileges at any time. This meant they could drop by and observe anything we were doing, ask any questions, or review any of the materials any time they wanted to. All protocols were forwarded to the committees for review and comment. They were encouraged to tear us up for anything they thought inappropriate about what we were doing. Until the project was closed at the end of 1995, no committee member complained of a single infraction, inferred or otherwise, in the operations of the lab. This should not be construed as implying that they didn't make any comments. On numerous occasions they had positive comments to make regarding the design of our protocols, or recommendations to tighten up areas where we could have run into trouble. Meeting remote viewing expectations within the boundaries of this kind of laboratory climate is extremely difficult—but doing so solidified the basis in reality for the kind of remote viewing I was doing. It not only strengthened my belief in PSI, it proved beyond a shadow of a doubt in many minds the facts of its existence.

When I hear people commenting about the reality of PSI, or whether or not it's just something happening in the imagination of the people involved, I wish they'd at least have the decency to read the history or actually review the data. There is so much proof extant for the existence of PSI, it's foolish to continue spending money, time, and effort "proving it" to the satisfaction of idiots. It's time to move on. Let's work toward figuring out why it's there at all, and how it works. It could be the single greatest understanding of humankind possible. It is my thought that it has everything to do with humankind's creative ability, our capacity for spontaneously healing ourselves and possibly others, as well as providing a new insight into the nature of our creator—what and who God is—the very origin of our species. Let's move on, for God's sake.

In 1990 the lab severed its long association with SRI-International and moved. Physically we only moved about four blocks down the street in Menlo Park to a new office, but nonphysically, we shifted our operations to Science Applications International Corporation (SAIC).

(Those who believe there was no real interest in remote viewing by the major intelligence agencies in Washington, D.C., need only look at the boards of directors, past and present, for SAIC, to understand that couldn't be further from the truth. Many of the past directors of those intelligence agencies work or have worked on SAIC's governing board. It is a multibillion-dollar company that provides support to a multifaceted array of interests in areas that range from geographic to defense.)

Prior to moving to SAIC, we were approached by an agency with an interesting question and task. Could we actually track an agent in the field using remote viewing, and was it possible to target what that agent might be doing? What makes these questions interesting is that the results of the simulations we did on behalf of this agency are some of the few declassified materials ever released that show the effectiveness of RV to do precisely what they were asking.

Furthermore, the targeting was controlled completely by the agency involved and no one in our lab was privy to the real information until the tasking had been completed. To my knowledge, this is the only real test of applications-level remote viewing available to the public today.

The way the operation worked was as follows:

The agency we were dealing with wanted to maintain complete control over the effort. While they didn't specifically say why they wanted to control all aspects of the simulation, one can assume either it was their intention to prove to themselves above and beyond extant proof that remote viewing could be a valuable collection asset capable of contributing to their efforts, or that this was their way of guaranteeing it was being accomplished without some form of cheating. In either event, our only concern was that they understood and ran the remote viewing targeting within the boundaries of protocol—in other words, that they kept the target protected and blind to all who were participating in the collection side of the house.

(We had long since acquiesced to operating with an assumption that anyone connected with remote viewing could be cheating, and to prevent such a possibility, subsequently designed all of our protocols to address these concerns. What is interesting is, even after doing so, people still demand to see for themselves and attempt to control the targets themselves, which only expands the numbers of people involved and hence the possibility for subterfuge or inappropriate manipulation of the results. Simply stated, it complicates an already complicated protocol.)

In order to simulate a real-world situation, they assured us that we would be targeted against a real agent (one of their own) and the targeting would take place on a date/time that would be fully dependent on the agent's actions, rather than a prearranged date/time, as used for normal experiments.

To facilitate this, I moved in with my friend Dr. Nevin Lantz, my normal remote viewing monitor, at his home in Berkeley, California. We spent time reading and otherwise doing things that kept us relaxed.

We received our first alert for targeting around midnight one evening in the middle of the week. We had all just gone to bed. He woke me up and we proceeded to the kitchen, where we set up on the kitchen table and I spent about thirty minutes speaking into a recording device and attempting to sketch the target location, at the same time taping Nevin's snoring, since he fell asleep at the table.

The targeting materials that I was given consisted of an unlined three-by-five-inch index card. Written on the card was a nine-digit Social Security number. Whoever called had given Nevin the number over the phone and he had written it onto the card. The only information I was given was "This is the number for an agent who is located somewhere in America. Describe the agent, describe where the agent is standing, and tell us what the agent is doing."

My results were very difficult to understand, as they had a very *Star Wars* quality. The information I was getting was so complicated as to be almost undeterminable. All the material seemed to have something to do with small particles of energy—packets of material, which were being moved around. Eventually, I gave up trying to draw the device I was sensing and simply stated that it was a machine for accelerating electrons. We were given no feedback until we completed the entire simulation of three separate sites.

The second targeting took place a few days later, sometime around midmorning. Again, I was handed the index card and asked to describe where the agent was standing. I stated that he was standing in the middle of a field of rolling hills. I described the field as containing large wind generators and some form of underground power grid.

The third time, I put the agent in the corner of a very complex area, which appeared to be industrial in nature. I said there were multiple buildings, some of which included underground areas and interconnecting underground corridors. I pointed out that the significant building of interest was a very large T-shaped building, seven stories in height, with a smaller building located on the roof. I stated that I felt the building was probably called or labeled "A building"— or at least that is what I would call it. I reported that the agent was standing on the upper floor, in the center of the front of the building in a main office area.

We were not provided feedback until after the entire mission was completed, but later found out that the first target location in which the agent was standing was inside the Stanford Linear Accelerator— a place where they accelerate electrons. The second target location was a large field of wind generators on hills in southern California and drawn with what the customer called near perfect accuracy. The last location was the main office building that is actually called "A Building" at the headquarters for Lawrence Livermore Laboratory. This drawing and description was accurate enough to provide a clear representation and identification of the location, making it possible to identify the Laboratory West Gate entry area and main building— all three of these being places I'd never seen before.

The results of all three remote viewing cases were forwarded to the agency that requested the information and an assessment of accuracy was independently performed by that agency.

This involved more than whether or not I said the right thing. In an operational mission scenario a lot could be said about a target that might not be pertinent to what is actually going on—and would therefore have no value. Or little could be said, which might change the very nature of the ongoing mission. To determine whether or not the information would have been of value as an intelligence collection tool requires a complex structure of analysis based on

> a. How much information could be said about the location that could have merit or value to the overall mission—what is actually important to know about the target location. (This list of questions is usually determined by the agency involved before any remote viewing. So that which is ultimately considered important to the mission is not what was specifically said by the

remote viewer, but is determined solely by what is necessary to fulfill the mission.)

b. How much of what I said actually provided answers to these previously determined questions.

c. How much of what I might have said was of no value or was not pertinent to the mission at hand, or might have even provided false leads or information that could be damaging to the overall mission.

All of this ensures a better measurement of the functional accuracy and reliability when trying to understand or measure relationships between what the agent was actually doing at the time, why he or she might have been doing it, and where or when he or she might have been doing it.

In this case, the agent's primary mission was to observe and collect data about the Linear Accelerator at Stanford, then proceed with a single stop (to rest) at the wind generation field, ending eventually at the headquarters building, Building "A" West Gate, of Lawrence Livermore Laboratory.

The agency's independent study was given with parenthetical numbers representing the value of each interest area of the target and how they valued it, or how important each of those elements was to their mission. A 1.0 was the highest value, or meant that it was critical information to have, while at the opposite end of the scale, a 0.25, was considered the least important to know. Therefore, of the gross elements they needed to know were (A) functions at the sites (1.0), (B) relationships between the separate elements at the site compared to the interests of the agent (0.75), and (C) the specific objectives of the agent in being at these sites (0.5). My results, by their calculation were:

SPECIFIC TARGET	ACCURACY	RELIABILITY
ACCELERATOR (1.0)		
Functions (1.0)	0.93	0.70
Relationships (0.75)	0.36	0.31
Objectives (0.5)	0.73	0.88
AVERAGE:	0.67	0.63

SPECIFIC TARGET	ACCURACY	RELIABILITY
WINDMILL FARM (0.5)	0.95	1.00
LLWG BUILDING "A" (0.25)	0.85	0.95
AVERAGE:	0.77	0.78

A further breakdown was made of the actual information provided relative to the accelerator and compared against the actual weight of need (1.0–0.25)—values predetermined about the possible site that could be important about the site to the agency involved. The accelerator was already labeled as being the most important end of the mission—the place where the agent started from. Instead of tracking him to a target, we had tracked backward from his supposed headquarters to the target. Based on what's called a fuzzy-set analysis, I received the following feedback:

Elements	Weights	Target	Response
FUNCTIONS (1.0)			
Directed energy	5	1	0.9
Electron accelerator	3	1	1
Beam ionizes air	1	1	0.6
Testing new form of laser	1	0	1
RELATIONSHIPS (0.75)			
Power source above beam line	1	1	0
Linear array of buildings	1	1	0.1
E&M radiation < 10 angstroms	1	0.1	1
Pipes into and out of sphere	1	0	1

Elements	Weights	Target	Response
OBJECTS (0.5)			
External electron beam	5	1	0
Tunnel	2	1	1
Loud noise	1	0.3	1
Hollow polished (internal) sphere	1	0	1

As can be observed in the statistics above, the ability to track an agent and report on where he or she is and what is going on nearby is possible to a remarkable degree of accuracy and detail.

The agency returned the following year and asked if we could do the same type of simulation, this time not only tracking the agent but telling them what was actually going on in his or her vicinity, in as much detail as possible.

This actually created difficulties for me, because I had not yet gotten specific feedback on my previous remote viewings that were relative to this agent, and I was still carrying around the images of what I had obtained in the previous three remote viewings. This created some degree of overlay, which I needed to clear from my system. I spent a considerable time doing that before providing the information they were requesting.

When I was able to put the information together, we had a description of an area in a desert location, isolated and hot. I described a machine that was being operated within a van (deliberately hidden), but that produced a wave front emission (I said it was operating at 6x4 centimeters—later determined to be inches), which meant it was operating in the microwave range. I said it was being targeted against other forms of electronic equipment. I described the wave front spread, distance to targets, and effective range of emission. I also talked about the general effects of this wave front and the overall evaluation of the equipment being assessed. The following represents an independent fuzzy-set analysis of my results based on reality at the target site—which turned out to be located in the middle of the hot and isolated desert testing facility at Sandia National Laboratory.

Elements	Weights	Target	Response
FUNCTIONS (1.0)			
High-power microwave production	5	1	0.8
Destructive testing of electronics	2	1	1
Ground focal area	1	0	1
Testing a concept—debugging	1	0.3	1
RELATIONSHIPS (0.75)			
Source enclosed in a trailer	5	1	0.7
Energy exit enclosure	3	1	1
Large, semicircular shape with block	1	0	1
Horn shape at end of 4 x 6 cm pipe	1	1	0.8
OBJECTS (0.5)			
Microwave generator (tubular 3 m)	5	1	0.7
Incoherent wave front	3	0.1	1
Buried sensors	1	0	1
Flat desert	0.5	1	1

This analysis resulted in an overall accuracy and reliability score of:

Target Type	Accuracy	Reliability
MICROWAVE GENERATOR		
Functions (1.0)	0.88	0.80
Relationships (0.75)	0.69	0.64
Objects (0.5)	0.82	0.63
AVERAGE:	0.80	0.69

Again, surprising accuracy and reliability, given that the agent could have been anywhere in the continental United States and engaged in a multitude of activities unknown.

Even more interesting—during the time that I was targeting the agent, I detected another target site, which I stated was not part of the site of interest, but was a site the agent visited as well. I described with some considerable detail a solar array field, where sunlight was being captured by large mirrors and reflected at targets on a tower location. I said they were using a computer system to control or manipulate the array. What is interesting about this information is that I was able to determine that while it too might be interesting to the agent and others, it was not part of the primary target and was therefore able to deduct this information from the overall information collected.

It turned out that in traveling to and from the actual target site located in the desert area, the agent was forced to drive past a Department of Energy solar array testing site where a field of computer manipulated mirrors were being used to target collectors on the tip of a tall tower. In fact, almost a year later, when I was allowed to actually go out and visit the site for feedback, we were stopped by a guard while they initiated and completed a solar test series at the Department of Energy test site.

The success of these two simulated missions resulted in producing a significant effect on the agency that had tasked us. It convinced them of the reliability and utility of remote viewing as a method for long-range intelligence collection against enemy agents in the field. This ultimately resulted in additional tasking and financial support to the lab.

Chapter Fifteen

Mind Trek and Searches

At the end of 1992, I began compiling materials for a book on my experiences with remote viewing. There was almost no information at all available to the general public, because most do not refer to or read the scientific journals where much of the information was being published. I felt that it was important that the public be made aware of how far remote viewing had been developed, as well as the fact that remote viewing could be used perhaps for solving crimes and attacking creative problems in industry. *Mind Trek* was published in 1993 by Hampton Roads Publishing Company.

After the exposure of the Star Gate program on *Nightline* in November of 1995, I was heavily criticized by a number of people who said that I should have written about the military use of remote viewing. Of course, these people would not have been facing severe disciplinary action and significant time in jail. I did make a point of sharing all that I was allowed to share—whatever was learned in the open or unclassified area of our lab efforts and studies. I also shared a great deal of information about remote viewing as well as some of my own theories about how it might or might not work. Some of these theories have proven to be more accurate than not, and some have been dead end issues.

With the publication of the book, I started getting a much larger influx of requests from companies and individuals in business regarding the use and applications of remote viewing. Since I promise total anonymity to my private customers, there is not much that I can share about the successes or failures there. I can say that it is statistically the same as the rest of my work over the past 23 years—right around a 70 percent rate of accuracy and reliability. This is not as high as some claims being made by others out there in the paranormal world, but then they haven't been tested under laboratory conditions, or within the severe constraints of blind and double-blind protocols either. Anyone who believes that my statistical averages are not significant should talk to a scientist who has tested me—of which there are many. I've been forced to demonstrate these percentages from year to year and they have remained relatively unchanged over the entire time.

I can talk generally about some of the work I've done within my company, and some of it has been very good. I've provided years of support to specific stock interests of individuals, and have given years of guidance to investment firms dealing in the exchange of world currencies. I've done projections on real estate investments for specific areas in cities, countries, and regions, and have provided advice on the types of real estate being considered. I've produced dozens of accurate locations for new and productive water wells in America, Belgium, France, Spain, Germany, and several African countries—by dowsing maps of these remote locations. And my company has been involved in the search for specific minerals, metals, and different types of stone used in building, finishing, or even for cosmetic purposes.

Most of the work I've been asked to assist in involves missing persons, which unfortunately is one of the most difficult areas to use remote viewing for. There are many reasons for this, but the major ones are:

> a. You can produce a near-perfect description of a location where a person is being held, is living, or within which a body has been hidden. But, if there are no local landmarks that are readily identifiable to a specific area or township, where in the world the location actually is, is quite difficult to pinpoint. (Unless of course you are using dowsing, and then there is a presumption that the map you might be using actually contains the location.)
>
> b. Sometimes the missing person is dead. If the body has been dismembered and spread throughout an area, it makes identifying the location more difficult.

c. However, the primary reason why locating an individual is most difficult is the reluctance of the authorities to use the materials provided. They either do not understand how to appropriately use them, or they write them off as meaningless because they come from a "psychic" source.

Often this isn't the authorities' fault. In many cases they are completely swamped with material originating from various psychics that has not been coordinated, and many times replicates bad information, and in any case has no baseline through which to gauge it. Many of the people sending in the information are very well meaning, but do not have a psychic bone in their bodies. Without some way of properly analyzing the information and/or applying it, all it does is clog the system.

I usually do not assist or provide information to authorities unless I have been formally asked to do so ahead of time. Over the years I've established relationships with different prosecuting and district attorneys' offices, police departments, and detective agencies. Without some guarantee that something will be done with the materials, and that whoever is going to use the materials understands the limitations of the materials, it is a waste of everyone's time and energy from the get-go.

As an example, in the winter of 2001–2002, in my own county of Nelson, a small girl was reported missing. I returned home from giving a talk at The Monroe Institute around 10:30 P.M., and within minutes received a call from a county resident who knows what I am capable of. I drove to the house of the missing girl, which is located in the middle of some of the roughest terrain you could find in the Blue Ridge Mountain area of Virginia. Unfortunately, in an election a few months earlier the local sheriff had been replaced by a new sheriff who had no previous knowledge of either me or my capabilities. The new sheriff established a police line at the scene of the house (which is normal procedure), which I was not allowed to cross. I explained to some of his deputies who I was and offered to help, but was continually denied entry as a matter of rule.

After standing in the cold till some time after 2:30 A.M., I saw an old friend pull in. He is one of the game wardens from the area. I explained that I wanted to help and asked him to intercede, which he attempted to do. He came back out and informed me that "my kind

The Stargate Chronicles

of help" was not appreciated. I gave him a map I had been able to get from one of the search and rescue (SAR) people on site, on which I had marked a starting place that they should begin their search. I indicated on the map that they would find both tracks and signs as to the direction in which the girl had gone. He said he would see that they got the map and I went home.

I was unable to sleep the rest of the night because I was having very clear visions of the young girl wandering in the woods. I was very sure that I could help, but no one wanted me to. I remained in my office working until I received a phone call around 9:00 A.M.. At that time, I was told that the head of the SAR teams wanted to speak with me at the girl's home.

When I got there they took me to the search trailer, where I was introduced to the man in charge of the search teams who had arrived from Richmond. He showed me my map and asked how I knew they would find signs of the girl in the location I had marked?

I explained what I had done in support of government agencies for many years and told him there was no pertinent explanation for what I could do, I was just able to do it. He said they found exactly what I had predicted in exactly the place I had predicted it to be. He then asked me where I had been the 24 hours preceding the girl's disappearance. I knew that he was checking my alibi, which was a reasonable request given I knew so much about where the girl had been previous to her disappearance. Since I had been accompanied by others for nearly two days prior, I was eliminated as any kind of a suspect. But what if I had no alibi? What then?

In any event, he took me to their large search map and asked me, "If you had to look for her right now—where exactly would you look?"

I put my finger on the lower right portion of the map.

"Here. Right here is where you will find her."

Well, that created a major problem. The area I had selected lay outside the overall grid of the major search area. In fact, it was almost two-thirds of a mile to the south and west of where they were searching, using dogs, helicopters, and about 175 people in teams of four to seven.

"We can't search in there yet," he stated. "We'll screw up the scent for the tracking dogs. We'll have to run a dog team through there, then we can go in with a search team. We'll also have to move our search grid to include that area and it will take a lot of time to do that."

I explained that I didn't think they had a lot of time. It had been down into the low twenties the previous night and the little girl was wearing a light blouse and otherwise had no protection against the elements. She had her dog with her, but the dog had wandered in earlier that morning exhausted and needing both water and food. They had not been able to backtrack the dog, or entice it to lead them to the girl. It just moved up under the house and refused to cooperate.

I asked if I could go in there alone. I knew that I could go directly to that spot on the map that I had pinpointed and leave very little trail going or coming that would mess with a dog team. In fact, the area they would have to enter from with the dog was up-wind and miles from the point of entry I wanted to try. I was told no.

Instead, they teamed me up with my friend the game warden and a couple of others and had us stand to the side and wait. We waited nearly six hours while the dog was taken through the area, and while they moved and did a regrid of the search maps they were using. I found out later that the dog team had in fact followed the easier route along a stream bed because they figured the little girl could not have gotten into the thick of it, being so little. They guessed that she would stick pretty much to a trail or somewhere easier to walk.

Eventually, they inserted two teams into the area that I had marked on the map. The team I was with entered from the west and north, and the other team was helicopter-lifted in from the top of the mountain to work its way outward toward our position.

Both teams converged on the body almost simultaneously. The mountain team found her body first and our team arrived at the location within ten minutes. The little girl was dead when she was found, and her body was within fifty to 75 feet of the location I had marked on the map.

I have no idea when the little girl actually died. There was evidence that she had fallen into a creek and completely soaked what clothing she had. Hypothermia would have been her greatest enemy from that point forward. I asked for a copy of the map that I had provided to the search teams the night before, and the request was refused. I asked to speak with the sheriff, in the hope of coming to some agreement about future incidents, but my request was denied. He didn't want to speak with me. Maybe I wouldn't have made a difference, but that is not what's material to this issue. What's material is the fact that people of proven and established talent can provide information through the use of psychic or remote viewing methodologies. When you haven't got any other kind of lead, it's the only lead!

It doesn't matter if the psychic's accuracy is 30 percent or 90 percent. If you haven't got a clue as to where to start, you take what you can to reduce the search area. If you have a 30 percent chance of reducing a search area and saving a life, you take it.

I've been involved with two other search and rescue operations in my own county. In all three cases, my information was the last information that was utilized. In a second case, they used my information because they were forced to. After 45 days of searching for a missing park ranger on the Blue Ridge, they terminated the search. In cleaning out the files they found my original map, which I had provided in the first 72 hours. A father and son team volunteered to pursue the map location just to close out the file. They found the park ranger's body precisely where I had indicated they would on the map.

In the third case, all I could provide was a general direction and there didn't seem to be anyone to find within the county. It turned out the plane they were looking for crashed outside the county boundaries quite a distance from our search area.

In the final years of the Star Gate project, I participated in a simulation for tracking nuclear materials. For some reason, I have a gift for finding such materials, and differentiating between real or not real targets. In my mind's eye, I can actually see a greenish glow around the real versus bogus materials.

In the simulation we did for a department within the Air Force, real nuclear materials were intermixed with bogus materials and they were moved from site to site. I was asked to first determine which were the real materials, and then put them at the appropriate site. An independent analysis of the simulation's results indicated that we had shown a capacity for identifying and locating nuclear materials with an accuracy and reliability in excess of 90 percent!

It's obvious that if you can reduce the search area within an hour or two by 90 percent, it's a method you might want to use. The point being that, regardless of your belief in remote viewing reliability, if you have 25,000 square miles to search anyway, you might as well take the chance that RV is going to work since you have to start somewhere anyway. It's a lot better than making a random choice. I don't think I'd much care about the ridicule I'd be forced to face when it comes to tens of thousands of American lives vanishing in a mushroom cloud. I somehow feel I could find the courage to live with the ridicule.

The problems I've been trying to convey are almost overwhelming. They involve overcoming a person's natural desire "not to be ridiculed." Many people earn their position, usually a position of implied trust, through their reputation (the value of which is usually self-conceived and not valid in the first place) or by votes. They will not voluntarily risk those positions even for the lives of others. In fact, when it comes to life and death, they will be overly cautious in consideration of a possible lawsuit. This is further complicated by the fact that there is no clearinghouse or testing agency that can verify or validate good from bad psychics (remote viewers), or when material should be used or when it should not be. It's far easier just to take up the tired old standard: "This is ridiculous. It doesn't work, and it's a bunch of bunk." Then there is no risk to face.

While it is difficult, I continue to provide assistance where and when I can with regard to missing persons—especially criminal cases. But, because my time is limited, and because the value given the information depends on the authority's positions or attitudes, I do not do so unless asked specifically by the authorities involved, or in those special or rare cases where I can be assured that something will be done with the information. I've never charged money for such work, which in most years constitutes the majority of my remote viewing.

Chapter Sixteen

Put to the Test—on Live TV

I'm not sure if it was a direct result of the publication of my book or not, but an amazing thing happened one day in July of 1995. I received a phone call from a Ms. Ruth Rivin, who was representing a production company called LMNO Productions. She came right to the point. Would I agree to do a live remote viewing under scientific controls for live television? I didn't hesitate—Yes.

As we talked, it became apparent that there was a lot of discussion about the growing myth of remote viewing. The special project was still buried deeply within the bowels of the government, but as a result of my book, and others (including many who were misusing the term) a lot of statements were being made in public about the accuracy of remote viewing. Most of them were nonsense and completely unsupportable. When she had asked me if I would do it, I felt it would be a good way of presenting RV in an appropriate light and underscoring what it was really capable of doing. It wasn't perfect and everyone should know it. When I agreed, I told them that there was as good a probability that it would fail as that it would succeed. I was up front about the possibility and suggested they should do as much homework as possible with my colleague Ed at the lab before attempting to replicate it live and with a camera.

To their great credit, they did their homework, sending someone to talk with Ed and pursuing the appropriate knowledge of the protocols and how to implement them. By the time they called me back, they were making lists of cities that were possible candidates for the shoot. They told me they wanted to take me to a city that I had never been to before. I agreed. After going through two complete listings of cities, we finally found one that I had never visited on the third list—Houston, Texas.

The RV segment was supposed to be one of three major segments in a one hour show that was going to be syndicated, called "Put to the Test"—an ABC special. The idea was to put people who were making incredible claims in front of the camera and let them demonstrate their claims or abilities live. Ruth later confided in me that they had called a dozen people before me, none of whom would agree to do whatever they did live. They would only participate if it were a "reenactment" of something they had previously done. She told me that I had stunned her into momentary silence when I had agreed.

I can understand the others and their hesitation. Up until that point, anything I'd ever seen on the television regarding the paranormal was always done tongue-in-cheek or with that slight edge of ridicule. But something in Ruth's voice led me to believe that she was nothing but up-front about what they wanted to do. So I had immediately agreed.

The woman they sent to the lab in California, Susan Elkins, a movie location scout, was briefed well on how to select targets that might be used in the random selection. She arrived in Houston two weeks early, with the intention of selecting only targets that were significantly different from one another. They had to be stand-alone targets as much as possible and she was directed to try to use places or positions that were not famous or significant attractions in their own right. This would ensure a very diverse and well-differentiated target pool from which to pick. She was also given permission to use all of the greater Houston area, which encompassed more than a thousand square miles of space.

She successfully located and photographed hundreds of possible locations throughout the Houston metropolitan area, carefully placing each one into a separate folder. She shared these locations with no one else on the production team staff.

I arrived the same day the shooting team and moderator arrived. We went straight to an embankment in front of the skyline and did an introductory piece and shot a few B-rolls, which are ultimately used for background. This was my first introduction to television and to a television crew. The moderator, Bill Macatee, introduced himself to me and said that he actually didn't believe in the paranormal. He was concerned that it might come across in our interaction and he didn't want to offend me. I told him that was okay, that I didn't either. I suggested we could just wait and see how it turned out.

From there we rode directly to the hotel, where I went straight to my room. I told them I didn't want to see anyone or talk with anyone before the actual remote viewing. I was nervous about them sticking to the protocol: I wanted to be as blind to the possible target as possible, and was afraid that in their exuberance they might believe that giving me hints or something would be beneficial. But in reality they had stuck to the agreement. The only person who knew anything about the targets had sealed the envelopes and was out of contact with the shooting team until after the remote viewing was finished.

While I waited in my room, they randomly selected four of the envelopes from the target pool and labeled them one through four to use during the following day's shoot.

A problem came up later that night that put kind of a comical twist on events. In their preshoot discussions, it had come up again that the person who had done the target selection for the target pool had been told specifically *not* to use a famous place or location within the Houston area.

This decision had been made based on a recommendation from Ed in California. He felt that doing so would create a major front-end loading problem for me, should I see or drive past one of their famous places, or might create doubt in the minds of the viewers. He rightfully believed that the more unlikely the actual spot chosen as a target, the more accurate the remote viewing would be. Being totally blind to the target is actually of great benefit. When it can be almost anything in a city, it leaves you no room whatsoever for making an educated guess. It leaves you with only being able to call on the remote viewing ability for an answer.

But they became more and more concerned that I might think they were going to use an important place as a targeted area within the city. So much so, they gave Ed a call and asked him what they should do. He said that since they wouldn't be using one of the more famous landmarks in the city, it would be okay to tell me that.

After a great deal of hesitation, they came to my room and knocked on the door. It was very late and I had to get out of bed to answer it. When they told me they wanted to share some information with me, I simply said I didn't want to know anything at all and shut the door, going back to bed. I didn't realize it at the time, but this really put them between a rock and a hard place. They were very concerned that I was going to opt to describe a famous landmark instead of going for the actual target. It really wasn't their fault; they just didn't understand that knowing nothing at all for me was better. In any event, with a huge amount of money and effort already expended, they all spent a rather sleepless night worrying about what might happen, while I slept like a babe under my covers.

I took all my meals in my room and did not leave it until they sent a police officer to escort me to the windowless room on the second floor they had chosen to use as a remote viewing room. On the way into the room, Ruth asked me if I would be put off if more than just the moderator, a cameraman, and sound guy were inside. I told her no, I didn't care who was there as long as everyone was blind to the target location. The room quickly filled with production people lining the walls. The tension was so thick you could cut it with a knife.

In a second room, next to the one I was sitting in, the moderator, Bill, was throwing a die and selecting the target from the previously randomly chosen four. Once they filmed the selection of the target, he passed the sealed envelope to the outbounder, Ms. Jessica Miller, from the Houston tourist bureau, who then departed with the second film crew. When Bill entered the RV room and sat down next to me, neither he, nor anyone else inside the room knew what the target might be. We were *all* blind.

After about fifteen minutes of cool down, where I do a small meditation with my eyes closed, I said I was ready to begin. At that point, Bill said the outbounder should be at the location by now, and he asked me to describe the location.

I quickly sketched a picture of the location on sheets of blank paper lying on the table in front of me. I'm sure that while I was drawing, Bill had no idea what it was that he was supposed to be doing, but now and then he interrupted with a question.

I drew a view looking downward onto the edge, or dock area, running alongside a river. I said that it was constructed of seawalls that were both finished and unfinished in parts, and that the river had been dredged in parts or places. I drew what looked quite a bit like a barge with a dredge or crane kind of machine on it. I also drew in curved lines and verticals of what I sensed was some kind of a bridge.

The Stargate Chronicles

But I mistakenly said that my sense was it was used only by people and not by cars. (In fact it was a major bridge crossing the river and was used in just the opposite fashion, mostly by cars and not by people walking.) Toward the end of the session, which lasted about twenty minutes, I said there was some kind of a large object that I couldn't quite make out, but that it had suddenly appeared in my vision from out of nowhere.

I told Bill at that point that there didn't seem to be any more pertinent information, at which time we terminated the session.

They stopped filming and Bill and I waited while they arranged the cars to take us out to wherever the actual site location was. During that time, Bill asked me what I thought the large object might be, and I responded probably some kind of a large ship.

We were escorted down to the limousine and were joined there by a cameraman and a soundman who continued to film us on the way to the actual target site. Our driver got the location via cell phone and as we drove I tried not to guess where we were headed. I sat in the backseat discussing the original drawings with Bill.

He was actually looking at the drawing of the barge when the limo pulled directly up to the edge of the river and stopped. When he dropped the drawing to see where we were, he was staring directly at the barge.

"Holy shit!"

It was the first and only curse word I'd heard Bill use in the entire time I spent with him.

"Cut! Cut!" The cameraman yelled. "Now we've got to go back out and arrive again, because we can't use that particular expletive over the air."

So, we drove a large circle and arrived back at the same point.

"Oh, wow! Look at that!" Bill said, smiling and holding up my drawing of the barge. He was clearly excited. In fact the entire crew was blown completely out of the box by what they were seeing. Everyone who had been in the filming room with me—who knew that there wasn't any way any of us could know what or where the site was—arrived and stepped out of cars with their jaws hanging open.

Later, at the river edge, I had to spend some time talking with the young woman who was the outbounder. She was clearly shaken by the experience and thought that the only way I could have done the drawings I did was by being inside her head and looking through her eyes. This was way beyond her capacity to understand and it frightened her severely. I told her what is true about RV, that probably that is not where the information comes from. I could no more be inside her head than she could be inside my own. After some time, I was able to calm her down.

Ruth asked me what I did to celebrate whenever I had such a good result and I immediately said that I would always go out and treat myself to a great meal. This really wasn't a lie. Ed, Nevin, and I would often go out and have a great lunch after a good RV back at the lab. We've always felt it was important to finish on a high note by giving ourselves appropriate feedback—emotionally, visually, and physically. As a result, they picked me up that evening and we all went out to a five-star restaurant in Houston to celebrate.

During the meal, Ruth and the senior producer from LMNO asked me how I could do what I did in front of a camera and not look at all nervous. I explained that it's easy when you don't have to do the remote viewing at the same time. This confused them a bit, so I explained that I hadn't really done the RV in front of the camera. I did it ahead of time in my room. I knew I might not be able to get into my cool-down in front of the camera because I'd never done it that way before, so I did my cool-down in my room the night before and did the viewing then.

They couldn't believe their ears.

"How could you do the remote viewing the night before, when no one knew what the target was going to be, not even the outbounder?" Ruth asked, clearly mystified.

"Time and space are illusions," I responded. "It doesn't matter when I do the remote viewing. I only have to target what I'm eventually going to see. That way, it never leaves my head."

There was a long silence at the table.

One of the executive producers looked over at me. "How do you tell it apart from the other targets we were selecting from?"

"Sometimes it's hard," I calmly responded. "But, in this case since they were so different it was easy."

They looked like they didn't believe me, so I mentioned that fact that I knew what the other targets were as well—ticking them off on my fingers— "a water slide, a wet arch, and I can't tell if it's a small tree house or some kind of a playhouse surrounded by large buildings somewhere in the heart of town."

The table was completely silent now, the executive producer staring at me incredulously. All he could say was "There is never a camera when you need one." And we all laughed.

I had an enjoyable time with the LMNO Production people and we have since developed a lasting friendship. They were my first taste of an exceptional group of people with high-order ethics in the media line of work. It shows in their responsible attitude toward their job as well. They went on to produce most of Bill Cosby's shows, and Joan London's *Behind Closed Doors*—high-quality broadcasting. I was told when the segment was eventually shown to the ABC executives that they were stunned by the results.

The ABC special—*Put To The Test*—was supposed to air sometime during the end of 1995. As we approached the release of the special, Scooter and I decided to spend some time together, and we took the first real vacation we had in six years, traveling to the beach at Kitty Hawk, North Carolina. But my first vacation in six years was going to be completely shattered.

Chapter Seventeen

The AIR Report

In the middle of 1995, at the request of Congress, the Central Intelligence Agency (CIA) considered assuming responsibility for the Star Gate project. As part of its decision-making process, it asked the American Institutes for Research to evaluate the research conducted since the National Research Council's (NRC) predominately negative 1986 report. At that time a supposedly blue-ribbon panel had been charged with evaluating the evidence bearing on the effectiveness of a wide variety of techniques for enhancing human performance.

This review was conducted by David A. Goslin, then executive director of the Commission on Behavioral and Social Sciences and Education (CBASSE), who by 1995 was the president of the American Institutes for Research (AIR). His report, *Enhancing Human Performance: Issues, Theories, and Techniques,* was published by the National Academy Press in 1988 and summarized by Swets and Bjork (1990).

They note right up front that while this panel found some use for guided imagery, "little or no support was found for the usefulness of many other techniques, such as learning during sleep and remote viewing."

What is fascinating here is what they don't tell you: We were under direct orders during the 1986 study *not* to talk to the members of the NRC blue-ribbon panel, and we didn't. Not only did they not talk with us, they were denied access to any of the project's remote viewing materials or historical files from 1979 through that study in 1986. These orders were intended to hide the effectiveness of the unit.

Even more fascinating, given the negativity toward remote viewing based on "nothing being provided" from the Star Gate project, they put the same man in charge of the AIR study—Dr. Goslin, already noted for his narrow-minded attitude toward remote viewing or anything else paranormal—a position even then a matter of record.

Regardless of these facts, the AIR initiated a study of the Star Gate program that was supposed to cover two issues:

a. Review the research program

b. Review the operational application of the remote viewing phenomena in intelligence gathering

To do this, another blue-ribbon panel of two individuals was appointed, consisting of "noted" experts in the area of parapsychology—Dr. Jessica Utts, a professor of psychology at the University of California/Davis, and Dr. Raymond Hyman, a professor of psychology at the University of Oregon. At the outset, Dr. Utts was considered to be pro and Dr. Hyman negative in their attitudes toward the paranormal, both having previously published in the area. To this, AIR added Dr. Lincoln Moses, an emeritus professor at Stanford University, for statistical advice; and Dr. Goslin, president of AIR, who served as the coordinator (and is previously mentioned as already having a bias).

This panel was asked to review *all laboratory experiments* and meta-analytic reviews conducted as part of the research program. They state within the AIR report that this consisted of eighty separate publications, many of which were summary reports of multiple experiments.

In the operational evaluation, they state that they first reviewed the relevant research literature to identify whether conditions applied during intelligence gathering would reasonably permit application of the remote viewing paradigm. Second, members of three groups involved with the program were interviewed: (1) end users of the information, (2) the remote viewers providing the reports, (3) the program managers. They also claim that feedback information obtained from end user judgments of the accuracy and value of the remote viewing reports was assessed.

The following was the finding based on these conditions:

FOR RESEARCH:

"A statistically significant laboratory effort has been demonstrated in the sense that hits occur more often than chance."

"It is unclear whether the observed effects can unambiguously be attributed to the paranormal ability of the remote viewers as opposed to the characteristics of the judges or of the target or some other characteristic of the methods used."

"Evidence has not been provided that clearly demonstrates that the causes of hits are due to the operation of paranormal phenomena."

FOR OPERATIONS:

"The conditions under which the remote viewing phenomena is observed in laboratory settings do not apply in intelligence-gathering situations."

"The end users indicated that, although some accuracy was observed with regard to broad background characteristics, the remote viewing reports failed to produce the concrete, specific information valued in intelligence gathering."

"The information provided was inconsistent, inaccurate, and with regard to specifics, required substantial subjective interpretation."

"In no case had the information provided ever been used to guide intelligence operations. Thus, remote viewing failed to produce actionable intelligence."

Their conclusions were quite general, stating that, "Even though a statistical significant effect has been observed in the laboratory, it remains unclear whether the existence of a paranormal phenomena, remote viewing, has been demonstrated." And, "Even if it could be demonstrated unequivocally that a paranormal phenomenon occurs under the conditions present in the laboratory paradigm, these conditions have limited applicability and utility for intelligence gathering operations."

Now for a reality check.

The entire idea behind the evaluation was that it should be open-minded and balanced. But, given the position already established by

Dr. Goslin in the NRC report of 1986, this was hardly the case. I was working in the project in 1986 and remember being ordered not to speak with any of the members of the NRC report investigators. Why? Because, the agencies we were working for didn't want them to know the success rate we were experiencing in the use of remote viewing for intelligence collection purposes. The members of the NRC lacked sufficient clearances for access to this information, as did also the later investigators representing the AIR who were tasked with reviewing the same level of information. So, no one in either blue-panel review group has ever seen the information they claim to have had access to.

In addition, of the vast collection of research studies, more than 75 percent of them were ignored, also due to classification. They make no note of this fact in reference to the purported large selection of data they supposedly had access to. There is also no explanation of how they were able to evaluate whether or not "conditions" present regarding operational targets could have effective remote viewing applied. How could they make such a recommendation when they had insufficient clearances to see the operational materials necessary to make such a decision and had no understanding of what might be required in order to apply remote viewing operationally in the first place?

Further, they state that they interviewed the end users, the remote viewers who produced the reports, and the program managers involved with the program. If they did this, they interviewed only those five individuals who were standing in the office during their visits. On at least five occasions I volunteered to be interviewed, and those interviews were denied. No one with more than a twelve-month history as a remote viewer was interviewed, and neither were the previous program managers. There was no attempt to seek out end-product users who actually used remote viewing materials, because they were considered by the panel to be *biased*. Then comes the goalpost shift!

They state that while there is obviously a significant statistical effect proven within the laboratory, it can't be directly related to paranormal activity—that is, remote viewing.

In other words, you can't tell us how or why it's happening! You can't provide us with a *cause*, so how can we accept it?

Now we suddenly find ourselves again defending the existence of the paranormal instead of defending the actuality of remote viewing or its effectiveness. And, if moving the goalposts isn't enough, we have a statement that *research methods do not apply to collection.*

But they do! They always have. If they want to point out the periods or times that remote viewing was not done within the framework of protocol, then they should have done so. But, there were significant numbers of intelligence targets that were handled within such protocols. In fact, in many cases the end users *guaranteed* those protocols by managing the collection targeting materials, as well as having independent evaluations done of the resultant materials. Obviously, none of these cases were reviewed—as perhaps it was intended that they should not be.

We are told that the information provided was *inconsistent, inaccurate,* and *with regard to specifics, required substantial subjective interpretation.* Now this is a surprise. This actually applies to every form of intelligence gathering and intelligence material I've ever been subjected to, evaluated, or had to make conjecture on. This not only well establishes a lack of expertise in evaluating intelligence-applied methods, it also underscores the planned ignorance in the design of the AIR evaluation. If I were one of the scientists asked to put my signature to such a document, I would be outraged. Not only did they cut them off from the materials necessary to make such considerations, they disallowed the appropriate expertise in support of their effort, denied them clearances for the level of material they were being asked to analyze, and restricted them to the worst twelve-month period in the 222-month period of the project.

Finally, they emphatically state, *"In no case had the information provided ever been used to guide intelligence operations. Thus, remote viewing failed to produce actionable intelligence."*

Had there been intelligence expertise involved in the final analysis, it would have been understood from the outset that there has probably only been a handful of cases in a hundred years where a single source of intelligence was utilized to guide intelligence operations. That is *never* the case, regardless of the form or method of intelligence collection utilized. No one in his right mind would make a decision without a plethora of indices driving him in one direction or another. In most cases, it boils down to a small-percentage-majority vote, then an entire folder of information being or not being discarded. There is no long discussion about the "method" of collection for any particular piece of information contained. Because information is discarded utilizing other methods of intelligence gathering, it is not abandoned without a full and fair evaluation. Remote viewing has never had the benefit of this open-minded view.

It's way beyond a reasonable doubt that the knives were out

when it came to a fair and open-minded evaluation of remote viewing—it just didn't happen. To state that there was absolutely no evidence that it provided materials of value flies in the face of more credible oversight committees on the research side of the house, and enthusiastic end users of the methodology who walked into Senate and congressional hearings held secretly year after year, presenting highly classified and sealed results of the effectiveness of remote viewing, arguing for its continued existence, use, and funding.

In reality, having been there for the entire period of its operation, I know it would be fair to say that in its final twelve months of existence there might have been some question as to the feasibility of continuing under the same plan of management. There might have even been a sufficient justification for tightening the controls and protocols under which the operational arm was performing. But these are material to how the project is being conducted from a managerial standpoint, not from a "does it work" standpoint.

It took decades to overcome resistance to the use of snipers. Every time war was declared, they had to reinvent the wheel and open a new sniper school to train them. This didn't happen because snipers couldn't shoot straight, or didn't always hit their targets. It happened because there was no effective historically established ethic for the training, use, and maintenance of a sniper-equipped and -qualified unit. It wasn't something "gentlemen" did to one another.

Regardless of how one might feel about the efficacy of using the paranormal for intelligence gathering, I can emphatically state that it works, it's here, and it will continue to be reinvented from time to time, until it becomes part of the established, historically accepted background. Wishing it can't, or won't, doesn't make it go away, and doesn't make it any less effective in the new understanding of modern warfare techniques.

I'll break the ugly silence with the unspoken question that no one ever wants to ask.

Is there a defense against remote viewing? Is that the real problem here?

Whether there is or isn't, isn't material here. I can appropriately state that not paying any attention to it is the same as burying one's head in the sand. Everyone should believe whatever s/he wants. Who really cares? What does it really matter?

Chapter Eighteen

Going Public

Scooter and I were enjoying a small cottage on the beach just south of Kitty Hawk when very early one morning I received a call from someone purporting to represent the program *Nightline*. I was asked a lot of questions about my participation in a black project called Star Gate. Up until that point in time, public knowledge of my existence or participation in the project was classified and protected. I have no idea who released my name to the program producer. I initially said that I had no comment regarding the existence of such a program and hung up the phone.

The situation was further complicated by the fact that the ABC special appeared within a week of the release of the report. It provided clear evidence that remote viewing worked and worked well, a point not missed by most of the media now wanting to talk to me.

I immediately called Ed May at home in California and asked him what was going on. He explained that someone had passed the AIR report, along with some very negative comments to a number of the news media, and it was growing into a very large story within just a few hours. We talked about whether or not we should admit to having been a part of the project that was reviewed, and having no guidance decided initially that we should seek advice from those in charge.

No one would return my calls.

In effect, official statements had been issued to the press by various agencies or offices of the government stating that while there had been some use of remote viewing, it was experimental and didn't work. These were flying in the face of the demonstration that was shown by ABC.

In fact, most of what we had been doing in the research side of the house was unclassified and open to public access. Much of our writing was published in numerous journals. In the case of events I've talked about in this book, for instance, I have prior authority and authorization for discussing them in unclassified company, or I wouldn't be talking about them at all. The intelligence simulations were specifically declassified for use in unclassified briefings and presentations. But, when seeking information about what could or should not be talked about with the media, the only word that was being given—and indirectly at that—was don't talk with anyone.

Meanwhile, we were being castigated within the media by some of our former users as somewhat over the edge, and guilty of having wasted millions of dollars in tax money, a comment repetitively levied over the phone to me by media representatives, which was not true.

Eventually, I received a call from the senior science adviser for *Nightline*, who asked me if I would agree to appear on the show. I was advised that there would be representation for the CIA, one of the end users who worked for the CIA, and others who supported the findings in the AIR report.

The room was beginning to smell bad. I agreed to appear, but only with the understanding that I would not speak to operations, only to the efficacy of using remote viewing for intelligence purposes. This was the beginning of a long involvement with the media that has sometimes been gentle, but for the most part has been testy under the best conditions.

Initially, the vast majority of the media was hostile and aimed toward one result—to ridicule. It was clear to me, if no one else, that there was a full-court press to paint the entire history of remote viewing in a negative and somewhat less than ideal light. The emphasis was on the number of dollars spent on the project over the eighteen and a half years of its existence—a figure of about eighteen to twenty million. I remember asking myself, "Now where in the hell did they get that figure?" It's actually a fairly accurate figure (general total) based on a compilation of figures taken from a multitude of financial support sources over a very long period of time and from a multitude of origins within the intelligence agencies of the U.S. government. The only way they could have gotten it was to have had it *tactically* slipped to them by someone *on the inside*. The fact that it was being used derisively also says all that has to be said about someone's possible ulterior motive.

The synchronicity of events leading up to and including my interview with *Nightline,* was also very telling. They flew Scooter and me in from the beach to Durham, North Carolina, by private plane for the interview. Initially, they took us to three separate locations to do the interview, but were unable to find an area quiet enough. In one case the interview was disturbed by a train, doing multiple-car decouplings and couplings, behind the bench we were sitting on. When we moved to a log house in the country the wind picked up to the point that the soundman had trouble standing up in the face of it. Eventually, we moved to the J. B. Rhine Center—which was crowded and had no room. A suggestion was made that we might be allowed to do the shoot at Ms. Sally Feathers' house. Sally is Dr. J. B. Rhine's daughter and was then the director of the J. B. Rhine Research Center. She agreed.

Her newly constructed house sits almost on top of her father's old house foundations, a place that one might even consider to be "the foundation" of paranormal research in America. I smile even now, when I consider the incredible synchronicity required to put me in a chair at that place for the first interview on the Army's Star Gate remote viewing project. Incredible.

Following the interview, which was shown in November of 1995, Star Gate was out of the bag. In spite of continued ill treatment from the majority of people representing magazines, newspapers, radio, and television, I persisted in giving as clear and accurate a response as allowable under the conditions of my security agreements. To this day, I have never violated them in any way. But the ridicule, tongue-in-cheek remarks, or comments clearly designed to criticize or embarrass me and others continued unabated. For those who have not had this experience, I will outline it for you.

No matter what you do, they have a story. If you agree to talk, you give them more to use any way they feel like using it. If you decide not to talk with them, then they have the grounds to backlight you as an unreasonable or nonresponsive person. Regardless as to how you respond or what you respond with, something will be written, and it will be edited in any fashion necessary to sell papers, airtime, or the magazine involved. They won't lie outright, as that would make them liable, but they will and sometimes do lie by omission. In other words, sometimes they will tactfully leave something important or pertinent out of the conversation to highlight your personal integrity in a bad way or dilute whatever point you are trying to make. It really doesn't matter what the truth is in most cases; it's what will people believe and how can it impact the most emotionally so it will sell.

In reality, the $20 million spent on Star Gate isn't even chickenfeed. It hardly deserves a line in a column of print. During either the Gulf War or the antiterrorist actions in Afghanistan, we spent more than that much after launching the first twenty cruise missiles.[16] To compare blowing up twenty mud-and-rock huts to an intelligence collection process that supported all the major intelligence agencies of the federal government for eighteen and a half years (inclusive of all of the research support involved) is completely ludicrous. If one were to actually go back and honestly look at the decisions that were affected by the intelligence provided, and how it might have saved lives, it's even more incredible that it would be viewed derisively.

It certainly wouldn't even reach the level one would have to ascend to to be considered "pork" attached to a real budget line item. Another fact that is always lost in the fine print is how much of that money was spent or distributed throughout the nation to colleges and universities doing subsidiary or supportive work to the RV research, or that which was shared with other national labs, renting their equipment. Easily half of the budget disappeared into those areas. It certainly wasn't spent helping intelligence officers down on their knees cleaning and scrubbing the floor of their own work environment.

Before my transfer to the special project, I spent ten times the entire eighteen-and-a-half-year remote viewing budget on a single stage of development for a prototype SIGINT device, which we weren't sure would work until it was finished.

But then I suppose it is big dollars to a guy on the street who is taxed to the limit and believes that remote viewing is an affront to God—many of whom called me as a result of the articles that were appearing.

My business, which had actually been doing very well for a number of years, began to rapidly taper off. It wasn't the negative reporting alone that was doing the damage. I quickly discovered that

---

[16] http://www.af.mil/news/factsheets/AGM_86B_C_Missiles.html - Unit Cost: AGM-86B, $1 million; AGM-86C, additional $160,000 conversion cost.

it was the fact that I was talking to someone (the media) in the first place. Many companies that had been using my services were now concerned about appearing suddenly in the public eye. What had been operating quite well beneath the mushrooms on the forest floor for many years might suddenly be exposed to direct sunlight. Fear set in quickly. They might actually get caught standing next to the person who was giving them a 15 percent edge on their competitors, or pointing out the inside track for a specific stock or currency, when the spotlight suddenly came on. Customers began to drop away like flies trying to squeeze through a heating coil. In spite of the fact that I have never violated a business confidence, decade-long relationships with some of my customers suddenly vaporized, as everyone suddenly seemed to be taking off on vacations. I started giving talks at The Monroe Institute just for something to do, and went back to contract building, and started a second book.

It might have been the stress, but my back, which I'd damaged severely in the helicopter crash in Vietnam in the late 1960s, finally gave out. I had surgery within a few weeks of my appearance on *Nightline*. The recovery took a lot longer than I anticipated, and while the pain in my lower back abated to some degree, it increased along the rest of my spine.

During the period between the end of 1995 and 2000, I added two chapters to my original book, *Mind Trek*, where I openly talked about the Star Gate project following its exposure. I wrote *The Ultimate Time Machine* (1998), which was intended to provide my own understanding for how I believe time works, and our place within it. I believe that we as humans are the "ultimate time machine." It contains dozens of predictions for the next 75 years, some of which have already come true and some of which have not. It wasn't meant to prove precognition, but to deliver a message about how time might work and why our place within it is important to the outcome. I also wrote *Remote Viewing Secrets* in 2000, attempting to establish a baseline for understanding how and why remote viewing might work, and how the average person might learn something about it and/or employ it—all published by Hampton Roads.

I continued to do live remote viewings on television as a way of demonstrating the fact that remote viewing works. I felt that if I couldn't control how things would be edited, then the most powerful thing I could do would be to demonstrate it.

During 1996 I traveled to London, where I appeared on a show called *The Paranormal World of Paul McKenna*—"Telepathy." Paul was a man known for his ability to use hypnosis in live demonstrations on Channel 4 in England. He asked me if I would do some demonstrations of live RV on camera for him and I agreed. We did two series of two.

The first two were very successful. He and his staff contacted Ed out in California and received instructions on how to set up a target pool and target me using an outbounder methodology. These two outbounder sessions were filmed live and worked, but with an interesting twist.

One of the things that people do not understand about RV is that how it is applied is almost as important as doing the actual remote viewing or collection of the data. As an example, in the first outbounder target they selected, one of their locally famous actors randomly chose a target from a pile of envelopes, then traveled there, arriving at a specified time, choosing as a target the very large coal-fired power plant located just outside the heart of London on the Thames River. When I entered the room of the hotel where we were going to do the RV, we sat and waited for nearly an hour, while the target selection process was done at the studio across town, and the actor fellow traveled to the target location. When it was time to begin, they sat me down at a table and handed me an envelope, which I opened, that contained a photograph of the actor.

"Have you ever seen this man before?" they asked.

"No."

"He should now be located at the target site. We would like you to draw a picture of where he is standing."

Which is what I did. I drew a lovely picture of a bridge spanning both a river as well as a roadway. I explained that he was standing just off the side of the bridge in the right-hand corner.

We all loaded into a London cab and headed out to meet the outbounder. When we arrived, I was elated. There he was, standing just to the side of the bridge that I had drawn in detail. However, when asked what the target was, he pointed across the river with a grin.

"It's over there. That large power plant."

The target was nearly a mile away. Everyone was disappointed, until I pointed out the fact that they asked me to describe where he was *standing*, not what he was *interested in*.

They learned a valuable lesson in that first RV. When you ask the viewer for something, that's exactly what you get. He hadn't been properly instructed to actually be standing on or in the target location. They asked me if I would do another one and I agreed. This time they did something even more foolish.

The following day, after guaranteeing that the outbounder was standing either next to or inside of the actual target, I was asked to describe it. The response went something like this:

"It's a place of dread. It's a dark place. It's a place of incarceration. It's a place no one is comfortable in." And that's pretty much how it continued. I was being overwhelmed with a foreboding sense about the target and a lot of warning bells were going off in the back of my head. I minimized my results and kept them as general as possible. I felt as though I were describing a secretive and dark area with heavily regulated access.

We all piled into another London taxi, which drove us again to the river's edge. We met with the actor standing on a small walkway along the edge of the river immediately behind a blockhouse kind of building—much like the rough sketch I did in the hotel room. As we approached with the camera crew, I noticed the dozens of cameras, which began to swing our way.

Well, it didn't take long for the group of "suits" to arrive, asking us what our business was. To which Paul McKenna announced very loudly that we were filming a live remote viewing with the ex-psychic spy from the United States. The building we were standing beside was the new British MI5 building—their equivalent of our FBI Headquarters.

When I returned a month later to the studio for the "chat show" portion of filming in the studio, I was told that we wouldn't be using any of the materials from the second target site location, which was no surprise to me. I was also hassled for nearly three hours entering customs. They kept badgering me for a Queen's permit because I was appearing on the television show and they wouldn't believe that I was making the appearance "unpaid." Or, at least that was their position. My sense was they were collecting their photographs and simply doing what good intelligence people do.

I've since done two more live RVs, both of which worked. I was filmed doing the remote viewing while sitting in a gazebo in Annapolis, Maryland, targeting where I would be in a couple of month's time on a future visit to England. In both cases, no one but me saw the films until I had actually visited the randomly chosen sites in England a couple months later. When I finished the RV in Annapolis, I personally removed the film clips and placed them along with the drawings and tapes inside a courier pouch, which was then sealed with a lead seal. I nailed both targets—although a Dr. Richard Wiseman argues over the judging of the second target. He is a researcher from Oxford who doesn't believe in the paranormal. He was the person who was asked to independently judge my materials and match them to one of four possible sites.

What I drew was a nearly perfect cube that I said had no windows, or very few. I said it had four massive engines that were creating a very high squealing sound—like high-pitched turbine noises.

When I got to England the actual target that was selected was another power station outside London in the countryside—a large cube of a building made from metal, inside of which were four very large power output generators driven by steam-driven turbines.

When they took us to the site for feedback, and filming, they wouldn't let us in. The general manager of the plant decided at the last minute that he didn't want his plant on television associated with psychics.

On the advice of Richard Wiseman, we went to a second site, which also happened to be a cube-shaped building—a museum containing four large locomotives. I argued that only the first site should have counted, and therefore the entire effort should be abandoned as a blown protocol. Richard said the second site had been his second-place match during the independent judging session and therefore it should count.

It was evident to the producer that since the locomotives were sitting there silent and I had specifically stated very loud turbine noises that there was something wrong with the protocol, but Richard refused to relent in his judging position. The producer abandoned the effort altogether, and I marked it all down as a failure.

I've done sixteen other live remote viewings on camera in Japan and America. Of the 22 total, seventeen have been successful. Of the five failures, two were protocol violations by the production companies (avoidable or not), so I asked them not to use them for that reason. I still consider them failures, however—at the very least, failure on my part to ensure they were properly instructed in how the protocol works.

One of the live RVs I did was at the J.B. Rhine Center for a group of students, which was also filmed by a production company for the

Discovery Channel. What I really liked about it was the fact that 29 of the 30 students and others present gave me a first-place match when comparing my drawing to a selection of five possible sites. (This means they chose the actual target from the five possible sites presented 29 out of thirty times.) The person who ran the protocol for that presentation was—Dr. Richard Wiseman, who happened to be visiting from England. Ed and I had dinner with him the night before and he incessantly argued that the protocols we used were not tight enough. So, we suggested that he take the materials and the target pool and run the protocol any way he chose the following day, which he did. I still got the 29 first-place matches and Discovery Channel got a wonderful piece for television. Richard has refused to discuss it since.

My first appearance on Japanese television was on a program called *Battle TV*, which has two panels taking opposing views of a controversial issue and arguing about it for the television audience. They brought me on to demonstrate RV.

I didn't know at the outset that the head of the panel opposed to the possibility of remote viewing was the head of the physics department at the University of Tokyo. I was told that at the beginning of the program that he had stood up and promised that if he couldn't demonstrate the "trick" I used to do remote viewing, he would resign his position at the university. The other part I didn't know was that they had asked him to stop somewhere on his way to the studio and have his picture taken with a Polaroid camera and not tell anyone about it.

When they announced this, I didn't point out the fact that it was a major violation of protocol, in that he would be sitting there, knowing what the target was, and could be giving me information simply by his body movements. It kind of upset me, but I didn't say anything. When they asked me to describe where he had his picture taken, I drew a descending ramp off the side of something I said was very large and made from concrete. I told them the descending ramp circled an open grassy area in the middle.

They asked him to show the picture he had in his pocket to the audience and it showed him leaning over the edge of a descending ramp coming off the side of a very large bridge. This really amazed the audience. The professor's comment was "He could have guessed. There are dozens of these ramps all over Tokyo."

My response was that there were also dozens of bowling alleys, temples, bridges, and other common places throughout Tokyo as well, but I didn't describe any of those.

His response was to sit silently staring back at me.

They then sent a young lady off with a camera team, and told the audience that she had three hours to go anywhere she wanted to in Japan. She had access to the bullet train, so that was almost true. They asked me what I was going to do, and I said that I was going to take a nap in the Green Room, which I did, stretching out on a tatami mat. Scooter told me they came in and filmed me snoring there a couple of times.

Three hours later I went back out onto the stage and sat down at a table and drew a picture of what I called a fake lake or pond with some sort of small, funny-looking tea-house sitting alongside it. I said it was strange because it felt as though it was all imitation. I was hoping not to offend anyone because they don't imitate much in Japan, as everything is original. When they called the young lady on her phone, they began transmitting from her location. She was standing in the middle of a small indoor pond, which had the funny little tea-house sitting toward the rear. Using the magic of technology, they even suspended my drawing of the small house over the actual picture and they were identical. It blew the audience away.

When they went to the professor and asked him what he thought, he was also obviously stunned. He hesitated, then blurted out that it was obvious to him that I was in collusion with the studio and that the whole thing had been prearranged. It was a stupid response and he knew it as soon as it came out.

They rushed the camera across the stage toward me, expecting me to be outraged, I suppose. Instead, I bowed very politely to the professor and said that since I had no help from the studio and everyone knew it, I could only take his comment as a compliment for the quality of my remote viewing. The audience roared its approval and the professor didn't say another word through the end of the program.

A few weeks after I returned home, the producer sent me an e-mail and said the professor had been back into the studio two days running after the show, looking at the films. He went over them again and again, trying to find out how I was somehow signaled or how I did the trick. Of course, he was unable to find something that wasn't there. So far he has failed to resign his position at the university, however.

When I first started doing remote viewings in front of the cameras, it was exciting and I felt it was also beneficial. But over time, I've found that it has probably done more damage than good.

Maybe it's human nature, but a lot of things have been done with my films that should not have been done. Many who are not remote viewers now point to my films as proof of how good remote viewing is, and use them to validate their own claims regarding their own abilities at remote viewing. It has already become a cliché that remote viewing can be taught to anyone and that anyone can be a world-class or expert remote viewer.

This is simply not true.

If it were true, the world would be filled with people demonstrating their prowess on national television stations against totally blind, randomly chosen targets.

It isn't.

Some examples are being shown that are "simulations of real events," but that isn't the same thing. It's easy to say you have done something and then re-create it for film. That doesn't mean it actually happened in the manner in which it's being presented. It may not be outright lying, but it certainly can be selective memory at work and things may not have gone as accurately as one might believe.

Numerous people call and tell me that my remote viewing examples are being used in presentations throughout the world. I have no problem with this, except in the cases where they then make claims based on that remote viewing in an effort to either sell themselves or some form of teaching. It isn't right, it isn't truthful, and as a result, in some cases people are being scammed out of a great deal of money. Remote viewing does work, but not as well as most want to believe.

As I've stated over and over again, just about everyone who walks the planet is psychic to one degree or another. The spontaneity of psychic functioning is exhibited across the land, in every country, wherever more than two people congregate. It is surprisingly common among populations with an open mind. However, when it comes to what might be termed "world-class" remote viewing, it is very rare, and while the rules regarding it might be teachable, the capability is not transferable by teaching.

There are a lot of claims made about one "method" of remote viewing versus another. A large percentage of these claims are outright fraudulent. The only way one can tell if they are true or not is if they can be demonstrated more than once, that is repetitively, under severely restricted controls—totally blind to anyone present when the remote viewing is being done.

While I keep reiterating this, many keep saying that this isn't absolutely necessary.

It may not be absolutely necessary within the form of applications they may be using it for. If it isn't, they shouldn't be calling whatever they are doing remote viewing. My statements regarding scientific controls while remote viewing are valid at all times—in and out of applications.

For a long time, I've stated that these comments should not be construed as derogatory of other forms of paranormal information production, such as being psychic, or dowsing, or reading cards. I mean that. They have their own rules and function in their own specific ways. But a lot of people have gone to an exceptional degree of trouble to design and develop the blind and double-blind protocols used when demonstrating remote viewing in order to establish the method as acceptable to science. The independent analysis, the way the analysis is performed, even the way the evaluation packet is presented to the evaluation team, are all specifically done to preclude fraud or to establish the veracity of remote viewing and remote viewing alone. And absolutely nothing that is done in the science of remote viewing is there to prove any other form of paranormal functioning. People who use it for these purposes may be doing it out of ignorance, or may know full well that it's inappropriate. In either case, it is wrong and damaging to all remote viewers who are attempting to develop their skills in an appropriate and ethical manner.

Chapter Nineteen

Curtain Call

During 1998, I began losing a lot of my energy and stamina. I also noticed that I was losing my breath on stairs. A visit with my cardiologist showed that my concerns about my heart seemed to be justified. The skip graft across the bottom of my heart muscle had ceased to operate effectively. While I had massively collateralized my heart muscle, there just wasn't sufficient blood circulation to the lower area, which was resulting in a great loss in energy. I scheduled myself for surgery in the summer of 1998.

I continued to work with the lab on the West Coast. Once the program had been exposed and terminated, the lab, which was previously located at SAIC, relocated to the Laboratories for Fundamental Research in Menlo Park, California. The new lab is actually just down the street from the old SAIC location. My longtime and dear friend Ed and I have continued to work as near full time as possible on the remote viewing research. For the past six years it has all been essentially unpaid work. Expenses are covered (for the most part), but there has been very little in the way of salary.

In July of 1998 I entered the hospital for a second open-heart bypass operation, which I was not looking forward to. I had reached a point where it took a great deal of effort and pain just to climb a set of stairs.

The operation turned out to be particularly scary for Scooter, because it was accompanied by complications. After cutting the wire-wrap retainers and cracking my sternum about half an inch, the surgeon (Dr. Irving L. Kron, the same surgeon who did the original work on me in 1985) discovered that my older bypass grafts had adhered to the scar tissue along the inside of my chest wall. Had he just opened my chest, I probably would not have survived. He spent hours carefully detaching the old grafts to gain entry to my chest for the second operation. Of course I was oblivious to this, because I was enjoying a walk in the out-of-body state along a peaceful brook in the Bavarian Alps at the time.

Because of my age, and the duration of the operation, it had a major impact on me. While I still returned home as quickly as I had from the first, it took a lot longer for me to regain sufficient strength to do what I considered a normal level of work.

The heart problem was really beginning to frustrate me. I decided that I would have to work even harder to regain my strength and vowed that eventually I would put it all behind me. In a sense, it caused me to drive myself even harder in many respects, much to Scooter's dismay. I think the second operation frightened her just as much as the first. I was very sensitive to the pain I was bringing to her, but there was little that I could do about it, except get through it. During this operation they used both the mammary arteries in the upper chest wall and a vein taken from my left lower arm area. Dr. Kron said they'd learned a lot since my first operation and this one would probably last a lot longer. The difference has been truly amazing. I still have a major heart problem, but it has been a lot easier to deal with.

Some of our research has carried us to other countries in the search for support and subjects. The research continues to be interesting and diverse, and Ed continues to publish most of the lab results in the appropriate journals, and I attempt to write about them.

One of my favorite remote viewings was done in private at the Eötvös Loránd University in Budapest, Hungary. Ed and I were visiting with the head of the experimental psychology department there, Dr. Eva Bányai, who is world renowned for her work in experimental hypnosis. She asked if we would do a demonstration of remote viewing for her, there in her office. We of course agreed. I was very honored to be asked by her, as I've read a great deal about her and her work and have a tremendous respect for her insightfulness and no-nonsense approach to the science of mind.

Ed and I carry a program in our laptop computers that includes a randomly generated selection method for doing remote viewing. It also contains a large target pool, photographs of a selection of possible sites across the world. The way it works is quite simple. Once you've entered your session data—name, date, place, etc., and it has been permanently recorded—you hit a button and it gives you a ready screen.

You then do the remote viewing by drawing something on a piece of paper, or writing out your thoughts that relate to the target, which you will see at some time in the future as feedback.

When the remote viewing is finished (and the remote viewing materials have been logged and recorded), someone can press another button and is then presented with a selection of five possible target pictures, one of which is the real target. Whoever is judging selects the one that most closely matches your results, followed by the second closest match, third, fourth, etc. Almost always this judging is done by a third party in order to keep the remote viewer from getting feedback on both the real target and the four randomly selected controls. Independently judging the results of a remote viewing also guarantees that the judge is not connected in any way to the collection of the material, keeping him or her blind to an expectation of a specific result. But in demonstrations, we usually leave the judging to the person we are demonstrating to, after I've left the room.

The target pool contains 300+ target photographs from all over the world and no two are alike. Although I've already seen many of them, it is impossible for me to know which will be selected randomly as a target at any given time. In fact, the more of them I see, the harder it gets because I have recall of those I've been exposed to in the past. It makes the actual viewing even more difficult.

There is one other catch, which I will explain in a moment.

We called up the program and showed her how we entered all the salient data. After this, Ed pushed the button and the screen went white. He asked me to do the remote viewing.

I started with what felt like a sweeping beach line across a white sheet of paper.

"A beach," I said.

I then added some palm trees and a cluster of buildings off to the left. I wrote "large buildings" over the cluster of blocks that I drew so she would know that's what I was describing by my rather crude drawing. I then drew what appeared to be the edge of a mountain running down to the sea to the right.

"Gee. This looks like Diamond Head, Waikiki Beach," I said, laughing. Then I added the title to the bottom edge of the drawing.

Handing it to her, I said, "Obviously Diamond Head." I reiterated that sometimes things might not be that exact, so when judging, she should use perhaps a bit less exactness. I then excused myself from the room while she and Ed did the judging.

After I left, Ed pushed the button and five pictures appeared. One of them was a typical photograph of Waikiki Beach and Diamond Head. She obviously had to give that a first-place match, followed by the other matching categories. When they were through, and the screen cleared of pictures, Ed called for me to rejoin them. He then asked her to punch the button, to show us what the actual target was.

The picture of Diamond Head appeared centered on the screen.

She smiled a bit nervously, thought for a very long moment, then proceeded to ask a lot of questions about leakage paths that might be possible as a result of how we just did the demonstration. Ed and I listened politely. Much of what she was saying were exactly the same comments or questions voiced by many scientists before her—all directed toward possible loops or problems in protocol that might have accounted for the accuracy of the remote viewing. Many of them are also quite true.

Only in this particular case, what neither Ed nor I told her from the outset was the following:

The target was not selected until her last button push!

The specific program set we were using at the time actually does not select a target until the end of the demonstration. Initially when the blank screen is shown, there has been *no target selected.*

I do the remote viewing, after which the *five possible targets* are selected for judging against what I've drawn.

Once the judging has been completed, the final time the button is pushed—in this case, when she pushed it—she *selected which of the five would be the actual target* or answer.

I essentially did a remote viewing for a target that was not selected until after it had been judged, a target that did not exist in time/space until after both the remote viewing was accomplished and the judging terminated.

The silence in the room after Ed explained this to her was incredible. I could not have asked for a more exceptional result, and it remains today one of the cleanest and finest examples of precognitive remote viewing I've ever done as a live demonstration. It's the kind of event that keeps me doing what I do; it's the reason I seldom lose interest.

I've received a number of honors from those I consider to be serious investigators into the paranormal. The Rhine Research Center in Durham, North Carolina, presented me with an award at their annual fundraiser on January 25, 1997. I was honored for my contributions to research and my participation in the exploration of remote viewing. I am a guest lecturer there during their summer student program, and visit quite often. I've also been included as a participant and sometimes consultant in some of their experiments.

A number of years ago, I was voted in as a full member of the Parapsychological Association. I am probably the only working psychic or remote viewer who's been honored in that fashion. I've written a paper, which was accepted and published in their *Journal of Parapsychology,* Vol. 61./No. 2, June 1997, titled "Perceptions of a Paranormal Subject." I've also participated in panel discussions during annual meetings. I am greatly humbled by the honor they've given me in this respect, something I never expected. The Parapsychological Association, Inc. is a member of the American Association for the Advancement of Science and our membership meets annually in various cities across the world.

I've given presentations or joint presentations on request to numerous universities including the University of North Carolina, North Carolina State University, Stanford University, and Harvard, for both faculty and the student body. I enjoy these lectures, especially when they stir open-minded debate and raise a lot of questions that may drive others into the world of paranormal research.

It does sometimes reach open-minded people who acknowledge, based on their own experience, the existence of PSI and what it can do in life. As an example, my wife and I were both recently honored with the titles "Dame's Cross" and "Knight Chevalier," respectively, in the Order of Saint Stanislas, by Prince Grand Master Count Juliusz Nowina-Sokolnicki GCCStS.

The Order of Saint Stanislas is an international order of chivalry, made up of honorable men and women of all races and creeds who are concerned with assisting those less fortunate than themselves. Although it has focus throughout the world, the current efforts of the order have been in Eastern Europe, where the order has a number of ongoing projects mainly based in Poland. One of the major charities in which the order is currently involved is the "Chernobyl Kids" project, which provides ongoing medical and financial support to the now second-generation victims suffering from a variety of cancers as a result of the Chernobyl disaster—these are children who otherwise have been abandoned by others.

I only point this out because it symbolizes how others feel concerning spiritual, moral, and cross-cultural attitudes necessary in any direct action contributing to the improvement of civilization and the relationships between diverse peoples of the world—something my wife and I have always attempted to exemplify through the appropriate application and use of remote viewing—a personal effort now extending over two and a half decades. It has never been easy identifying the moral high ground, and attempting to operate from that point of view, especially in a world as complex as today's. We are very honored to have been recognized for our efforts to help others in this respect.[17]

Some people have begun to ask me when I'm going to retire from remote viewing. Or, put another way, don't you get tired of it?

The honest answer is yes. I do get tired. It's not the remote viewing that makes me tired. It's the frustration and sometimes rage I feel when I see my work being used to validate a scam, or when I observe the media mixing apples and oranges—one specific subject matter in with another—such as blending remote viewing in with remote influencing—one having at least an acceptable set of standards and the other none at all. I get tired of the deliberate and destructive nature of some of the people on both sides of the issues who do terrible damage to the credibility and work so many have spent a lifetime trying to establish across the entire field of paranormal research. I get tired when the media or critics don't even take the time to read the literature.

I don't want to be misunderstood here. It's okay to disagree with

---

[17] Anyone who would like to contribute to the charitable goals of this order is welcome to contact me for further information, or the Order directly—The Order of St. Stanislas, Dame Commander Lorraine Ambrose-Boothsy, P.O. Box 351, Edgewater, Md. 21037.

Joseph McMoneagle

the literature, but if you are going to do so, you need to put at least as much thought into the disagreement as went into the argument in the first place. Putting it down to the work of the devil, calling into question the integrity of the researcher (without any proof), or going on a destructive binge with someone's reputation just to darken the skyline over the subject matter is not comic relief—it's criminal.

I suppose my plan is really a simple one. I don't believe in retirement; I do believe in contributing something as long as it continues to be of value to someone. I have just completed my twenty-second remote viewing that was done live on camera and under controls for national television in Tokyo, Japan. I believe it will be my last. It's always good to stop doing something on a good note, and it was about as good as it gets.

The Japanese production team arrived at my house in January 2002. Originally they were going to fly me to Japan to do the remote viewing, but decided it would have more impact for me to do the viewing from my home in the mountains of Virginia, and then fly to Japan for the studio portion and results.

I did four targets for them—three while they were in the States and one, which was a surprise to me, while filming in the studio.

Two of the targets involved missing people, which as I said before, are the most difficult targets to complete, especially in a short period of time. At the time of targeting for the first two targets, I was given no information, doing them as I always like to do them—blind.

My wife and the producer put the name of the missing person in a sealed envelope, which was then brought into the dining room, where I had agreed to do the remote viewing. Attached to the envelope were two questions written on a yellow Post-It note:

"Describe the person and their current health or condition."

"Describe the location of the person."

The crew handed me the sealed envelope and asked me to provide an answer to the questions on the envelope. I did not know at the time that it was a search for a Mr. Noriyuki Ito's mother, who, if still alive, would be 48 years old. Mr. Ito, who had been abandoned by his mother when he was a year old, had no idea of her location. In fact, she had not been seen in 27 years. Without resorting to any information, even the mother's date of birth, I provided the following, on film:

- The missing person is a female, middle aged, and alive.
- She currently lives in a metropolitan area of six million to seven million people (I specified the location as definitely not being Tokyo).
- The city has a bay and four man-made islands.
  I felt her presence strongly in the southwestern area (which they originally assumed to be Nishinomiya in Osaka).
- The population definitely does not exceed 300,000 (for that specific prefecture).
- A river divides the city and a much larger city to the side.
- I felt her residence lay in a delta area between the river and the center of the city proper.
- There was a large parklike area near her residence.
- There was a round monument-like structure in the center of the city area there.
- She lives in one of the rooms of a three-story apartment containing six rooms.
- I said that her residence was the backmost room.

On returning to Japan, the crew agreed that the place must be Nishinomiya Prefecture of Osaka. But they found that Nishinomiya had no river as part of its border, and a small delta along the river couldn't be found. Checking in with the local real estate office, they were told that according to the description it couldn't be Nishinomiya.

They made a decision to modify the search based on my data. The population was specifically stated to be less than 300,000. They discovered that Nishinomiya was 390,000. Looking for a city within Osaka with a population less than 300,000, they discovered there was only one such prefecture. For purposes of protecting the individuals concerned, they refer to this prefecture as City X. It was shown as having a population of 280,000.

A full investigation of City X was begun immediately. Surprisingly, they found that a river served as a border to the area, and a small delta as described was located, as well as the large round monument. The large park they felt I was referring to most likely was the small Cessna airport, one of the very few small airports located within a major city anywhere in Japan.

Combing the area within the delta that was described as most likely the location of her residence, they found a three-story apartment building, with twelve rooms, rather than the six I had said. Checking the nameplate on the mailboxes though, lo and behold, they discovered the *maiden name of Mrs. A.* That specific mailbox belonged to the *backmost room* of the first floor. But the nameplate on the door held nothing.

Suspicious, the crew searched to find signs of someone inside, but there was originally no response. The crew asked some residents on the second floor, and learned that a woman in her fifties lived in that room. At that moment a man appeared from the room and was questioned by the crew. The man refused to speak, claiming he knew nothing. He quickly left on his motorcycle.

Sensing it might be dangerous to intrude any further, the crew instead went to the local city hall to check the records. They found that *indeed, that room was her residence.* (Mr. Noriyuki Ito has since written his mother a letter but has not yet received a response.)

The second missing person was a Mr. Saburo Tanaka. Again, the target's name was placed within a sealed envelope with the same questions attached.

I accurately described Mr. Tanaka and said that he lived in Tokyo. It was my perception that he was making himself hard to find because of money he owed from a debt incurred due to stock losses at a company he worked for.

Based on the information I provided, they have narrowed the search to a specific group of apartment complexes within a specific prefecture of Tokyo and are now searching that area. It is a continuing investigation.

Subsequent to the show's broadcast, a viewer phoned the studio to report the missing man as being his neighbor, living under an assumed name—in the apartments identified through remote viewing.

At the beginning of the show, the detective who is searching for Mr. Tanaka was asked if he believed in using psychics to hunt for people, and his response was a definite "no." It was his feeling that it was a waste of time.

During the filming of the show, he stated that he was totally surprised to hear me describe the missing man exactly and, with great detail, the reason he was being sought. He had in fact worked for a securities firm and there was a great deal of debt incurred as a result of bad investments. What he didn't know, however, was that his brother and the rest of his family had made good on these debts and just wanted him to come home. He stated that there was previous evidence that he had cashed checks in the area in which I had placed him.

The detective is now committed to a very detailed search of that area, and gave me his card after the show, inquiring as to my availability to help on future cases. He is now convinced that, used properly, remote viewing information can assist in at least providing new leads or narrowing down a search area dramatically.

The third case, an unsolved murder of a family of four—father, mother, daughter, and younger son, remains sealed since it involves an ongoing murder investigation. In that case, using photos of the victims, I gave an accurate description of the murder sequences in detail, a description of the killer, what he was wearing, and a motive for the murder. I also provided a beginning search area and suggested places for picking up a lead to finding the suspect. I guess in time I'll hear something.

At the end of the show, they asked a panel member to stand up. He had had his photograph taken on the way into the studio. They asked me if I could describe where he had been standing when the photograph was taken.

After a great deal of trouble, I finally said it wasn't going to be very detailed, because it appeared to be just a large, open space. I described the entry to the large open space as being a somewhat ornate tunnel-like passage.

When I saw the picture, I immediately realized they, like many others, had asked the wrong question. The individual was standing in the very empty courtyard of a large enclosure, circled by buildings. It was a very famous shrine in Tokyo. He had been kind enough to take a picture of the way into the open-spaced enclosure, which was through a complex shrine constructed of interlocking poles and beams—much like my drawing.

If only they had asked me to describe the actual target within which he was surrounded! I guess no one ever reads the literature.

There have been a lot of comments made regarding the September 11th events in New York City and Washington, D.C. Could remote viewing have prevented it from occurring?

There is evidence that precognitive information can be—and has been—given in the past about violent incidents that were about to occur. The problem is that it is almost impossible—at least in most cases—to positively identify the location without a great deal of effort and multiple remote viewings. In the case of New York, I believe there would have been sufficient details to identify both the city and the target beforehand.

Would that have stopped it from happening?

The real answer is that we will never know and, even more truthfully, probably not. The reason has to do mostly with belief. Someone has to believe that the complex course of actions that allowed it to happen are foreseeable and, therefore, preventable. I happen to agree with these statements, but most don't. I have to believe that, because that's how I make remote viewing work. I believe it is possible—and for me it is and always will be. I know that remote viewing is far from the perfect capability that many on the radical edge want to paint it as. I know that it is a continual and uphill battle just to find enough funding to keep the electricity going in the few labs that study it—never mind salaries. But, I also know from time to time it works, and surprisingly well.

It works when you have an open mind and aren't afraid to approach it—albeit with caution and respect. It works when you don't get all your information off the Internet, but take the time and trouble (and money) to hire the experts—the scientists who have spent a quarter of a century investigating it, using it, and testing it. You have to invest the time reading the appropriate literature, the stuff you find in the scientific journals.

The saddest part of all is that a lot of people out there are applying "remote viewing" right now who don't even understand what it is. They are calling what they do remote viewing because it sells—it opens the door to their fifteen minutes of fame.

It could be used in some small way, some controlled way, to assist in the defense of the country, to aid in the hunt for terrorists, to prevent or reduce the destruction and death of human beings. It can be used to investigate the creative mental endeavors we may require in meeting the future challenges to our survival as a species.

All it takes is an open mind—a disciplined nature—and a reasonable degree of personal ethics or responsibility.

Final Words

Understanding there are differences that exist between the terms "psychic" and "being psychic within remote viewing protocols," in the end, as in the beginning, we are still left with questions.

Can someone be trained as a psychic and remote viewer, like a lawyer or a carpenter? Or by necessity is there a natural talent present from the beginning?

Does it take a special kind of person to be a psychic? Does it have to be someone who has a predisposition for it from the outset?

Do psychic people have an advantage over the norm? Or is it the norm?

Should they profit from the use of their talent? Or should they donate their talent, reject personal wealth and fame, and live their lives as saints?

Is being psychic and a world-class remote viewer a gift from God? Is it the work of the devil?

Can one refuse the gift? *Should* one refuse the gift?

I've had to deal with many of these questions for well over two decades now. I'm still not sure about some of the answers. The only way to really understand the answers is to understand the context in which the questions were asked or the circumstances in which the answers were learned. To do that, one needs to have a very good feel for what it's like to be psychic, and even more difficult, what it's like to be psychic within the constraints of a valid remote viewing protocol. And the best way to accomplish that—other than being psychic and a remote viewer—is to have direct access to the mind of a psychic who is a remote viewer.

I have tried to present these issues herein. To do so, I did what I said I never would do—I opened a door to my own experience and reality as I've observed it. I also did this in a way I've never wanted to, by opening a doorway to my mind as well as my soul.

So this book was about me, my mind, my thoughts and experiences. It was a description, or perhaps only my perception, of how many steps it took to go from a being a child born in Miami, Florida, to an Army intelligence officer, then to psychic spy, Remote Viewer #001 of the United States Army Star Gate program.

But, it also became more than that.

I discovered, in digging through my past, nuggets of understanding for an entire process in my development. Being psychic, and especially a remote viewer, is a long-term growth process. The "gifts" someone is endowed with are derived from the essence of the soil—the person—in which the elements have been planted. It involves the kinds of fertilizer—or lack thereof—that encourage growth or stunts its process at critical points in development. It points to survival at a basic or possibly subliminal level as a necessary ingredient, and points out the very clear necessity that a person submit at times, not to logic, not to reasonable expectation, but to something even more primal that comes from somewhere deep within.

The journey hasn't been an easy one, as should be evident from the content herein. Certainly the path was never clearly marked. No signs said that my inner voice was more correct one minute than the next, and sometimes the feedback did not arrive before the next decision point. At times I wasn't even sure I was still on the path I had chosen. Even so, this journey has occupied my every moment for nearly two and a half decades, and, unconsciously, since birth.

I have now written it down to the best of my recall, in the hope that it may prove of value to those who follow. I've walked this jungle. Others on their own paths are facing the same kinds of threats and confusion in the tangled undergrowth one finds beneath a triple canopy of trees. Even in daylight, shadows shift, and it's difficult to spot the mines. I related my own experiences, the way my own mind has developed, birthed out of my experiences and exposure to the paranormal. It is the way that seems to work for me. I fervently hope that it will be of value to others.

Had I been asked if I was psychic, or thought that I could perform under the rigors of remote viewing, prior to the latter part of 1978, I would have said no. Like most humans, I believed, in spite of many experiences, that I was "normal," which dictates that psychic functioning does not occur. *Can* not occur. It's automatically thought to be a violation of reality, or how we understand reality to work. And if you can't be psychic, you most certainly can't do remote viewing.

But if that's true, then how was I hooked? Where and when did the conversion of a no-nonsense, fairly hardened career soldier take place?

Is it possible I was psychic all along? That I was supposed to be a remote viewer? Or did I learn how to be psychic? Did it occur over a long period of time, one change stacked atop another, or was it akin to being electrocuted—suddenly struck—as though by lightning?

And, as if these questions weren't hard enough, more suggest themselves.

Aren't some things a military remote viewer may be required to do morally objectionable? Can someone be psychic, be a remote viewer, when the very actions in which they participate are offensive or, at best, amoral?

Should we assume that someone who demonstrates a higher-than-expected level of functioning as a psychic and remote viewer represents what is "best" within the human race—that somehow such a person represents what we should strive for in human growth and understanding?

Should we place such people on a pedestal?

Should we always expect more from someone like that?

On the other hand, does admitting that one is psychic and a remote viewer demonstrate mental instability or self-delusion? Are some psychics crazy and some sane? Does one walk a fine line between the two, as though in a gray haze, somewhere between those who appear rational but maybe aren't and those who are solid through and through?

As a psychic and remote viewer, how do you know when you are slipping from sanity into insanity? Who do you go to to find out whether you are deluding yourself? Do you seek out another psychic? A friend? A scientist?

Are all scientists open-minded? Can't a scientist be deluded as well?

In the end, as in the beginning, we are left with questions.

Appendix A

Parapsychology in Intelligence: A Personal Review and Conclusions

Winter Issue—1977, *Studies in Intelligence,* an internal newsletter published within the Central Intelligence Agency. By Kenneth A. Kress, Ph.D., a senior analyst charged with reviewing the paranormal effort taking place at SRI-International on behalf of the CIA in the early 1970s, using psychics as spies against the Soviet Union.

Parapsychology in Intelligence

A Personal Review and Conclusions

—Dr. Kenneth A. Kress

The Central Intelligence Agency has investigated the controversial phenomenon called parapsychology as it relates to intelligence collection. The author was involved with many aspects of the last of such investigations. This paper summarizes selected highlights of the experiences of the author and others. The intent is not historical completeness. Files are available for those interested in details. Instead the intent is to record some certainly interesting and possibly useful data and opinions. This record is likely to be of future benefit to those who will be required to evaluate intelligence-related aspects of parapsychology.

The Stargate Chronicles

The Agency took the initiative by sponsoring serious parapsychological research, but circumstances, biases, and fear of ridicule prevented CIA from completing a scientific investigation of parapsychology and its relevance to national security. During this research period, CIA was buffeted with investigations concerning illegalities and improprieties of all sorts. This situation, perhaps properly so, raised the sensitivity of CIA's involvement in unusual activities. The "Proxmire Effect," where the fear that certain Government research contracts would be claimed to be ill-founded and held up for scorn, was another factor precluding CIA from sensitive areas of research. Also, there tend to be two types of reactions to parapsychology: positive or negative, with little in between. Parapsychological data, almost by definition, are elusive and unexplained. Add a history replete with proven frauds and many people instantly reject the subject, saying, in effect, "I would not believe this stuff even if it were true." Others, who must have had personal "conversion" experiences, tend to be equally convinced that one unexplained success establishes a phenomenon. These prejudices make it difficult to evaluate parapsychology carefully and scientifically.

Tantalizing but incomplete data have been generated by CIA-sponsored research. These data show, among other things, that on occasion unexplained results of genuine intelligence significance occur. This is not to say that parapsychology is a proven intelligence tool; it is to say that the evaluation is not yet complete and more research is needed.

Attention is confined to psychokinetics and remote viewing. Psychokinetics is the purported ability of a person to interact with a machine or other object by unexplained means. Remote viewing is akin to clairvoyance in that a person claims to sense information about a site or person removed from a known sensory link. Anecdotal reports of extrasensory perception (ESP) capabilities have reached U.S. national security agencies at least since World War II, when Hitler was said to rely on astrologers and seers. Suggestions for military applications of ESP continued to be received after World War II. For example, in 1952 the Department of Defense was lectured on the possible usefulness of extrasensory perception in psychological warfare.[18] Over the years, reports continued to accumulate.

---

[18] A. Puharich, "On the Possible Usefulness of Extrasensory Perception in Psychological Warfare," delivered to a 1952 Pentagon conference, *The Washington Post*, August 7, 1977.

In 1961, the reports induced one of the earliest U.S. government parapsychology investigations when the chief of CIA's Office of Technical Service (then the Technical Services Division) became interested in the claims of ESP. Technical Project Officers soon contacted Stephen I. Abrams, the Director of the Parapsychological Laboratory, Oxford University, England. Under the auspices of Project ULTRA, Abrams prepared a review article, which claimed ESP was demonstrated but not understood or controllable.[19] The report was read with interest but produced no further action for another decade.

Two laser physicists, Dr. Russell Targ and Dr. Harold E. Puthoff, reawakened CIA research in parapsychology. Targ had been avocationally interested in parapsychology for most of his adult life. As an experimentalist, he was interested in scientific observations of parapsychology. Puthoff became interested in the field in the early 1970s. He was a theoretician who was exploring new fields of research after extensive work in quantum electronics.

In April of 1972, Targ met with CIA personnel from the Office of Strategic Intelligence (OSI) and discussed the subject of paranormal abilities. Targ revealed that he had contacts with people who purported to have seen and documented some Soviet investigations of psychokinesis. Films of Soviets moving inanimate objects by "mental powers" were made available to analysts from OSI. They, in turn, contacted personnel from the Office of Research and Development (ORD) and OTS. An ORD Project Officer then visited Targ who had recently joined the Stanford Research Institute (SRI). Targ proposed that some psychokinetic verification investigations could be done at SRI in conjunction with Puthoff.

These proposals were quickly followed by a laboratory demonstration. A man was found by Targ and Puthoff who apparently had psychokinetic abilities. He was taken on a surprise visit to a superconducting shielded magnetometer being used in quark (high energy particle) experiments by Dr. A. Hebbard of Stanford University Physics Department. The quark experiment required that the magnetometer be as well shielded as technology would allow. Nevertheless, when the subject placed his attention on the interior of the magnetometer, the output signal was visibly disturbed, indicating a change in the internal magnetic field. Several other correlations of his mental efforts with signal variations were observed. These variations were

---

[19] S. I. Abrams, "Extrasensory Perception," Draft report, 14 December 1965.

never seen before or after the visit. The event was summarized and transmitted to the Agency in the form of a letter to an OSI analyst[20] and as discussions with OTS and ORD officers.

The Office of Technical Services took the first action. With the approval of the same manager who supported the ESP studies a decade previously, an OTS Project Officer contracted for a demonstration with the previously mentioned man for a few days in August, 1972. During this demonstration, the subject was asked to describe objects hidden out of sight by the CIA personnel. The subject did well. The descriptions were so startlingly accurate that the OTD and ORD representatives suggested that the work be continued and expanded. The same Director of OTS reviewed the data, approved another $2,500 work order, and encouraged the development of a more complete research plan.

By October, 1972, I was the Project Officer. I was chosen because of my physics background to work with the physicists from SRI. The Office of Technical Service funded a $50,000 expanded effort in parapsychology.[21] The expanded investigation included tests of several abilities of both the original subject and a new one. Curious data began to appear; the paranormal abilities seemed individualistic. For example, one subject, by mental effort, apparently caused an increase in the temperature measured by a thermistor; the action could not be duplicated by the second subject. The second subject was able to reproduce, with impressive accuracy, information inside sealed envelopes. Under identical conditions, the first subject could reproduce nothing. Perhaps even more disturbing, repeating the same experiment with the same subject did not yield consistent results. I began to have serious feelings of being involved with a fraud.

Approximately halfway through this project, the SRI contractors were invited to review their results. After careful consideration of the security and sensitivity factors, the results were shared and discussed with selected Agency personnel during that and subsequent meetings. In February, 1973, the most recent data were reviewed; thereafter, several ORD officers showed definite interest in contributing their own expertise and office funding.

The possibility of a joint OTS/ORD program continued to

---

[20]H. E. Puthoff, Stanford Research Institute, Letter to K. Green/OSI, June 27, 1972.

[21]Office of Technical Service Contract 8473, 1 October 1972 (CONFIDENTIAL).

develop. The Office of Research and Development sent new Project Officers to SRI during February 1973, and the reports that were brought back convinced ORD to become involved. Interest was translated into action when ORD requested an increase in the scope of the effort and transferred funds to OTS.[22] About this time, a third sensitive subject, Pat Price, became available at SRI, and the remote viewing experiments in which a subject describes his impressions of remote objects or locations began in earnest. The possibility that such useful abilities were real motivated all concerned to move ahead quickly.

The contract required additional management review before it could be continued or its scope increased. The initial review went from OTS and ORD to Mr. William Colby, then the DDO. On 24 April, Mr. Colby decided that the Executive Management Committee should pass judgment on this potentially sensitive project. By the middle of May, 1973, the approval request went through the Management Committee. An approval memorandum was written for the signature of the DCI, then Dr. James Schlesinger.[23] Mr. Colby took the memorandum to the DCI a few days later. I was soon told not to increase the scope of the project and not to anticipate any follow-on in this area. The project was too sensitive and potentially embarrassing. It should be tabled. It is interesting to note that OTS was then being investigated for involvement in the Watergate affair, and that in May 1973, the DCI issued a memorandum to all CIA employees requesting the reporting of any activities that may have been illegal and improper. As Project Officer, clearly my sense of timing had not been guided by useful paranormal abilities!

During the summer of 1973, SRI continued working informally with an OSI officer on a remote viewing experiment which eventually stimulated more CIA-sponsored investigations of parapsychology. The target was a vacation property in the eastern United States. The experiment began with the passing of nothing more than the geographic coordinates of the vacation property to the SRI physicists who, in turn, passed them to the two subjects, one of whom was Pat Price. No maps were permitted, and the subjects were asked to give an

---

[22]C/TSD; Memorandum for Assistant Deputy Director for Operations; Subject: Request for Approval of Contract; 20 April 1973 (SECRET).

[23]W. E. Colby; DDO; Memorandum for Director of Central Intelligence; Subject: Request for Approval of Contract; 4 May 1973 (SECRET).

immediate response of what they remotely viewed at these coordinates. The subject came back with descriptions, which were apparent misses. They both talked about a military-like facility. Nevertheless, a striking correlation of the two independent descriptions was noted. The correlation caused the OSI officer to drive to the site and investigate in more detail.

To the surprise of the OSI officer, he soon discovered a sensitive government installation a few miles from the vacation property. This discovery led to a request to have Price provide information concerning the interior workings of this particular site. All the data produced by the two subjects were reviewed in CIA and the Agency concerned.

The evaluation was, as usual, mixed.[24] Pat Price, who had no military or intelligence background, provided a list of project titles associated with current and past activities including one of extreme sensitivity. Also, the codename of the site was provided. Other information concerning the physical layout of the site was accurate. Some information, such as the names of the people at the site, proved incorrect.

These experiments took several months to be analyzed and reviewed within the Agency. Now Mr. Colby was DCI, and the new directors of OTS and ORD were favorably impressed by the data. In the fall of 1973, a Statement of Work was outlined, and SRI was asked to propose another program. A jointly funded ORD and OTS program was begun in February 1974.[25] The author again was the Project Officer. The project proceeded on the premise that the phenomena existed; the objective was to develop and utilize them.

The ORD funds were devoted to basic studies such as the identification of measurable physiological or psychological characteristics of psychic individuals, and the establishment of experimental protocols for validating paranormal abilities. The OTS funds were to evaluate the operational utility of psychic subjects without regard to the detailed understanding of paranormal functioning. If the paranormal functioning was sufficiently reproducible, we were confident applications would be found.

---

[24]K. Green; LSD/OSI; Memorandum for the Record; Subject: Verification of Remote Viewing Experiments at Stanford Research Institute; 9 November 1973. (SECRET)

[25]Office of Technical Service Contract, FAN 4125-4099, Office of Research and Development Contract, FAN 4162-8103; 1 February 1974 (CONFIDENTIAL).

Before many months had passed, difficulties developed in the project. Our tasking in the basic research area proved to be more extensive than time and funds would allow. The contractors wanted to compromise by doing all of the tasks with less completeness. The ORD scientists insisted that with such a controversial topic, fewer but more rigorous results would be of more value. The rigor of the research became a serious issue between the ORD Project Officers and SRI, with myself generally taking a position between the righteousness of the contractor and indignation of the researchers. Several meetings occurred over that issue.

As an example of the kinds of disputes, which developed over the basic research, consider the evaluation of the significance of data from the "ESP teaching machine" experiments. This machine was a four-state electronic random number generator used to test for paranormal abilities. SRI claimed the machine randomly cycled through four states, and the subject indicates the current machine state by pressing a button. The state of the machine and the subject's choice were recorded for later analysis. A subject "guessing" should, on the average, be correct 25 percent of the time. SRI had a subject who averaged a statistically very significant 29 percent for more than 2,500 trials.

I requested a review of the experiment and analysis, and two ORD officers quickly and skeptically responded. They first argued that the ESP machine was possibly not random. They further argued the subjects probably learned the nonrandom machine patterns and thereby produced higher scores.[26] During this review, it was noted that whether the machine was random or not, the data taken during the experiment could be analyzed to determine actual machine statistics. The machine's randomness was unimportant, because the subject's performance could then be compared with actual machine performance.[27] The ORD Project Officers, however, did not believe it would be worth the effort to do the extra analysis of the actual data.

I disagreed. I had the Office of Joint Computer Services redo the data analysis. The conclusion was that during the experiment "no evidence of nonrandomness was discovered" and there was "no solid

---

[26]L. W. Rook; LSR/ORD; Memorandum for OTS/CB; Subject: Evidence for Non-Randomness of Four-State Electronic Random Stimulus Generator; 12 June 1975 (CONFIDENTIAL).

[27]S. L. Cianci; LSR/ORD; Memorandum for OTS/CB; Subject: Response to Requested Critique, SRI Random Stimulus Generator Results; 12 June 1975 (CONFIDENTIAL).

reason *how* he was able to be so successful."[28] I further ordered the subject retested. He averaged more than 28 percent during another 2,500 trials. This information was given in written and oral form to the ORD Project Officers, who maintained there must be yet another flaw in the experiment or analysis, but it was not worth finding. Because of more pressing demands, the issue could not be pursued to a more definite conclusion.

Concurrent with this deteriorating state of affairs, new Directors of ORD and OTS were named again. Since neither Director had any background or experience in paranormal research, the new Director of ORD reviewed the parapsychology project and had reservations. I requested a meeting in which he said he could not accept this reality of paranormal functioning, but he understood his bias. He said that inasmuch as he could not make an objective decision in this field, he could simply follow the advice of his staff. The ORD Project Officers were feeling their own frustrations and uncertainties concerning the work and now had to face this unusual kind of skepticism of their new Director. The skepticism about the believability of the phenomenon and quality of the basic research adversely affected the opinions of many people in OTS. Support for the project was vanishing rapidly.

As these pressures mounted, the first intelligence collection operation using parapsychology was attempted. The target was the Semipalatinsk Unidentified Research and Development Facility-2 (URDF-2, formerly known as PNUTS). The experimental collection would use our best subject, Pat Price. From experience it was obvious that Price produced bad data as well as good.

Borrowing from classical communications theory concepts, this "noisy channel" of information could nevertheless be useful if it were characterized. An elaborate protocol was designed which would accomplish two characterization measurements. First, we needed assurance the channel was collecting useful data. I reviewed the photos of URDF-2 and chose two features, which, if Price described them, would show the channel at least partially working. Referring to Figure 1a, these features were the tall crane and the four structures resembling oil well derricks. It was agreed that if Price described these structures, I would be prepared to have him sign a secrecy agreement, making him witting, and collect more relevant intelli-

---

[28] G. Burow; OJCS/AD/BD; Memorandum for Dr. Kress; Subject: Analysis of the Subject-Machine Relationship; 8 October 1975 (CONFIDENTIAL).

gence details. Secondly, after a working channel was thus established, a signal-to-noise or quality characterization was required. This would be done by periodic tests of the channel—that is, periodically Price would be asked to describe features of URDF-2 which were known. The accuracy of these descriptions would be used to estimate the quality of the data we had no obvious way of verifying.

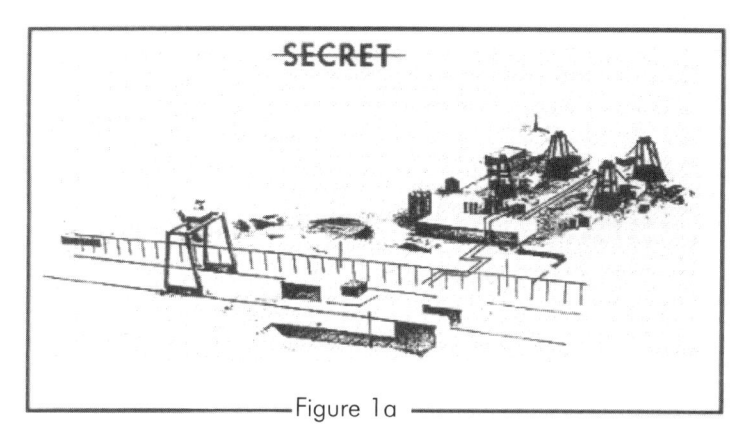

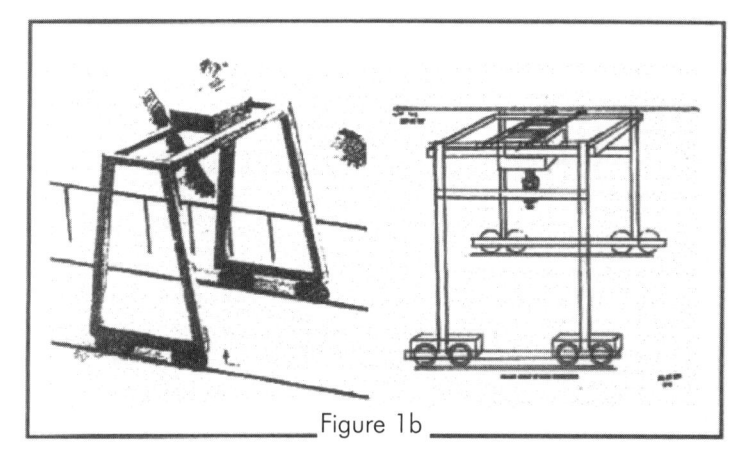

Figure 1a

Figure 1b

The experiment began with my Branch chief and me briefing Targ and Puthoff in a motel. Later, at SRI, Price was briefed by Targ and Puthoff. Since Targ and Puthoff presumably knew nothing about URDF-2, this protocol guarded against cueing and/or telepathy. Initially Price was given only the geographic coordinates, a world atlas map marked with the approximate location of URDF-2, and told it was a Soviet RD&E test site. Overnight, he produced the drawing on

The Stargate Chronicles

the bottom right of Figure 1b. Price further mentioned that this was a "damned big crane" because he saw a person walk by and he only came up to the axles on the wheels (note sketch, Figure 1b). This performance caught my attention; but with two more days of work, we never heard about the derricks. Eventually, a decision was needed. Because the crane was so impressive, my Branch chief and I decided the derricks description requirement should be relaxed and we should continue.

When the decision was made to make Price witting, I decided to test him. My Branch chief and I sat in a conference room while Targ and Puthoff brought a smiling Pat Price into the room. I was introduced as the sponsor, and I immediately asked Price if he knew me.

Yes.

Name?

Ken Kress.

Occupation?

Works for CIA.

Since I was then a covert employee, the response was meaningful. After having Price sign a secrecy agreement, and some discussions, I confronted him again. I rolled out a large version of Figure 1a and asked if he had viewed this site.

Yes, of course!

Why didn't you see the four derricks?

Wait, I'll check.

Price closed his eyes, put on his glasses (he "sees" better that way) and in a few seconds answered "I didn't see them because they are not there any more." Since my data were three or four months old, there was no rejoinder to the implied accusation that my data were not good. We proceeded and completed a voluminous data package.

In a few weeks, the latest URDF-2 reconnaissance was checked. Two derricks were partially disassembled, but basically all four were visible. In general, most of Price's data were wrong or could not be evaluated. He did, nevertheless, produce some amazing descriptions, like buildings then under construction, spherical tank sections, and the crane in Figure 1b. Two analysts, a photo interpreter at IAS[29] and a nuclear analyst at Los Alamos Scientific Laboratories, agreed that Price's description of the crane was accurate; the nuclear analyst wrote that "one: he, the subject, actually saw it through remote view-

---

[29]W. T. Strand; C/ESO/IAS; Memorandum for Director, Officer of Technical Service; Subject: Evaluation of Data on Semipalatinsk Unidentified R&D Facility No. 3, USSR; 20 August 1974 (SECRET).

ing, or two: he was informed what to draw by someone knowledgeable of URDF-2."[30] But, again, because there was so much bad information mixed in with the good, the overall result was not considered useful. As proof of remote viewing, the data are at best inconclusive. The ORD officers concluded that since there were no control experiments to compare with, the data were nothing but lucky guessing.

I began to doubt my own objectivity in evaluating the significance of paranormal abilities to intelligence collection. It was clear that the SRI contractors were claiming success while ORD advisors were saying the experiments were not meaningful because of poor experimental design. As a check on myself, I asked for a critique of the investigation from a disinterested consultant, a theoretical physicist with broad intellectual background. His first task was to evaluate the field of parapsychology without knowledge of the CIA data. After he had completed this critique, I asked him to acquaint himself with the CIA data, and then to reassess the field. The first investigation produced genuine interest in paranormal functioning as a valid research area. After being acquainted with CIA data, his conclusion was, "a large body of reliable experimental evidence points to the inescapable conclusion that extrasensory perception does exist as a real phenomenon, albeit characterized by rarity and lack of reliability."[31] This judgment by a competent scientist gave impetus to continue serious inquiry into parapsychology.

Because of the general skepticism and mixed results of the various operational experiments, a final challenge was issued by OTS management: OTS is not in the research business; do something of genuine operational significance. Price was chosen, and suggestions were solicited from operational personnel in both OTS and the DDO. An intriguing idea was selected from audio collection systems. A test to determine if remote viewing could help was suggested. The interiors of two foreign embassies were known to the audio teams who had made entries several years previously. Price was to visit these embassies by his remote viewing capability, locate the coderooms, and come up with information that might allow a member of the

---

[30] D. Stillman; Los Alamos Scientific Laboratory; "An Analysis of a Remote Viewing Experiment of URDF-2"; 4 December 1975 (CONFIDENTIAL).

[31] J. A. Ball; "An Overview of Extrasensory Perception"; Report to CIA, 27 January 1975

audio team to determine whether Price was likely to be of operational use in subsequent operations. Price was given operationally acceptable data such as the exterior photographs and the geographical coordinates of the embassies. In both cases, Price correctly located the coderooms. He produced copious data, such as the location of interior doors and colors of marble stairs and fireplaces that were accurate and specific. As usual, much was also vague and incorrect. Regardless, the operations officer involved concluded, "It is my considered opinion that this technique—whatever it is—offers definite operational possibilities."[32]

This result was reviewed within OTS and the DDO, and various suggestions for potential follow-on activities were formulated.[33] This package of requirements, plus the final results of the current contract, were reviewed at several meetings within OTS and ORD. The results of those meetings are as follows:

1. According to the ORD Project Officers, the research was not productive or even competent; therefore, research support to SRI was dropped. The Director of OTS felt the OTS charter would not support research; therefore, all Agency funding in paranormal research stopped.

2. Because of the mixed results, the operational utility of the capability was considered questionable but deserved further testing.

3. To achieve better security, all the operations-oriented testing with the contractor was stopped, and a personal services contract with Price was started.

4. Since I was judged to be a positively biased advocate of paranormal functioning, the testing and evaluation of Price would be transferred to a more pragmatic OTS operations psychologist.

---

[32] S/AOB/OTS; Memorandum for the Record; Subject: Parapsychology/"Remote Viewing"; 20 April 1976 (SECRET).

[33] Chief/Division D/DDO; Memorandum for C/D&E; Subject: Perceptual Augmentation Techniques; 24 January 1975 (SECRET); AC/SE/DDO; Memorandum for C/D&E; Subject: Perceptual Augmentation Testing; 14 January 1975 (SECRET); C/EA/DDO; Memorandum for Director of Technical Service; Subject: Exploration of Operational Potential of "Paranormals"; 5 February 1975 (SECRET); C/Libya/EL/NE/DDO; Memorandum for OTS/CB; Subject: Libyan Desk Requirement for Psychic Experiments Relating to Libya; 31 January 1975 (SECRET); CI/Staff/DDO; Memorandum for the Record; Subject: SR I Experiment; 12 December 1974 (SECRET).

The OTS psychologist picked up his new responsibilities and chose to complete an unfinished DDO requirement. The origin of the requirement went back to the fall of 1974 when several OTS engineers became aware of the parapsychology project in OTS and had volunteered to attempt remote viewing. They passed initial remote viewing tests at SRI with some apparent successes. To test these OTS insiders further, I chose a suggested requirement to obtain information about a Libyan site described only by its geographic coordinates. The OTS engineers described new construction which could be an SA-5 missile training site.[34] The Libyan Desk officer was immediately impressed. He then revealed to me that an agent had reported essentially the same story. More coordinates were quickly furnished but were put aside by me.

The second set of Libyan geographic coordinates was passed by the OTS psychologist to Price. A report describing a guerrilla training site was quickly returned. It contained a map-like drawing of the complex. Price described a related underwater sabotage training facility site several hundred kilometers away on the sea coast. This information was passed to the Libyan Desk. Some data were evaluated immediately, some were evaluated only after ordering special reconnaissance. The underwater sabotage training facility description was similar to a collateral agent's report. The Libyan Desk officer quickly escalated the requirement to what was going on inside those buildings, the plans and intentions, etc.[35] The second requirements list was passed to Pat Price. Price died of a heart attack a few days later, and the program stopped. There have been no further CIA-sponsored intelligence collection tests.

Since July, 1975, there has been only modest CIA and Intelligence Community Staff interest in parapsychology. The Office of Scientific Intelligence completed a study about Soviet military and KGB applied parapsychology.[36] During November of 1976, Director George Bush became aware that official Soviets were visiting and questioning Puthoff and Targ at SRI about their work in parapsychology. Mr. Bush requested and received a briefing on CIA's investigations into parapsychology. Before there was any official reaction, he left the Agency.

---

[34] OTS/SDB; Notes on Interviews with F. P., E. L., C. J., K. G., and V. C., January 1975 (SECRET).
[35] DDO/NE; Memorandum for OTS/BAB; Subject: Experimental Collection Activity Relating to Libya; 8 October 1975 (SECRET).
[36] T. Hamilton; LSD/OSI; "Soviet and East European Parapsychology Research," SI 77-10012, April 1977 (SECRET/NOFORN).

The Stargate Chronicles

Various intelligence community groups, such as the Human Resources Subcommittee on R&D, have exhaustively reviewed parapsychology in CIA, DOD, and the open research, but have failed to conclude whether parapsychology is or is not a worthwhile area for further investigation. Several proposals from SRI and other contractors were received by CIA but none were accepted. There are no current plans for CIA to fund parapsychology investigations.

POSTSCRIPT

At this point, I have traced the action and reaction of various elements of CIA to what is certainly an unconventional and highly controversial subject. Also of interest are the concurrent reactions of other agencies to parapsychology. In August, 1973, parapsychology was discussed with several members of DIA. The DIA people were basically interested in the Soviet activities in this area, and expressed considerable interest in our own fledgling results. Numerous meetings have occurred during the past several years. DIA remains interested on a low priority basis.

The Army Materiel Command learned of CIA interest in the paranormal. We discovered the Army interest was generated by data which emerged from Vietnam. Apparently certain individuals called point men, who led patrols into hostile territory, had far fewer casualties from booby traps and ambushes than the average. These point men, needless to say, had a loyal following of men and, in general, greatly helped the morale of their troops under a brutal, stressful situation. The Army gave extensive physical and psychological tests to a group of unusually successful point men and came to no conclusion other than perhaps that paranormal capabilities may be the explanation! The Army was most interested in CIA results and wanted to stay closely informed. After a few more follow-up meetings, the Army Materiel Command was never heard from again.

The Defense Advanced Research Projects Agency (DARPA) reported that they had not only a showing of interest but a hostile response as well to the subject area. At one time, we felt we had the strong interest of some people at DARPA to discuss our data. The SRI contractors and I went to a briefing where we had a several-hour confrontation with an assemblage of hostile DARPA people who had been convened especially to debunk our results. After a long, inconclusive, emotional discussion, we left. Contacts with DARPA stopped for several years. The Navy reviewed part of the work and became interested. Some groups developed strong interest, and minor funding was provided to SRI by Navy to replicate one of SRI's earlier experiments under more controlled conditions. The experiment was replicated. Then the Navy asked SRI to repeat the same experiment under different conditions. An effect was observed, but it was not the same as the previous observations. About this same time, the Navy became very concerned about this research being "mind warfare"-related. Funding was stopped.

The active funding for parapsychology now has shifted to the Air Force's Foreign Technology Division with the addition of modest testing being completed by another group at DARPA. These investigations are not yet completed, but a second phase is funded by the Air Force. The Air Force project is attempting to evaluate whether signals and communications can be sent and received by paranormal functioning. Also aircraft and missile intelligence which can be verified is being gathered and evaluated. To date the results are more consistent than those seen during the CIA research, but still they are mixed. Some simple experiments seemed very impressive and conclusive. The more complex experiments are difficult to assess.

In the non-government world an explosion of interest in unclassified parapsychology research occurred after the first publication of CIA-sponsored projects. Books have been written, prestigious professional societies have had sessions on parapsychology, and several national news reports have been broadcast and printed.[37] Director Turner revealed publicly that CIA has had operational interest in parapsychology.[38] The open publication of these investigations is generally

---

[37] R. Targ and H. Puthoff; "Information Transfer Under Conditions of Sensory Shielding"; *Nature*, CC LII, 602-607 (October 18, 1974); H. Puthoff and R. Targ; "A Perceptual Channel for Information Transfer Over Kilometer Distances; Historical Perspective and Recent Research"; *Proceedings of the IEEE*, LXIV (March 1976, Number 3, 329-354); R. Targ and H. Puthoff; "Mind-Research Scientists Look at Psychic Ability"; Delacarte Press (1977); J. Wilhelm; "The Search for Superman"; Dell (1974); IEEE Conference on Man; Systems and Cybernetics; Washington (1976 and 1977); NBC Nightly News; 4 and 5 August 1976; NBC Today; 9 August 1976; J. Wilhelm, "Psychic Spying?"; *The Washington Post*, Outlook Section, August 7, 1977.

[38] J. O'Leary, "Turner Denies CIA Bugging of South Korea's Park," *The Washington Star*, 9 August 1977.

healthy and helpful. It shows a reduction of associated emotionalism and bias. These publications will also stimulate other scientific investigations into parapsychology.

There is a less positive aspect to open interest and publications. Before adequate assessment was made by the CIA and others, we may have allowed some important national security information out into the public domain. It is my opinion that, as it relates to intelligence, sufficient understanding and assessment of parapsychology has not been achieved. There are observations, such as the original magnetic experiments at Stanford University, the OSI remote viewing, the OTS-coderoom experiments, and others done for the Department of Defense, that defy explanation. Coincidence is not likely, and fraud has not been discovered. The implication of these data cannot be determined until the assessment is done.

If the above is true, how is it that the phenomenon remains controversial and receives so little official government support? Why is it that the proper assessment was never made? This state of affairs occurs because of the elementary understanding of parapsychology and because of the peculiarities of the intelligence and military organizations which have attempted the assessments. There is no fundamental understanding of the mechanisms of paranormal functioning, and the reproducibility remains poor. The research and experiments have successfully demonstrated abilities but have not explained them nor made them reproducible. Past and current support of parapsychology comes from applications-oriented intelligence and military agencies. The people managing such agencies demand quick and relevant results. The intelligence and military agencies, therefore, press for results before there is sufficient experimental reproducibility or understanding of the physical mechanisms. Unless there is a major breakthrough in understanding, the situation is not likely to change as long as applications-oriented agencies are funding parapsychology. Agencies must commit long-term basic research funds and learn to confine attention to testing only abilities which at least appear reproducible enough to be used to augment other hard collection techniques (example: use parapsychology to help target hard intelligence collection techniques and determine if the take is thereby increased). Parapsychology, like other technical issues, can then rise or fall on its merits and not stumble over bureaucratic charters and conjectures proposed by people who are irrevocably on one side or the other in the controversial area.

Appendix B

"Psi Conducive States,"
Journal of Communications, pp. 142–152 (1975)
—William Braud[39]

According to findings from research into different areas of study, including altered states of consciousness, cognitive psychology, hemispheric studies, Eastern and esoteric philosophies, mystical tradition, and parapsychology, he suggested that what he called a "Psi-conducive syndrome" did indeed exist, and that it "has seven major characteristics. Some of these characteristics (or "syndromes") are physiological, some are psychological, and others are phenomenological."

While these depict specific psi-conducive states and not specific remote viewer characteristics, they do indirectly provide us with things we should be paying attention to or that might be necessary in a remote viewer. These are:

a. Subjects should be physically relaxed.

b. There is a reduction in physical arousal or activation.

c. There is a reduction in sensory input and processing.

d. Subjects should have an increased awareness of internal processes, feelings, and images (including dreams and fantasy).

e. Psi functioning should decrease with "action mode/left hemi-

---

[39] William Braud at the time was an associative professor of psychology at the University of Houston, Texas.

spheric functioning" and increase with "receptive mode/right hemispheric functioning."

f. Subjects should have an altered view of the nature of the world.

g. The act of psychic functioning must be (at least) momentarily important.

To the above criteria Fred Atwater added that within the military structure other possible indicators might be:

a. The person would be successful at whatever the task.

b. They would be liked by their peers but considered to be different from the norm.

c. Generally operate outside normal boundaries.

d. Be willing to pursue new avenues of approach.

e. Open to whatever works.

f. Capable of critical thought and unafraid to voice an opinion.

g. Highly and uniquely creative.

Appendix C

Legion of Merit and Certificate

THE UNITED STATES OF AMERICA

TO ALL WHO SHALL SEE THESE PRESENTS, GREETING: THIS IS TO CERTIFY THAT THE PRESIDENT OF THE UNITED STATES OF AMERICA AUTHORIZED BY ACT OF CONGRESS 20 JULY 1942 HAS AWARDED

THE LEGION OF MERIT

TO CHIEF WARRANT OFFICER TWO JOSEPH W. MCMONEAGLE
UNITED STATES ARMY

FOR distinguishing himself by exceptionally meritorious conduct in the performance of outstanding services during his Army career, culminating in his assignment as Special Project Intelligence Officer with the 902d Military Intelligence Group from 1 August 1974 to 1 September 1984. He was instrumental in developing a new, revolutionary intelligence project. He resourcefully supported national-level agencies with critical intelligence, often performing operations single-handedly. Chief Warrant Officer Two McMoneagle's distinguished performance of duty throughout this period represents outstanding accomplishments in the most cherished traditions of the United States Army and reflects utmost credit upon him and the military service.

GIVEN UNDER MY HAND IN THE CITY OF WASHINGTON
THIS 18th DAY OF May 19 84

Major General, USA
Commanding

SECRETARY OF THE ARMY

CW2 Joseph McMoneagle has brought great distinction upon himself, INSCOM and the United States Army throughout his military career by total dedication to the highest ideals of service and selfless commitment to our nation. From Aug 1974 to Sep 1984, he served as an Electronic Warfare Detachment Commander, Field Station Augsburg, for which he was hand-picked to successfully restore an ailing organization to operational health, and which he successfully accomplished; Operations Sergeant at Field Station Augsburg, where he was instrumental in achieving smooth functioning and efficient mission accomplishment; and Senior Emitter Location Identification Techniques Officer, DCSOPS, USAINSCOM. During this time he was a primary designer of the new, much-heralded AN/TSQ-114 Trailblazer tactical direction finding system, and participated in the modification of the AN/TRQ-32 DF system as well as the development of the AN/TSQ-112 emitter locater system's operational deployment concept. He served most recently as Special Project Intelligence Officer for SSPD, SSD, 902d MI Gp, as one of the original planners and movers of a unique intelligence project that is revolutionizing the intelligence community. While with SSPD, he used his talents and expertise in the execution of missions for the highest echelons of our military and government, including such national level agencies as the Joint Chiefs of Staff, DIA, NSA, CIA, and Secret Service, producing critical intelligence unavailable from any other source. His adept management skills and leadership were instrumental in establishing this project's unique capabilities and impressive reputation. Additionally, he fulfilled vital responsibilities as ADP officer. Under his initiative, guidance and supervision, a 160 mega-byte data and word-processing system was obtained, programmed and assimilated into the project. His procurement of this system not only revolutionized procedures and expedited mission accomplishment, but allowed development of capabilities otherwise impossible to achieve. CW2 McMoneagle's broad knowledge of new technologies, intuitive ability to "cut through" extraneous details to the true heart of complex issues, and his unsurpassed knack for accomplishing tasks impossible for individuals of lesser scope and imagination have all helped make him virtually irreplaceable. CW2 McMoneagle was in the demanding position of carrying the entire operational load himself--a responsibility he accomplished with great acumen and resolve. CW2 McMoneagle's drive, high moral fiber, consummate skills, and ultimate accomplishments serves as a model for the ideal soldier. His many valuable contributions in service to this nation will be felt for years to come.

Works Cited

ABC *Nightline,* November 1995.

Abrams, S. I. "Extrasensory Perception." Draft report, 14 December 1965.

Ball, J. A. "An Overview of Extrasensory Perception." Report to CIA, 27 January 1975.

Battle TV. Japan.

Braud, William. "Psi Conductive States." *Journal of Communications,* 1975, 142–52.

Burow, G. OJCS/AD/BD; Memorandum for Dr. Kress; Subject: Analysis of the Subject-Machine Relationship; 8 October 1975 (CONFIDENTIAL).

C/TSD; Memorandum for Assistant Deputy Director for Operations; Subject: Request for Approval of Contract; 20 April 1973 (SECRET).

Chief/Division D/DDO; Memorandum for C/D&E; Subject: Perceptual Augmentation Techniques; 24 January 1975 (SECRET); AC/SE/DDO; Memorandum for C/D&E; Subject: Perceptual Augmentation Testing; 14 January 1975 (SECRET); C/EA/DDO; Memorandum for Director of Technical Service; Subject: Exploration of Operational Potential of "Paranormals"; 5 February 1975 (SECRET); C/Libya/EL/NE/DDO; Memorandum for OTS/CB; Subject: Libyan Desk Requirement for Psychic Experiments Relating to Libya; 31 January 1975 (SECRET); CI/Staff/DDO; Memorandum for the Record; Subject: SRI Experiment; 12 December 1974 (SECRET).

Cianci, S. L. LSR/ORD; Memorandum for OTS/CB; Subject: Response to Requested Critique, SRI Random Stimulus Generator Results; 12 June 1975 (CONFIDENTIAL).

Colby, W. E. DDO; Memorandum for Director of Central Intelligence; Subject: Request for Approval of Contract; 4 May 1973 (SECRET).

DDO/NE Memorandum for OTS/BAB; Subject: Experimental Collection Activity Relating to Libya; 8 October 1975 (SECRET).

Encyclopedia of the U.S. Military. New York: Harper Business, 1990.

Goslin, David A. *Enhancing Human Performance: Issues, Theories, and Techniques.* Summarized by Swets and Bjork, Washington, D.C.: National Academy Press. 1990.

Green, K. LSD/OSI; Memorandum for the Record; Subject: Verification of Remote Viewing Experiments at Stanford Research Institute; 9 November 1973. (SECRET)

Grose, Peter. *Operation Rollback: America's Secret War Behind the Iron Curtain.* Boston: Houghton Mifflin Co., 2000, p. 61.

Hamilton, T. LSD/OSI; "Soviet and East European Parapsychology Research," SI 77-10012, April 1977 (SECRET/NOFORN).

http://boojum.hut.fi/triennial/squid.html

http://www.af.mil/news/factsheets/AGM_86B_C_Missiles.html

http://www.remyc.com/squid.html

IEEE conference on Man; Systems and Cybernetics; Washington (1976-1977)

Kress, Kenneth. "Parapsychology in Intelligence: A Personal Review and Conclusions." In *Studies in Intelligence.* Winter, 1977.

McMoneagle, Joseph. *Mind Trek.* Charlottesville, Va.: Hampton Roads Publishing, 1997.

———. *Remote Viewing Secrets: A Handbook.* Charlottesville, Va.: Hampton Roads Publishing, 2000.

———. *The Ultimate Time Machine*. Charlottesville, Va.: Hampton Roads Publishing, 1998.

———. "Perceptions of a Paranormal Subject". *Journal of Parapsychology* 61:2.(1997).

Mickolus, Edward F., Todd Sandler, and Jean M. Murdock. *International Terrorism in the 1980's: A Chronology of Events, 1980–1983*. Ames, Iowa: Iowa State University Press, 1989.

NBC Nightly News; 4 and 5 August 1976.

NBC Today; 9 August 1976

O'Leary, J. "Turner Denies CIA Bugging of South Korea's Park," *The Washington Star*, 9 August 1977.

Office of Technical Service Contract 8473, 1 October 1972 (CONFIDENTIAL).

Office of Technical Service Contract, FAN 4125-4099, Office of Research and Development Contract, FAN 4162-8103; 1 February 1974 (CONFIDENTIAL).

OTS/SDB; Notes on Interviews with F. P., E. L., C. J., K. G., and V. C., January 1975 (SECRET).

McKenna, Paul and Giles O'Bryen. *The Paranormal World of Paul McKenna—"Telepathy."* in London: Faber and Faber, 1997.

Puharich, A. "On the Possible Usefulness of Extrasensory Perception in Psychological Warfare," speech delivered to a 1952 Pentagon conference. Reported in the *Washington Post*, August 7, 1977.

Puthoff, H. E. Stanford Research Institute, Letter to K. Green/OSI, June 27, 1972.

Puthoff, H. and R. Targ; "A Perceptual Channel for Information Transfer Over Kilometer Distances; Historical Perspective and Recent Research"; Proceedings of the IEEE, LXIV (March 1976, No. 3, 329-354)

Rook, L. W.; LSR/ORD; Memorandum for OTS/CB; Subject: Evidence for Non-Randomness of Four-State Electronic Random Stimulus Generator; 12 June 1975 (CONFIDENTIAL).

S/AOB/OTS; Memorandum for the Record; Subject: Parapsychology/"Remote Viewing"; 20 April 1976 (SECRET). Parapsychology in Intelligence: A Personal Review and Conclusions.

Stillman, D.; Los Alamos Scientific Laboratory; "An Analysis of a Remote Viewing Experiment of URDF-2"; 4 December 1975 (CONFIDENTIAL).

Strand, W. T.; C/ESO/IAS; Memorandum for Director, Officer of Technical Service; Subject: Evaluation of Data on Semipalatinsk Unidentified R&D Facility No. 3, USSR; 20 August 1974 (SECRET).

Targ, R. and H. Puthoff; "Information Transfer Under Conditions of Sensory Shielding." *Nature*, CC LII, 602-607, October 18, 1974

Targ, R. and H. Puthoff; "Mind-Research Scientists Look at Psychic Ability." Delacarte Press, 1977

Wilhelm, J. "Psychic Spying?" *The Washington Post*, Outlook Section, August 7, 1977.

Wilhelm, J. *The Search for Superman*. Pocket Books, 1976

Index

902nd Military Intelligence Group, 72
   conference room, 75
ABC special, 231, 236, 243
Abrams, Stephen I., 271, 289
Abrams XM-1, 96
African Congo, Zaire, 114
Air Force Intelligence Agency (AFIA), 132
Air Force's Foreign Technology Division, 283
Alexander, John, 143
Alexander, Secretary of the Army Clifford, 92
altered states of consciousness, 285
American Association for the Advancement of Science, xxiv, 259
American Embassy in Tehran, Iran, 109
American Institutes for Research (AIR), 237
   report, 160
Analects of Confucius, 50
Apocrypha, 50
Archbishop Curley, 19
Army Intelligence and Security Command (INSCOM), 132
Army Materiel Command, The, 282
astral projection, 139
Atwater, 1st Lt. Frederick "Skip,"
   as the viewer, 91
   counterintelligence officer, 72
   introduction of, 67
   monitor, 87, 163
   operations officer, 101, 109
   temporary departure of, 132
   TMI relationship, 139, 148-150
   See also Monroe Institute, The
Augsburg, Germany, 56, 58-62, 64-65, 113
automated data processing (ADP), 66
automatic ridicule, 73
background investigation, 73
Bad Aibling, 46
Bahamas, 37, 53
Bangkok, 53, 55
Bányai, Dr. Eva, 256
Barney, 66, 136, 176-178
Battle TV, 251, 289
Bee, Lt. Col., 161-162, 183
Bell, Capt. Kenneth (Ken), 102, 207, 209
   counterintelligence officer, 77
   introduction of, 77
   observer, 87
Blavatsky, Madame, 50
border site commander, 46-47, 56, 60
Bosch, CW2 Gary M., 158
"Branch,"
   calls from, 107, 157
   negotiations with, 132
   Special Action members, 154
   support of, 128
Braud, William, 289
bright cone of light, 40

293

British MI5, 249
Buchanan, Lyn, 163
Buckley, William, 208
Buddhism, 50, 53
Building 2560, 95
Building 2561, 94
"Bullseye," 41
Bureau of Alcohol, Tobacco, and Firearms (ATF), 132
Bush, George, 281
Carlos the Jackal, 119
Carter, President Jimmy, 113-114
Castaneda, Carlos, 50
Castorr, Brig. Gen L. Robert, vii, ix
Central Intelligence Agency. See CIA
CHEC unit, 169-170
    See also Monroe Institute, The
checks and counterchecks, 191
CIA,
    claims, 115, 237
    experiments, 90-91
    Office of Technical Service, 271
    Public Affairs Office, 159
    research, 159, 271, 283
    sponsored investigations, 273, 281
    supporting the, 132
    tasking, 110
clairvoyance, xii, 270
classified documents, 76
clearance, 74, 92, 144
code word materials, 71
cognitive psychology, 285
Colby, William, 273-274, 290
collection missions, 90, 110, 158
combat racquetball, 125
combat vets, 148
Commission on Behavioral and Social Sciences and Education (CBASSE), 237
Communist Party, 74
counterintelligence, 63, 74, 79, 88, 154
Cowart, Robert, v, 134, 149, 160
crane, 71, 233, 276, 278
Crawford, Daniel, 199
Dames, Capt. Ed, 163
David Francis Hall, 152

    See also Monroe Institute, The
DCI, 273-274
DDO, 273, 279-281, 289-290
Defense Advanced Research Projects Agency, The (DARPA), 282
Defense Intelligence Agency (DIA), 111, 132
deputy chief of staff, 66, 115, 158, 174, 179
derricks, 276, 278
Desert One, 111
Dhammapada, 50
Director of the Parapsychological Laboratory, 271
disbelief, 80, 82
Discovery Channel, 251
double-blind condition, xi
Dozier, Brig. Gen., 115-117, 119-120, 208
Drug Enforcement Agency (DEA), 132
eleuthera, 37-38, 40-41
Elkins, Susan, 231
Encyclopedia of the U.S. Military, 88, 290
Enhancing Human Performance, 237, 290
espionage, 74
Europe,
    bases closing in, 61
    NDE in, 80
    terrorism in, 133
extrasensory perception (ESP), 272, 275, 279, 289
    in psychological warfare, 270, 291
"false awakenings," 204
father,
    and alcoholism, 5, 15, 21
    childhood of, 8-9
    death of, 147
    lesson from, 11
    marriage to mother, 5
    religion, 14
    the gentleman, 8, 11
Feathers, Sally, 54, 245
Federal Bureau of Investigation (FBI), 132

Flynn, Brigadier General, 63, 113-114, 132
Ford, Angela, 210
Foreman, Gemma, v, 160
Fort,
  Benjamin Harrison, 66
  Huachuca, 134
  Jackson, 28, 30-31, 94
  Meade, 72, 75
Franks, Lieutenant Colonel, 134, 136-138
Freeze, General, 68, 73
Friede, Eleanor, 181
frightening, 2, 50, 79, 141
functional accuracy and reliability, 217
Gary, 158, 189, 209-210
Gates, Robert, 122
Gateway at the Institute for INSCOM officers,
  See RAPT program
Gateway Seminar, 140-141, 143, 151, 165
  See also Monroe Institute, The
general background, 80
general traits, 73
Ginsberg, Samuel, 74
Gods that People Play, 181
Gorsuch, Dr., 194
Goslin, David A., 237-238, 240, 290
Graff, Dale, 119
"great guess," 82
Great Skill, 158
grief, 131, 142, 178, 194
Grill Flame,
  See also Star Gate
  project name change, 98
  project office, 101
Grose, Peter, 74, 290
Hammid, Hella, v, 189
Harvard, 259
Hebbard, Dr. A., 271
Hemi-Sync, 141, 148, 152
  See also Monroe Institute, The
Hepatitis B, 55
Higgins, Lt. Col. William, 172, 176-177, 184, 207
Hitler, 270

Hodgkin's disease, 130
Homestead AFB, 41-42
Honeycutt, Bud, 188
Honeycutt, Nancy,
  marriage to, 188-189
  meeting, 140
  TMI director, 198
  TMI trainer, 167
House Committee, 74
Houston, Texas, 231, 285
Human Intelligence Collection, 161
human superskills, 72
human use requirements, 91
HUMINT, 174-175, 179
Humphries, Beverly, 189
Hungary, 256
hurricane Betsy, 38
Hyman, Dr. Raymond, 238
individual intelligence problems, 133
informational boundaries, 83
insanity, 78, 157, 268
Intelligence and Security Command (INSCOM), 65, 132
intelligence,
  branches, 74
  -related aspects of parapsychology, 269
Intuitive Intelligence Applications, Inc., 184
intuitive nature, 31, 45-46
Iranian affair, 110
Iranian revolutionaries, 109
Italian ANSA news agency, 117
Ito, Noriyuki, 261, 263
  mother, 261
J. B. Rhine Research Center, 245, 250
Jager, Melissa, 140
Japan, 250, 252, 261-263, 289
Jimmy, 16, 28
Journal of Parapsychology, 259, 291
Karanja, 170
Keenan, Major, 76-78
Keith, Jackie, v, 112, 130, 189
KGB, 281
Kimbrough Army Hospital, 94, 127
Kress, Dr. Kenneth, 71, 269, 290
Krivitsky, Walter G., 74

Kron, Dr. Irving L., 256
LaBerge, Dr. Stephen, 199
Lantz, Dr. Nevin, 189, 215
Lawrence Livermore Laboratory, 216-217
Legion of Merit, viii, xxv, 179, 287-288
Litsa Guba, 123
live demonstration, 82, 259
live television, 230
LMNO Productions, 230
LSD experiments, 91
lucid dream state (LDS), 200-206
"luck," 12, 64, 82
M.I.A.S., 152-153
Maahs, Ralph, 67-68, 73
Macatee, Bill, 232
Maher, Richard, 65
Marciano, Rocky, 10
May, Dr. Edwin, xxi, 189
McKenna, Paul, 248-249, 291
McMoneagle, Elizabeth, 15
McMoneagle, Joseph
  1998 surgery, 54, 255-256
  accident on the Beltway, 135
  Aunt Margaret, 1
  disability pay, 129
  disc injury, 126
  divorce, 57, 61, 81, 157, 187
  divorce, effects of, 131
  Elizabeth, sister. See McMoneagle, Elizabeth
  employee of the SRI lab, 185
  exhaustion, 126, 133, 148
  health, ix, 21, 110, 125, 261, 302
  heart attacks, 192-195
  high school, 5, 18, 21-25, 42, 58, 146
  Kathleen, sister. See McMoneagle, Kathleen
  Margaret, sister. See McMoneagle, Margaret
  marriage, first. See Sue
  marriage, second. See Murphy, Margaret Mary
  marriage, third. See Honeycutt, Nancy
  Mary, sister. See McMoneagle, Mary
  near-death experience, 54
  parents. See father; mother
  pets. See Barney
  son. See McMoneagle, Scott
McMoneagle, Kathleen, 16, 29-30
McMoneagle, Margaret, 4, 7-8, 13-16
  and mother's death, 141
  shares secret, 18
McMoneagle, Mary, 12-13, 15
McMoneagle, Scott, 52-53, 56, 58, 145-146
McMoneagle, William Thomas, 11, 27
McNear, Tom, 134, 160, 208
MEG (magnetoencephalograph), 211
Meritorious Service Medals, 64
"method," 253-254
  definition, xi
  for learning, 137
  Ingo's, 163
  of collection, 241
  SRI, 163
  training, xii, xvi
Meyer, Army Chief of Staff General, 92
Miami, 24, 25, 168
microparanormal events, xiv
military,
  intelligence, 31-32, 51, 56, 67, 72, 159
  labs, xiii
  service, 74, 173
  veterans, 129, 173
Military Intelligence Excepted Career Program, 158
Military Personnel Center office, 107
Miller, Jessica, 233
mind control, 91
Mind Trek, ii, viii
  published, 223
  Stargate chapters, 247
  targets found in, 86, 150
mind-boggling, 79

missing,
  persons, 224, 229
  Soviet aircraft, 114
Monroe Institute, The (TMI),
  CHEC unit, 169-170
  David Francis Hall, 152
  Gateway Seminar, 140-141, 143, 151, 165
  introduction to, 139
  lectures, 225, 247
  M.I.A.S., 152
  trip to, 148
Monroe, Robert, 139, 149, 152, 192, 200
Mooney, CW3, 157
Moscow, 29, 75
Moses, Dr. Lincoln, 238
mother,
  and alcoholism, 15, 18
  complexity of, 4
  conversion to Catholicism, 14
  death of, 141
  feelings toward, 5
  illnesses suffered by, 21
  marriage to father, 5
Munich, 46-47, 49-51
Murphy, Margaret Mary, "Peggy,"
  dating, 61
  divorce from, 157, 187
  marriage to, 62
  meeting, 59
  worsening relationship, 97, 136
National,
  Laboratory at Los Alamos, 209
  Security Agency, 46, 52, 132
  Security Council (NSC), 111, 132
Naval Intelligence Command (NIC), 132
Navy, 11, 27-28, 36, 41, 76, 88, 283
Near Death Experience (NDE), 48, 54, 80-81, 140, 179
Necessary Evil, A, 197
nefarious work, 74
negative reaction to women, 77
Nelson County, Virginia, 178
"New Land," 145, 152, 192
New Testament, 50

New York, 71, 162, 186, 198, 208, 210, 290
Nightline, xiv, 122, 223, 243-245, 247, 289
North Carolina State University, 259
"not believe," 1, 80, 270, 275
NPIC (National Photographic Interpretation Center), 88
NSC, 111, 114, 121-124, 132
Odom, Maj. Gen. William E., 113, 132
Office of,
  Research and Development (ORD), 271
  Strategic Intelligence (OSI), 271
Office of the,
  ACSI, 154
  Army Assistant Chief of Staff for Intelligence, 90, 128
old cook's school, 94
one-line sound bites, xiv
Operation Rollback: America's Secret War Behind the Iron Curtain, 74, 290
Order of Saint Stanislas, 259
our own home, 198
"outbounder," 78-79, 86-92, 233-235, 248-249
Out of the Body Experiences (OBEs), 50, 139
Oxford University, 190, 250, 271
Padua, 118, 120
pain,
  control, 129
paranormal,
  event, 80
  functioning, 80, 274, 276, 283-284
Paranormal World of Paul McKenna-Telepathy, The, 248, 291
Parapsychological Association, xxiv, 259
parapsychologists, xiv
Parapsychology in Intelligence, viii, 269, 290-291
Passau, Germany, 47
Peggy. *See* Murphy, Margaret
Penn, Judge Carleton, 187

phenomena, xiv, 159, 212, 238-239, 274
Pleiku, 43-44
Poland, 260
power station, 250
premature stages, 73
Price, Pat, v, 71, 78-80, 85, 273-274, 276-281
proactive investigation, 76
Project ULTRA, 271
protocol, xi-xii, xv-xvii, xxiii
"Proxmire Effect," 270
pseudo random number generator, 190
PSI, viii, xvi, 7, 191-192, 212-213, 285-286
Psi Conducive States, 285
psychic,
  ability, xv, 43, 283, 292
  development, 7
  functioning, 4, 72, 74-76, 78, 162, 286
  methodologies, xv
psychokinetics, 270
public demonstrations, 82
Pulling the Plug, 196-197
"Put to the Test," viii, 230-231, 236
Puthoff, Dr. Hal, xxiii, 78-79, 84-86, 271-278, 291-292
quark experiment, 271
Qur'an, 50
RAPT program, 152-155
Red Brigades, 115-117
remote viewing,
  "circus entertainment," xiv
  funding, 69, 98, 134, 184, 212, 265, 283-284
  live, 247-248, 250
  "magic stunt," xiv
  method. *See* method
  protocol, xi-xii, xvi-xvii, 267
  various numbers, 186
Remote Viewing Secrets: A Handbook, ii, xvi, 247, 290
Rhine Research Center, award from, 259
ridicule, v, xiv, xvii-xviii, 73, 92, 124, 130, 182, 231, 270

Rig Veda, 50
Riley, S. Sgt. Melvin (Mel), 77, 80, 90, 98, 163, 165
rise-time, 85, 87-88
Roberts, Jane, 50
Roberts, Steve, 40
Rolya, Brig. Gen. William, 65, 92, 113, 168
Russia, 29, 120
Russian analyst, 124
Russian Northern Fleet, 123
RV. *See* remote viewing
"S-2," 62-63
Sable, Patricia aka Kim Baker, 167
Saint Mary's Catholic School, 14
Sal Corrado, 37
Salyer, Jim, v, 189
Sandia National Laboratory, 219
Schlesinger, Dr. James, 273
Schleswig am Zee, 60
Schul, Bill, 155
Science Applications International Corporation (SAIC), 214
scientific evidence, 82
Scientific Oversight Committee, 213
Scooter. *See* Honeycutt, Nancy
Secret Service (SS), 132
security leak, 113
self-selection process, 78
Semipalatinsk Unidentified Research and Development Facility-2 (URDF-2), 276
senior projects officer, 66
separation, 57, 131
Seth, 50
severe sunburn, 40
Severodvinsk, 121, 123
shaman rituals, 53
signal line, 96, 118
signals intelligence, 32, 66
Signals Intelligence and Electronic Warfare, 66
Skylab, 97-98
slanted tubes, 122
Smith, Capt. Paul, 162
solar array testing site, 221

Soviet, 75, 114, 269, 271, 277, 281-282, 290
nuclear test site, 71
Soyster, Maj. Gen. Harry, 181
"special switch," 90
specific threat assessments, 76
"spooks," 73
spoon-bending parties, 154
SQUID (Superconducting Quantum Interference Device), 211
SRI-International, xv, 71, 98, 181, 214, 269
St. Louis, Missouri, 156
Stanford,
　Linear Accelerator, 216
　Medical Center, 79
　Research Institute, v, xi, 71, 79, 171, 274
Stanford University, 86, 199, 238, 259, 271, 284
　Art Museum, 86
　sleep lab, 199-206
Star Gate, v, xiv-xvi, xviii, 73, 122, 223, 228, 243, 267
Star Wars, 215
State Department, 132
Stilson, Adrian, 199
structure of analysis, 216
Stubblebine, Maj. Gen. Burt, 132, 143, 154, 162, 181, 198
Studies in Intelligence, 71, 269, 290
submarine, 121-124
Sue, 42, 46-47, 53, 58
Swann, Ingo, 71, 85, 134, 162, 164, 189
synchronistic, 78
Tanaka, Mr. Saburo, 263
Tanakh (scripture heading), 50
Targ, Russell, 78, 84, 189, 271, 277, 281, 291
target,
　material, xi
　unknown, 101
Technical Services Division, 271
terrorism, xvii, 133, 291
terrorist activities, xiv, 133
Tet holidays, 44

Thailand, 53-55
Thompson, ACSI General, 98, 108, 113
Thompson, Maj, Gen. Ed, 90
Thompson, Martha, v, 189
tracking nuclear materials, 228
"training method," xii, xvi
treasured secrets, 78
Trent, Hartleigh, v, 88, 130
"tricks," xvi
Typhoon Class, 123
U.S. Army in Europe, 46
Udon Thani City, 53
Ultimate Time Machine, The, ii, 247, 291
UnAmerican Activities, 74
Uncle Red. *See* McMoneagle, William Thomas, 11, 27
underground devices, 71
United States,
　Army, ix, xix, 44, 56, 72, 80, 112, 144, 267
　Coast Guard (USCG), 132
University of,
　Moscow, 75
　North Carolina, 259
　Tokyo, 251
unsolved murder, 264
Utts, Dr. Jessica, 238
verification, 72, 271, 274, 290
Verona, Italy, 115
Vietnam, 26, 33, 42, 53, 126, 188, 247, 282
Vint Hill Farms Station, Virginia, 52
Walter Reed Army Medical Center, 130
WANG system, 161
"war room accouterments," 75
Watt, Major Scotty, 67, 81, 87, 94, 104, 114, 131
weight and conditioning, 127
wind generators, 216
Wiseman, Dr. Richard, 250-251
World Trade Center,
　February 1993, 208
　September 11, 2001, xiii

Hampton Roads Publishing Company

... for the evolving human spirit

Hampton Roads Publishing Company
publishes books on a variety of subjects including
metaphysics, health, complementary medicine,
visionary fiction, and other related topics.

For a copy of our latest catalog,
call 800-766-8009,
or send your name and address to:

Hampton Roads Publishing Company, Inc.
1125 Stoney Ridge Road
Charlottesville, VA 22902
U.S.A.
e-mail: hrpc@hrpub.com
www.hrpub.com